Sybille Bedford is a Vice-President of PEN, and a Fellow
of the Royal Society of Literature. She was awarded the
OBE in 1981. Her books include *The Sudden View* (*A
Visit to Don Otavio*), *A Legacy*, *The Best We Can Do*, *The
Faces of Justice*, *A Favourite of the Gods*, *A Compass
Error*, a two-volume biography of Aldous Huxley, and
Jigsaw, which was shortlisted for the Booker Prize in 1989.
She lives in London.

AS IT WAS

Pleasures, Landscapes and Justice

SYBILLE BEDFORD

published by Pan Books

First published 1990 by Sinclair-Stevenson Ltd
This Picador edition published 1992 by Pan Books Ltd,
Cavaye Place, London SW10 9PG
1 3 5 7 9 8 6 4 2
This edition © Sybille Bedford 1990
The right of Sybille Bedford to be identified as author of this
work has been asserted by her in accordance with the
Copyright, Designs and Patents Act 1988.

The following are reprinted with kind permission of:

'A Look at Judges at Work' – *Observer* 1965
'Notes about a Journey in Portugal' – *Vogue* 1959
'The Anchor and the Balloon' – *Encounter* 1954
'Auschwitz. The Worst That Ever Happened' – *Post* 1966
'The Trial of Jack Ruby for the Murder of Lee Harvey Oswald
Part I' – *Life* 1964
'Idem Part II' – *Life* 1964
'Venice in Winter' – *Venture* 1968
'A Journey in Yugoslavia' – *Venture* 1966
'The Trial of Lady Chatterley's Lover' – *Esquire* 1959–60
'A Look at Judges at Work' – *Esquire* 1965
'Portrait Sketch of a Country' – *Esquire* 1962
'The Quality of Travel' – *Esquire* November 1961

The author and the publishers have used their best endeavours
to trace the holders of the original copyrights
in the contents of this book. If any copyright holder has
been inadvertently omitted or misidentified, this can
be rectified in any future edition.

ISBN 0 330 31888 8

Printed in England by Clays Ltd, St Ives plc

TO
LESLEY
from her nervous passenger

CONTENTS

I

EUPHORIA
❧ Travels ❧

II
RIGHT & WRONG
❧ *Law at Work* ❧

I

EUPHORIA

❧ *Travels* ❧

Depuis huit jours, j'avais déchiré mes bottines
Aux cailloux des chemins. J'entrais à Charleroi.
– Au *Cabaret Vert*: je demandai des tartines
De beurre et du jambon qui fût à moitié froid.

Bienheureux j'allongeai les jambes sous la table
Verte je contemplai les sujets très naïfs
De la tapisserie. – Et ce fut adorable,
Quand la fille aux tétons énormes, aux yeux vifs,

– Celle-là, ce n'est pas un baiser qui l'épeure! –
Rieuse, m'apporta des tartines de beurre,
Du jambon tiède dans un plat colorié,

Du jambon rose et blanc parfumé d'une gousse
D'ail, – et m'emplit la chope immense, avec sa
  mousse
Que dorait un rayon de soleil arriéré.

Arthur Rimbaud

THE QUALITY OF TRAVEL
France and Italy
1961

A PART, a large part, of travelling is an engagement of the ego v. the world. The world is transport, the roads, the clerks behind the counters who deal out tickets, mail, messy money, keys; it is the porters, the waiters, the tourist industry, the natives, the weather. The world is hydra-headed, as old as the rocks and as changing as the sea, enmeshed inextricably in its ways. The ego wants to arrive at places safely and on time. It wants to be provided with entertainment, colour, quiet, strong coffee, strong drink, matches it can strike and change for a large paper note. It wants to find a room ready, warmth, cool, hangers, the right voltage, an ashtray and enough clean towels. It wants the shops to be open and dinner at six-thirty or at half past ten p.m. It wants to be soothed, reassured, attended to, left in peace. It doesn't want to be stared at. It wants to be made to feel competent, generous, knowledgeable and of accepted looks. It wants to find everything just as it expected, only rather better. It also wants to find the unexpected, but it wants that to be manageable. And whatever it wants, it wants it NOW.

It is not a pretty state, but one that is not easy to resist. Foreign travel is a precipitant: as home and office and familiar responsibilities recede, the man outside the ego, unless he is a gipsy, of saintly detachment or a travelling statesman, becomes the baby or the monkey in the pram, he *is* a bundle of wants at the mercy of his environment. To himself he is alone. To the world he is myriad. For every traveller who goes disgruntled, there will be tomorrow's car load, bus load, train load. If *he* does not come back, someone awfully like him will. The traveller is expendable.

The dice have always been loaded. In most centuries travel was simply frightful. The first movements of mankind across the surface of the earth were blind massed wanderings, beset with dim perils, liable to end in extinction. Nobody in those times stirred alone. Later on, displacement became more conscious and more organized: navigation, messengers from Rome, legions on the march. The professionals moved, the seasoned, the dedicated, the passionately curious, the greedy. As travel became more individual, it became more heroic, the aims more high-flown – India, the Tomb of Christ, the Boundaries of the Universe, Gold . . . The hardships, the uncertainty, the odds against arrival were staggering. In ship, on horse, in armour, trudging beside the donkey and the sack of Bibles, racked on wheels, the knight, the pilgrim, the conquistador, the itinerant quack, the trader swaying with the caravan, the Jesuit embarked for China, the slave in the hold, the showman to the fairground, the bold, the privileged, the meek, all stood to brave the portent of the sudden cloud, the speck on the ocean, the swirl of wind in the sand, the threat at the crossroads. All were prey to filth, disease, rapacity and the routine ferocity of man to man. Those who were not garotted for their purse were likely to be knifed by a fanatic. Those who were fleeced at the inn might find themselves sold into captivity as well. No one was sure to wake to a new day.

By the eighteenth century rigours and perils had hardly abated. Voltaire's *Candide*, though a professed work of fiction, is a realistic travelogue of the time. So were, in due course, *Childe Harold* and *Don Juan*. Yet the scope of travel, if not its mechanics, was softening, was getting humanized as it were. Men travelled to enlarge their education, to look at the world not to seize it; they travelled to seek health and took their families; to buy and carry home works of art – they were travelling at last for pleasure. Poets were crossing the Alps, Milord was in his carriage with his valet and the bulldog and the brace of marmosets under the coachman's seat: the era of the amateur traveller, the traveller for travel's sake, was on its way.

Gradually, very gradually, at least within a tamed circle of Western Europe, the starker dangers diminished. The discomforts remained. Mud, snow, dust, the rutted road, the bolting horses, the axle giving way; dirt, exorbitance, the doubtful bed; the delays, the waiting, the *distance*. It took eighteen days from Paris to Rome – if you were in a hurry, that was, and under favourable conditions. The Napoleonic wars did not help; yet they did not hinder. Curious as it may seem to us, war in the past was never an entire obstacle to private travel. Then steam came and all was changed. For the first time in the lives of men and beasts, locomotion, the assisted way of getting from place to place, was quick, almost safe, cheap; and no sooner was it quick and cheap than it became luxurious. When it was technically possible to satisfy it, there was a large – though by contemporary standards limited – and discriminating demand. The nineteenth-century well-to-do lived well at home, they were not going to live less well now wherever they were or went on land or sea. Ingenious commercialism and the opulent new appetites built the transatlantic liners, the Grand Babylon hotels, railway sleeping-cars, Monte Carlo, Torquay, Saratoga Springs. Plush, mahogany and conspicuous space in public places, pilastered halls, the champagne bucket, roasts cradled in silver trolleys wheeled along the well-set tables d'hôte, the subdued, well-trained servants in place of the hordes of ruffianly soup-stained waiters – such were the complements of the steam-engine and industrial change, the props of the brief gilded age of travel that flourished until 1914.

Would *we* have enjoyed it? First of all, would many of us have been *able* to enjoy it? It seems to be axiomatic now that the pleasures of good living then were only for the substantial rich. Yet I think that dollar for dollar, pound for golden sovereign, the answer to the second question is, yes. The many of us who today are able to travel at all, would also have been able to afford a helping from the Edwardian fleshpots. It is tricky to determine what anything really cost at any given time. Did the bottle of five-star brandy at five shillings take longer or less time to earn than the bottle at £3–10–0 in 1961? But it would not be wrong to assume that highball for imperial pint of Veuve Clicquot, ocean passages, hotel rooms, restaurant meals and drink took if anything a rather smaller slice out of a person's yearly income than it would today. But then the full price of any commodity cannot be reckoned solely by the cash that comes out of the consumer's pocket. Smooth travel was possible largely because many people contributed their services to it for small pay. The great chefs of the age, in London, on the Riviera, in Switzerland (if we are to believe Arnold Bennett, who went thoroughly into such matters, and my own father who frequented cooks and sat in kitchens in the way other gentlemen of his time frequented jockeys and the paddock) commanded the kind of salaries we associate with bull-fighters and opera stars. Head-waiters and hall-porters retired into sunny villas on their amassed tips. But the many, who polished the boots, carried the trunks and wiped the plates of the relatively few, worked, according to the economic structure then prevailing, long hours and for wages that were – relatively *and* absolutely – low.

The other big reason for the traveller's steady comfort was of course that the supply still exceeded the demand. There were fewer people on the planet, and fewer of them, for good cause or bad, moved about. Hotels, restaurants and liners were seldom full up. The traveller was the customer and the customer ruled the roost. 'Kitchen's shut', 'I'm afraid we can't, sir', '*Monsieur, c'est trop tard*', '*Chiuso!*', were words he never heard. Instead, *he* said: 'My consommé is weak.' (See the travel manuals.) 'This truffle has not a good colour. The sauce is too thin. There is shot in these quail. The cream in this pudding has not set. The claret is too warm/too cold/is corked. Take it away.' 'Very good, sir.' And the sommelier at the Majestic knew, and the manager knew, and the share-holders knew, that if another bottle of Pichon-Longueville '04 was not swiftly forthcoming the chances were that this guest would be dining at the Hôtel Splendide tomorrow night.

Well then, *would* we have enjoyed it? Now, being what we are, and used to what we're getting now, very much indeed in some respects and rather less in others. There would have been less occasion for frustration, disappointment, anxiety. Take departure. It would *not* have been a long traffic-bound drive to the airport or to the railway station. There would have been no herding, channelling, queuing, standing, waiting, hanging about. The trains at least *left* on time. At 11.04 your ordeal, if you happened to suffer from travel fever, was over. (Sooner, if you had chosen to occupy your place half an hour before.) There you were, with your luggage stacked above your head and nothing more to worry about than your neighbour's cigar. You didn't have to live through the take-off, you didn't have to think about the landing. Wind and weather, except in the extremes of blizzard, were none of your concern. You could open your magazine, book a seat in the dining-car, unstop a flask: you could, in today's so cherished word, relax.

The hotels (where there were hotels) were well-built, the bedrooms were larger, the wardrobes deeper, a door shut stayed shut. The Victorian plumbing across the corridor was first-rate, but in the room itself there was likely to be a stand with a pitcher and basin, slop-pail and carafe. Horror of present horrors: no running water.

As for the food. Was it really so very good? What did it taste like? Like lobster? Or like a sauce glued to some substance? I do not know because, like most of us, I never ate it. Like the voice of Adelina Patti, Edwardian dinner-parties are now the stuff of legend. Not entirely yet, as there are survivors and we have the menus and the cookery books. The recipes are as we know elaborate. (They are also of a high technical excellence of their kind, the product of a prodigious amount of hard work, thought and skill; and the material called for was the best there is, *fresh* butter, *fresh* vegetables, new-laid eggs, home-raised meat. Only the game was high.) The elaboration itself was a natural enough development; there is always a point where prosperity touches again on barbarism, where sober opulence turns to variations for variations' sake, to refinement, to over-refinement, to vulgarity. After Greece, Rome (and the Roman banquet). After the massive façade, baroque; after baroque, papier mâché. On the gastrological level, a society had been eating solid food through the bulk of a century, now it wanted to ring some changes: it turned to rich food, rich food with frills. Instead of the twelve-pounder boiled turbot, roast mutton and suet pudding, it was *Turbotin Daumont*, *Selle d'Agneau Edouard VII* and *Bombe Médicis*. *A la Daumont* means with mushrooms, crayfish, force-meat of whiting, Chablis and cream; *Edouard VII* is lined with foie gras and marinaded in Marsala. Well may we sigh. It is a bit preposterous. But was it, or was it not, perfect of its kind? I should say sometimes yes, more often no. Because one trouble with that kind of cookery is that the effort, the care, the sheer honesty demanded are more than flesh and blood and avarice can stand without an occasional recourse to short-cuts, kitchen-aids, the steam-table, the bottled essences. I have dabbled in *haute cuisine* myself and know; not only that it takes all day but the kind of a day it is. So one does suspect that even in 1910 some of the processes were often scamped; there must have been already more than a hint of mass-production in the dishing up of the triple choice of sixteen courses, particularly in the very large hotels, in the not so large hotels which aped them and in royal palaces. The food in these is said to have never been quite hot. King Leopold I of the Belgians used to rise from his own table, plate in trembling hand and shout, '*La soupe du Roi est froide.*'

What *we* would have found most irksome travelling fifty years ago were the clothes that went into those trunks (and had to be put on in dining-room and beach), the starch and studs, the cloth and silk, the *hats*. On every dressing-table in every hotel room there was a washing list printed in five languages:

. . . Jupons/ petticoats/ unterröcke/ enaguas/ sottanini
. . . Gilets blanc/ dress waistcoats/ weisse westen/ chalecos de etiqueta/ panciotti

That. And what went with it. Smoking in the smoking-room. Ladies without escorts went in pairs. When they ordered drink it was in half-bottles, preferably Sauternes; spirits never. To us, with our drip-drys and quick-drys, our pack of Camels, our mixed rounds of daiquiris, who have dined in shorts and polo shirt on the Costa Brava, it would have been intolerable.

THERE WAS perhaps after all one golden age of travel. It was brief, as are such ages, and even while it lasted the compass was not large. It unfolded during what we now may see as the early-middle period of the automobile. The Model T had done its good work and was being left behind. Balloon tyres and self-starters had come in, and reasonable speeds; comic breakdowns were a thing of the past. Cars were cheap enough, manageable enough, worked well enough to be bought and *used* with insouciance. One could take a chum, a girl, a suitcase, set out of a fine morning, start in the cool of night, *comme le coeur vous en dise* . . . Suddenly there was choice; the world had opened up, even the world twenty miles beyond one's doorstep. The Iron Horse had abbreviated the distance between A and B. With the new toys of freedom one could dash to F, see X, dance at Y and get to B as well. In its minor way it was a dawn, and to have been in it, and alive, was good. Less than a hundred years after Puffing Billy, travel was back again where it began, on the roads. But this time (for a time) with the stings taken out, private, fancy-free – our own.

The 1914 war was over, five years, ten years, fifteen . . . In Europe the stringencies of social custom had, and remained, slackened. If Maxim's and the Beaurivage Palace still flourished, the traveller also stopped at the Nautique, the Post, the Sol, the Commercio and the Rendez-Vous des Pêcheurs. The car took him into market-towns, to the waterfronts, to the rock-pool in the next bay, to the village where they'd found the fresco, into the mountain woods to the inn by the stream. He ate chez Jacques, at the Greek's and chez la Mère Gros, at Luigi's, da Cesare, chez Nine, chez Paul, zum Ochs, at le Bon Coin and at l'Auberge de la Forêt du Dom. He drank in wine-shops and in taverns and in cafés, and in cool dark narrow new places called American Bars. He sat in the sun and in shade, on city pavements under the chestnut trees, in summer gardens, in piazzas, by lake-sides, on quays, below arbours of vine and awnings flapped by mistral, in tap-rooms redolent of pinewood and late on terraces above swift nocturnal water. Sometimes there was sawdust under his feet and his elbows touched oilcloth or marble; the napkins were floppy and blue and red, the bottle was brought to him by the patron or a boy or a woman, and the food was the food of the country. Wherever he went he was welcomed and, within a charmed circle, he went wherever he pleased.

Not for long. The golden circle, never large, was narrowing early. The first countries to drop out were the ones struck by phantasmagorical inflations. If it is a rule of golden travel that the living and the moving and the pleasures must be happily within the traveller's means, there is also one which says that the traveller's joys must not be – to any gross degree – at the guest country's expense. He may live off the land only if those who own the land live off it with him. The playground must be a tolerably happy one; and he may only take pleasure, *share* pleasure, where pleasure is, not grab and buy it where it is provided in a vacuum of greed and need. To be a, most likely very profitable, guest who lives more agreeably than he might at home is one thing and a very nice one too; a difference in degree is a difference in kind. The idyllic traveller cannot be a parasite, a marauder battening on misery; whatever living at the Hotel Adlon for 2/6 a day including Beluga Malossol and Johannis-berger Schloss Spätlese for lunch may have been, it was not golden travel.

When economics go wrong, politics do not lag far behind. Italy went next. The Blackshirts marched on Rome; the country for all the world remained a travel country – no one who loved Italy could bear to stay away, nor in those days stayed for long – but it was no more inside the magic circle. Meanwhile the years were ticking on, if we knew it or not, ticking on towards 1929, 1933, 1936; towards 1939.

The Wall Street Crash thinned out the travellers themselves; Germany again, and inexorably now, became a condemned playground; the Spanish Civil War broke out; Austria fell. Those who still could, travelled all the harder. Where was there to go in those brief last summers? There was Scandinavia, Holland, Switzerland, unfailingly; Greece for a few; there was Yugoslavia; but of the great spellbinders of travel there remained only France. Between the Mediterranean, the Seine and the Gironde lay the last golden enclosure. It was almost enough.

The French are both soft and stoic. They are above all resilient. Their losses in the 1914 war were on such a tragic scale that it left them with a private and a national sense of irreversible bereavement. If they managed to keep a glow on life it was because of their sensuous vitality, their readiness to enjoy what life had to offer, or what they made it offer; their cultivated and articulate capacity for taking life physically: their passion for food, their due regard for bed, that perennial saving streak which is also an undoing. The French, goodness knows, had plenty of troubles. There was much political bitterness, much corruption, power-seeking, distrust, self-interest, ill-will, right-wing and left-wing fanaticism, as well as the usual dose of sheer fatuous imbecility. People and parties howled at each other, even shot at each other, as people and parties will when they have nothing total to fear, but as régimes went in Europe the French were bird-free. Their tycoons were as predatory as they come, their budget never balanced, persons who had to live on salaries and pensions were often wretchedly ill-off, but a very large number of individual French were comfortable and pros-perous and able to stuff themselves, and their mattresses, with paper money, in the then still time-honoured way of a nation of small shopkeepers and peasants fattening and selling calves and vegetables for and to each other.

It was the French themselves who in those days discovered what they were quite content to label *le tourisme*, much in the same way as some twenty years later on this supposedly most conservative of people suddenly took to foreign travel. (Before, no sensible French person who could help it set foot outside the borders, and certainly not in the name of curiosity or pleasure.) They adored it. They never stopped talking about it. They doted on everything that went with it. The roads, the Renaults, the

11

Peugeots, the Citroëns with the new front-wheel drive cornering down the N6 at ninety-five an hour, *les voitures américaines* (*t'as vu la Buick de Jean?*), the mileage, the tree one nearly went into, Michelin, the posters (apéritifs and gasolines), the maps, the road-signs (AGINCOURT 5 km), the guide-books, the mobilo-gastro chatter, the STOPS. '*On peut déjeuner?*' 'Mais oui, Monsieur – Madeleine: deux couverts! – vous auriez notre jambon fumé pour commencer avec de la terrine, puis une brandade de morue si vous la desirez, puis il y a du poulet aux morilles, de la salade de cressons, du cabécou, de la tarte aux abricots . . .' '*On peut dîner?*' 'Justement ils nous arrivent des langoustes – Gaston: fait voir le 11, une chambre à grand lit – et ces Monsieur-Dames ont-ils envie de manger du gibier?' Ah, the stops – the stops were the heart, the life-blood, the marrow, the primum mobile of *le tourisme*.

Everybody had their own place up their sleeve (allez-y de ma part), there were adventurers, dissenters, pioneers, but the heavens of the tourist trade moved according to the overall belief in the Michelin Guide's star system – ☆ worth a visit, ☆ ☆ worth a detour, ☆ ☆ ☆ worth the journey. The entire country played at it: what to eat, where to eat, what to drink with what to eat (quand même pas un Alsace sur la langue de veau!), what one ate last night, where to eat next Sunday, what one drank, what one paid, what was said: the patron liked to see the customers, the customers liked to see the chef, the sommelier leaned against the table and expressed his views (un Corton c'est toujours un Corton, mais pour moi le '23 vaut pas le '26), the brother-in-law would come over for a drink – on les fait manger; ils nous font manger; *on mange*. . . .

AND NOW* – now that we are all so much cannon-fodder for the travel industries? Is there anything we can do to improve our

---

* *That* now – 1961 – is no longer the now (to become transient in turn) of 1990. It is for the reader to decide what essentially is unchanged and what is changed: changed for better, for worse, for much worse, for monstrous worse.

  (This not is applicable to much in this book.)

regimented lot? Travellers of the World, Unite. You have nothing to lose but your holidays. Well no one can say that there are not enough of us. (And only that many fine months, that many free days in the year, that many flights, roads, rooms, tables against the wall to go round.) The dice, indeed, are once more loaded. It's a sellers' market. Take it or leave it, and if you don't take it *now* it'll be gone. So in February we buy our tickets for September. Yet the quintessence of good travelling is still freedom. Here today: meet a friend in the square, see a beach – stay on tomorrow. But No: the *Reservations*. The Excelsior on the 9th, Stockholm the 12th, Edinburgh . . . Here is where they get us, tied hand and foot, playing our fears (*not* without cause) of finding ourselves without bed or a booking. It rains in Florence, the galleries for some sprung-up national holiday are going to stay shut, the schedule has us down for another forty-eight hours. We do manage to slip off to Venice on our own, the sun is shining, the food is delicious, why not skip Stockholm this trip? UNI-AIRCRAMP says No. Travellers of the World Divide. Disperse, narrow your compass, go underground.

It was in that spirit that I decided to make a journey, an unambitious journey, to Italy through France without a time-table or a single reservation. The thing is to choose one's territory (no vast distances, but manoeuvre-room), get oneself across the Atlantic or the Channel, take a car or hire one, count one's days, and make sure of a booking home. Within that framework, the choice – up to a point! – is ours.

The new day comes when at last our feet are firmly on the continent of Europe, and our hands upon the wheel. We may not feel as unworn as Venus risen from the sea, but hope springs eternal. What's behind is behind: the fifty-nine things to do, the getting off. It is at least *possible* to have had a smooth flight from Chicago, to step off bronzed and rested from the SS *Espérance*; the same cannot be said of the various methods of Channel crossings as still practised. The air-ferries are not bad (if one discounts the ridiculous expense, time and paper fuss involved in covering 21 miles), but they are grounded during every puff of gale or fog. What is wanted of course is not the Tunnel or a

Channel bridge, but a tunnel *and* a bridge, several tunnels, a whole span of bridges, anchors to make the island know at last its place. The citizens of Calais are said to be preparing for this unlikely event by setting up profitable amenities, in England it is still looked on as science fiction. Never before in history has England moved as fast as she has been moving backwards in these last few years.

My fellow travellers at the airport (English side) looked shirt-sleeved and dishevelled. Tea slopped in the saucers, ash-trays overflowed, the counters stayed unwiped. The food displayed was predominantly shredded processed cheese on margarine and white. There were also on sale some of those dead-meat pies, the full soggy weight of which has to be eaten to be felt. We stood in line – cheerful – to be served. The service was absent-minded rather than snarling. The beer, it happened to be one of the one hours out of three in which one is allowed to drink some, was, need I say it, warm. My fellow travellers (French side) looked shirt-sleeved and trim. Floors, counters and glass cases shone with polish. There was Chanel scent for sale. The barman (*clean* white jacket) was not above cutting a slice of ham. There was champagne by the glass. Not very good champagne, but iced and dry. There were also, besides several kinds of French beer, Danish beer, Dutch beer, English beer and stout. The French and Danish beers were chilled, the Dutch and English cool. Everything cost about twice as much as it did on the other side.

The extreme north of France is not inviting. The country is flat, the roads uneven and impeded by level crossings, good places to stop at few; it is as if the population could hardly wait to be rid of the new-landed visitors and get on with their drab agri-culture of turnip and sugar-beet. My own idea was down to Rouen, quickly, and a very good lunch. The first. Luncheon on the quay, of mussels and sole. The choice, I said, would be ours. True enough, if ours includes the car's. Bad cars break down, good cars exercise a subtler despotism. Nothing, no death-rattle of a poor old crock, is as compelling as the moral blackmail levied by a new car. Mine, as expressed by its glossy service manual, had to have a special oil changed for another very special oil at a certain number of miles. That number was up *now*. The manual also informed one where this operation had best be executed in this part of the world. Accordingly I headed to a not very attractive town in the Department of the Somme. The garage was in the dingy but machine-loud outskirts where such establishments are usually to be found. A number of namesakes of my car were standing about in various stages of disembowelment. The mechanics had not finished their lunch; I had not begun mine. It is my habit, however, to carry iron rations. The manager's wife invited me to a chair in her kitchen, spotless and somnolent. I unwrapped what I could. Danish rye, a hunk of cheddar, eggs. Iron was the word. The woman eyed me like something in the zoo.

'Vous êtes danoise?' she said.

I denied this.

Her eyes stayed on the bread; when she saw how black it was, she squealed. I explained that in my opinion the bread in England was not fit to eat.

'You come from Denmark?' she said.

I said that Danish bread was to be had in London like Camembert and Bombay duck. 'C'est *noir*,' she said. I dared her to eat a piece, she shrank with giggles; further communication failed.

I spent that first night in Normandy at a place which is rather typical of one new kind of French country hotel. It is the converted small château or manor house, converted with taste and perhaps not quite enough money spent on the plumbing, and run with only relative amateurishness by people not originally brought up to the trade. This particular one, standing in beautifully kept grounds, is an eighteenth-century house overhanging a small green-banked river. The French lay much stress on reception, *l'accueil*, and it is accorded special marks in their many guide-books. Quite rightly so. The tone, the level of intelligence, of the welcome, the speed with which the traveller is enabled to put his car at rest and find himself *with* his belongings behind a shut door and *alone*, makes all the difference at that weary hour.

I am not prejudiced in favour of Normandy. In winter it is bleak, in summer pretty. Anyone inalienably attached to the Mediterranean landscapes, to olive and ilex, to the bleached bare spaces of Provence and the terraced Tuscan hills, is not captivated long by hedgerows and apple-trees. Normandy is a cider, not a wine region, which makes for a broody, sullen, suicidal form of drunkenness. But cider and calvados are innocuous compared to the Norman affluence of butter and cream. Eating, over-eating, is not always the amiable weakness we like to think it: gluttony and rapacity go often hand in hand. Cream and butter are quite literally the Normans' Golden Calf. During the Occupation even one-cow farmers grew to Cadillac riches from black-market butter; and so in 1944 the populace threw stones at the advancing Allied soldiers because liberation from the Germans put an end to that.

The *accueil* at that Norman hotel was perfect. Entering my room was like walking into a Monet painting: the window *was* the river and one might almost touch the live, leaf-reflecting water. Alas, as I knew before the night was out, the room was also damp and there were many serious things wrong with the woodwork, the pipes, the flooring . . . This is not a complaint, only a statement of the facts of life. One cannot have everything. Old houses such as these can only be lived in as they are, or destroyed; to do them over at impossible expense would put an end to them as twelve-roomed hotels. A matter of choice.

We (I had been joined by friends from Paris) went down to dinner. The menu was large, that is, it was on a large sheet of cardboard. I watched out for the cream. It *was* in evidence. But looked at as a whole that menu was sound and unpretentious: two made dishes, one of chicken, one of duck; red meat grilled to order; fresh trout, lobster, also cooked to order; and that, with a terrine, one soup, vegetables, and some puddings, was the lot. The chicken, a *spécialité de la maison* of course, was simply a good deal of white chicken (a decently bred fowl) presented with mushrooms and a sauce stiff with cream (not flour) flavoured with calvados; it was one of those fool-proof dishes doted on by the French because they are so rich and by Anglo-Saxons because they seem so hard to get at home. I doted on them myself until I was about twenty-five. This one was as good as they can be. The entrecôte I had was a thick cut of first-rate meat – firm texture, well-flavoured – it was properly grilled and served with a large piece of butter (nothing amiss with the quality) and fresh watercress. The fried potatoes were burning to the fingers, slender and crisp and left no trace of grease. The balance was marred by the haricots verts, brown-green and softened into a blotter for butter, a standard treatment of vegetables in France.

Wine. It much depends on who does the buying with what standards and from whom. Do the patron and his wife know their stuff or do they order according to the blandishments of the shipper's salesman? It takes a lot to keep a fair wine-list. As for the customer, there is no longer such a thing as a *safe* wine. Those Anglo-Saxons who are wine drinkers are usually spoilt because standards of export are high. Transport and duty costing what they do, it is foolish to ship muck across the seas. I drink better claret in England than I can hope to find during a casual trip through France. There, the home market is so huge – in the one street in Paris where I usually stay there are a dozen people, five of them women, who are known to drink up to their ten litres of red a day – and has become so indiscriminate that cheap production for high yield, inferior grapes, inexpert handling and adulteration, pay.* This goes for the *ordinaires*, the current wines, splashed out by the litre, as well as for the named and bottled mainstays of good daily drinking: the Anjous, Beaujolais, Bordeaux Blancs and Médocs Supérieurs; the Grands-Crus, real ones, are still to be found – at a price – and in Paris, Nice and Bordeaux as well as in Boston, London, Brussels, San Francisco. We stuck to the mainstays, and were lucky. A Muscadet without sharpness, a passable Châteauneuf. It is not hard really to tell sound wine – your insides, from five minutes to the morning after, are the judge.

Not so now: one marked change for the better.

The coffee, too, was fair (they still *will* mess with those filters). They tipped us with liqueurs. We chose calvados; it did not make us sullen. To sum up, the place was good of its kind. By other standards, those of very expensive London restaurants or the run of reputed Paris restaurants or those of some famed places on the tourist routes, the quality and honesty of the cooking and materials here, the individual attention, were remarkable. What keeps it so? The right patron (some people like to give their best, others are born cheaters), discriminating customers, competition. Outside the summer and the Easter seasons there is not much transient trade (foreign transients seldom praise and never complain); the backbone are regulars, local families eating out, Sunday Parisians, people who will come again *or* stay away. In this fertile valley it is but a stone's throw to the next *spécialité de la maison*.

Full marks, too, for the get-off. We decided on an early start, a very early start. You don't have to break it to them, *they* put it to you: Breakfast – six o'clock? seven o'clock? ten o'clock? Miserable hours for the staff? Not at all. Madame is up on her own, bent over a gas-ring in her dressing-gown. Tea, coffee, or chocolate in piping jugs, hot croissants from the baker, honey, two kinds of jam. I am not mentioning the other stuff. The bill is ready too, and there is change. Not a small bill, but expectedly so, and scrupulous. The car is still waiting under the trees; unlocked. Nobody has touched the luggage.

One good way to drive down to the South of France, if one wants to avoid the over-crowded and over-priced National roads Nos 7 and 6, and I always do except in the dead of winter and great hurry, is to go roughly by Chartres, Blois, Bourges (or through the Loire), Moulins, or Montluçon, through the Auvergne, over the Cévennes and into the Ardèche by Clermont-Ferrand, Le Puy, and come out into the Rhône Valley anywhere between Valence and Avignon. The roads, like pretty nearly all first and secondary roads in France, are very good and except for the Sunday-luncheon traffic half empty most of the year. Getting South takes a bit longer, but only if you count in hours, as there is rather more winding and climbing and the road often passes through villages, but the actual mileage is the same. The country is varied and most beautiful, and there are of course a great many things to see. The Auvergne alone, to mention only the less obvious, is rich in Romanesque churches of astonishing originality, the painted basilica at Issoire, Auzon, Brioude, Fontannes, the stupendous Benedictine abbey on top of a rock at La Chaise-Dieu . . . But I am concerned here with the material framework of travel, not its contents.

The Auvergne is another region of abundance; mountainous, well to the south of centre, it is still cow pasture (blue cheese, Cantal) and also swarms with pigs, barnyard-fowls, game-birds and sturdy vines.

We stopped at an inn near Riom, a charming place, a traditional establishment of the old school (beds provided so that those who dine may sleep) and starred by Michelin. That system flourishes as much as ever. Meals in such places are set meals; you *can* eat à la carte, there's nothing inflexible about arrangements, but somehow you never do as well. The form is three set meals, three menus. *Le Menu à 7NF Le Menu à 16NF* and *Notre Menu Gastronomique*. Before looking at any you know that you will have to take the 16 francs one. The cheap menu will have been made to appear so unexciting, so mingy (by contrast) that you feel you cannot bear to dine off just soup, omelette, lamb chops, salad, ice-cream; while the gastronomic one is sheer show-off, a shop-window, not designed for human consumption. Besides it costs 32 Nouveaux Francs, c/s/b – cover/service/drink – *not* included. So you also shy from *Les Délices des Anges* – *Le Pintadeau Entier Sous Cloche* (2 Pers.) – *Le Soufflé G'd-Marnier* (40 mins), and get down to business. The manageable menu offered us a choice between something hot in pastry and two pâtés. We chose – being two at that stage – one terrine de canard and one pâté de gibier. The range of quality in pâtés is wide, at the extreme ends of the scale they have nothing in common but a name. These were far removed from the starchy-filler and grey-pulp variety, and they were served as they should be, not on a little plate with a tired leaf but in their earthen terrines left on the table with a good knife, plenty of hot toast and bread. It is easiest to say what a good pâté should not be – fat, too close or gelatinous in texture, too salty, under-seasoned, all peppercorns and gristle, over-herbed, soused in cheap brandy, stale, too high, too fresh, worst of all not made of plenty of sound meat. Ours were none of these things: they were made of duck and pork and hare and couldn't have tasted better.

On arriving I had asked for some white wine to drink, and they had given me a glass of a local one to try. I liked it and ordered a half bottle for apéritif and it went on drinking itself well. It was a most pleasant discovery. The name is St-Pourçain, it was fairly dry and not a bit thin, one could feel at once that it was wholesome and it had that fleeting taste of earth and fruit and flint that one loves to catch in a white wine. I have since learnt that it can be got in London, but have not had the heart to try. Here it costs 3 F. 60, a bottle, restaurant price. We ordered some more with our terrines and the second course, which was either trout or *Lotte à l'Américaine*. I don't think trout out of a tank is worth eating, because its muscles and so its flesh will have gone flabby, while trout straight out of a cold river is so good that it should be had by itself, in suitable quantities, with melted butter and perhaps some boiled potatoes, and not shoved between two high flavoured courses, so we chose the *lotte*, a fish* which ought to be able to stand up to the *américaine* treatment: cayenne pepper, tomato concentrate, herbs, flared brandy . . . The dish that arrived was not quite like that, the sauce that covered it was thickened with starch (gluey) and had a smooth brown uniformity that betrayed a semi-mass-produced origin in a stock-saucepan. Next (with *red* St-Pourçain, nicely robust and no disappointment) one of us had chicken done with morels under a bubbling crust: a bit of a virtuoso dish, but neatly turned out, and the morels, the firm black nightshade so like a species of sea fauna in appearance, with the hot white chicken and their compounded essences was delicious.

The alternate main course, irresistibly described as *Jambon*

---

*Our new friend, the monkfish.

sous la cendre, was a come-down. Whatever merits the ham may have possessed were smothered not under hot ashes but a drenching of our old acquaintance the smooth brown sauce, gingered on this time by a lacing of Madeira – cooking Madeira, no other is purveyed in the French provinces. There came also a panful of new potatoes right off the stove in their parsley and butter; these were pure and good and horribly out of place. What was wanted if anything was a spoonful of plain rice. (Which the French mysteriously are unable to make. A Pilaff, just; à l'impératrice, yes; plain steamed rice, never.) Salad, dressed to order – cheeses – fruit – fruit tarts and ices for who wanted them – the filtres – a presentation bottle . . . The place indeed had many virtues: everything set before us had been in most generous amounts, to me an essential for good faith. They were very friendly, commercial friendliness, but dispensed with good-nature; the bill was moderate. Two-thirds or less than it would have been in Normandy, or the Côte d'Azur for that matter, and this holds good for most of provincial France off the main tourist track.

I went into the details of this dinner because it was so typical of both the good things and the defects one may expect to find elsewhere. Nearly everywhere we went, we found the same inequality: one dish outstanding, the next a travesty. Much of French cooking is based on methods which mean long slow work by hand. There aren't enough people anymore to do it, nor is it economical; the family may help, but the family may not be numerous or have other ideas for themselves. Not every young man, even in the Dordogne, will want to spend his life stirring *sauce grand-veneur*. At the same time, it's a question of prestige and prejudice. The French still *believe* in sauces. If it's without a sauce, or not flamed or puffed, or encased in crust or wrapped or stuffed with something else, it may be very good – it may be a great deal *better* – but it's not *la cuisine*. *La cuisine* was (*is* they would say) one of the glories of France. Nobody else knows anything: the Italians live on macaroni, the Germans on potatoes, the English cook exclusively in tepid water, the Americans do not cook at all. French cookery stands like an ageing beauty

– forward ho, nobody is going to notice the little bit of rouge and dye, nobody is going to notice the little bouillon cube.

How did I fare in general? As far as hotels went, very well. We drove across the Rhône and back into the main-stream, spent some days at Aix, a week between Bandol and Nice. Easter came and went. We did not sleep in the car, nor in the cold-water pension nor on the billiard table in the station hotel. (I am now convinced that this free-wheeling is perfectly practicable ten months of the year for anyone unencumbered by small children. Only July and August need a different approach.) French hotels are getting better and better. The really monstrous plumbing of my golden youth is giving way to tiled and glistening shower-baths and WCs. You may even wash these days with comfort and hot water at some gas stations. (The discrepancy between the near-Swiss domestic cleanliness of the French and the filth of their public places has always puzzled me.) Nor are hotel rooms expensive, in fact they cost less than anywhere else in Europe except Portugal; but of course the bill catches up with one on the food. And the food, after the first flush of arrival, fails to stand up all too often. Great pretensions breed great expectations. I recall some nadirs: the starred *auberge* where at least three courses of the dinner were built round batter – fishy fritters, pancakes encasing béchamel and cheese, pancakes encasing béchamel and vanilla essence – and where the wine pressed upon one was an acrid rosé in a dolled-up bottle. The well-frequented place not far from Cannes where the red mullet was not fresh and the escalopes had been pre-cooked and re-heated (the first *can* happen, the second is pre-meditated). The famous restaurant by the sea where the dinner produced for us – a table of four – was so shocking that I prefer to believe that it can only have been due to a chain of chance mishaps. The disgraceful rot-gut served without batting an eye-lid by far too many places in the South, and about which one can do nothing as the 'better wines' in such places are sure to be neither well-chosen nor well-kept. And yet at times one does eat beautifully in the Midi, as indeed one should. I remember an hors-d'oeuvres of home-cured small black olives, anchovy, firm butter and radishes just pulled from the earth. I remember sardines grilled dripping from the sea; a little dish of veal cooked with new artichokes and sorrel. Striped bass, fish-soup, *oursins*. A stew of wild boar; rabbit done with peppers in a flat black pan at a Spanish place at Aix; green almonds, the first apricots, a round hard goat cheese eaten with fresh figs and the red Rhône Gigondas. Other wines, obscure and world-travelled: Château Simone, grown in upper Provence; Cassis, still one of the best of oyster wines, but beware, there is not much of it and not all of its shippers are true; a nice natural tough red wine made by a peasant near St Tropez and a nice natural white wine made by a peasant near Grasse; a vintage champagne light like fine silk, and a sequence of exquisite wines at a luncheon given by an American woman. I even remember *one* meal at a star place where the whole menu was held in impeccable bounds and was from first fork to last spoonful delicious. It was a Friday and we ate *maigre*. We (a party) began with a salmon from the Loire accompanied by the lightest cucumber mayonnaise, a coolness of pink and pale green; the central dish was simply a hot stew of sea-food, and it was as good as it sounds.

The French are prosperous again – ça marche – and the young, disillusioned or not, feel free. People probably work less, care less . . . They certainly earn more, drink more; standards are lower, workmanship more shoddy, the new *things* look hideous, but the people look thriving. Virtual dictatorship, near police-state, plastic bomb throwing – the general political precariousness of the country is hair-raising, but then whose is not? The French dash off for their *vacances*, pour into the Mĭdi: there is an exhilarating vitality at large, and with it a sense of live and let live, of individual ease, and it stays with one from border to border.

LET US look at Italy. If one were wafted straight from our shores on to the Via Aurelia at Ospedaletti (Roma = 676 km), our first shock of pleasure might be the cypresses and fig-trees, the pink- and blue-washed houses, the dazzling sea. When the transition is by motoring in from France, the first shock is the mad driving. It is driving that scares the French. Each time, one finds that it has got more impossible. It is not that Italian driving does get worse, it stays the same and they drive very well, extremely well, too well, every man boy jack of them; it is that each year there are more cars to drive. Italian motoring is like the nationalism of a very young nation, but there is more to it than that, there is also a natural affinity: the automobile must be God's special gift to the Italians. He even created it noisy. The Fiat, the Lancia, the Alfa are the young man's fine feathers; at the wheel, he is a bird of paradise displaying a dance of courtship – love my car, love me. Courtship in the animal kingdom is competition. So it's a battle-field. On narrow roads. Plenty of blind corners. And precipices. Tanks, too: doubledecker buses, oil-trucks triple-linked.

One gets used to it. To the point of feeling dazed by the slow pace during the first hour out of Italy. But one never gets used to the coast-road between Nice and Pisa. From the frontier to Genoa, squeezed between the Sea-Alps and the sea, twined with a busy railway, tunnelled, quarried, tram-lined, the road is frustrating and murderous. Once again one swears to oneself that next time one will come in by way of Switzerland and Milan. At Alassio, we stopped to break the tension. Alassio has pretty arcaded streets full of those shops where they will make you a pair of sandals or a silk shirt in twenty minutes, and for the Riviera it has a good beach. We found that it had become a German enclave. Things are like that in Italy (an occuppee mentality formed by history: layers of soft yielding, nonchalant compliance, below bedrock). Florence used to be English (when we were still able to spread ourselves), the Americans have chosen Rome, Venice is an international city; the Germans, a modest choice one must say, have taken over Alassio. I am not distressed by the sight of a good many people on a holiday. People must go somewhere; there are only so many places in the sun; that we *are* so many is not the fault of these actual generations; I hope they, we, we'll all enjoy ourselves. What does distress me are the unbecoming, commercial, but stupid commercial, monkey-tricks practised by the natives. God knows the French are great tourist-trappers, but they have kept some dignity. Look at this Italian in his doorway, waving a napkin, 'Nicy spaghetti!'; he is behaving like a *silly* prostitute. Alassio is plastered with notices in German touting *asti spumante* and whipped cream, mis-spelt, grotesquely worded, as if they had been taught by some tipsy joker in the small hours, as in fact they very likely were. And so, in English, in French, in anything, is the whole of Italy, it's the new polyglot illiteracy. The grammar or lack of it doesn't matter, not a scrap, only the fact that the people who utter those invitations turn themselves into parrots, cut the link between thought and speech . . .

When Italian food shops are good, which they are in all the towns and all the resorts of the North and Centre, they are very very good. To me the first one after absence is almost unbearable. The cleanness, the smell of Parma ham and sometimes of truffle, the order, the reasoned abundance – I am moved to transports of appreciation. Look at the whole cheeses in their beautiful black rinds, look at the hanging provolone, the fiaschi, the salami, they *have* fresh fior di latte *and* mascarpone, the cooked ham looks good too, and the tunny fish . . . But I buy our picnic with restraint. Prosciutto di montagna, smoky and mild; a few olives; bread, not the rolls which are often sad stuff, but a cut of a coarse baked loaf; a wedge of parmesan, the hard *grana*: a morsel is prized off and tendered on the tip of the knife – yes, this one; and one soft cheese, a ball of mozzarella.

Cherries off a stall in the street. A wine-shop. What they chiefly drink here comes from Piedmont and the Val d'Aosta just above, Barbera and Barbaresco, frank reds, rather strong. I take a flask of the lighter Bardolino from the Veneto because it is an agreeable wine to drink. The good wines of Italy are easy and companionable. Soave, the undenatured Chiantis, Valpolicella, Bardolino, the rosé from Ravello . . . You can do with them what you never would with a hock or claret, trundle them about in the car, opened and all, fling in a handful of ice, drink them without a glass, drink them at all hours, with any food, in carefree quantities.

After Genoa the road rises, the curves sharpen, the traffic becomes *more* lively; from now until La Spezia one forgets about the frustration and concentrates on the murderous. In between, we spent the night at Portofino. This is now one of the most, probably the most expensive place on the entire Mediterranean coast between Torremolinos and Maratea. (There are 1051 inhabitants and 1039 of them are said to have tucked away a minimum each of $10,000 in the last few years.) These few feet of land between hill and sea could not be more fashionable or over-run. Which only goes to show what good taste people have. For that constellation of harbour, small township and castello is ravishing, and remains so as the law forbids anyone to alter as much as the shape of a window. When we were there it was out of season and in moonlight; one cannot ask for more.

We dined. The first dinner in Italy – will it stand up? is anything ever as good as one remembers? It did, and it was. We ate a light curled pasta that lay like a nest on the plate, with the green genovese dressing of pounded basil and garlic, and then we ate a firm grilled fish, a sea-bream, charred and nutty, seasoned only with a thread of limpid Tuscan olive oil and some lemon. With it we drank the wine of the neighbourhood, white Cinqueterre I had never had before and it was most pleasant. Later on the waiter made us a salad of young sprigs and leaves, a salad such as you can only get in Italy and in Italy only in the spring. Then there was fruit, and cheese, melting stracchino and parmesan full-flavoured and crumbly, and with these we drank each a quartino of Valpolicella. Everything tasted simple and strong. Everything had been made honestly, quickly, without frills, but as it should be. It was wholesome, life-giving . . . We had eaten well, we felt well. As we sat in the piazza inhaling our black half-inches of double espressi, I felt very happy.

After Portofino one comes a bit down to earth. Not for long though. One is soon at Pisa. Who – however road-worn, tired, outraged by his last encounter with a Vespa – can forbear from feeling a pang of child-like pleasure at the sight of that extraordinary assemblage of felicitous architectural absurdities standing on that tidy strip of grass?

I have often slept at Pisa, in comfort and in squalor, but I can't say I have ever eaten very well. My luck and fault entirely. Restaurants in Italy all look much the same, so if one's not tipped off one knows it may be hit or miss. Putting one's nose inside helps, but that needs the resolution to walk out again. A place being half empty is no indication either way, the inhabitants of Cremona may not stir out on Mondays or after 8 p.m. Of course there are the guidebooks, even Michelin now, but by the time a place gets into one it often has already passed its prime. The kind of integrity that makes Italian cooking is built largely on innocence and popular eating habits; it tends to go off when confronted by foreigners and success. Not that you can go so terribly far wrong, you will always eat. The Italian range is not so very large, excellence at one end (an excellence achieved by texture, the goodness of materials and their startling freshness), innocuous dullness at the other. The worst you can expect is a bellyful of ready-made spaghetti followed by a pallid bit of veal. I've lived in Italy off and on since I was a child, I've had some starkly bare food in the poor south and in other remote places, but never once in my memory have I been given something that had gone off (a very common experience elsewhere), nor can I recall any outstanding instance of *grande cuisine manquée* even in the internationally-minded hotels.

I forgot: there *is* a skeleton in the culinary cupboard, and it is made of fishbone. It is the national illusion about the fish-soup, *il cacciucco*. They love it, they drive miles to the Ligurian waterfronts to order it, they even think they can eat it. The Italian fish-soup has been described for all time in its crazy glory by Norman Douglas in *Siren Land*, and I can only say here that the soup is all he says it is, fishes' heads, coruscating colour, over-powering spices, spikes, sharp little bones and uncrackable little crabs, and that the serving of it still flourishes.

After Leghorn we dawdled down the straightened coast-road towards Rome, half-consciously postponing an arrival which to me is always tinged with awe, looking at Etruscan tombs, stopping here and there, at Castiglione della Pescaia, at Porto Ercole . . . In Italy when the weather is right it is joy itself, when it fails the single wet day is dismal and dead; just so, existence in this unique country is at times Elysian and at others like a sojourn inside a power-driven mincing machine. Like other travellers, we were alternately floating along in elated bliss or reeling off the streets felled by combat fatigue. There are always marvels, always pin-pricks . . . Here stands Diana's temple, it is a private moment, '*Postacards? Cartes postales?*' The uninvited guide continues at your heels, talking, talking, you do not want to mar the day by the loud word that may even fail to send him off. You turn into the Square, the Palazzo Pubblico, a first glimpse of arches, colonnades . . . you stop to park the car: from the kerb there rise four human leeches.

The best of coffees is yours everywhere for the price of three or four of those light new coins. You sit down, order an ice, too, with a swirl of cream: the radio, off-station, starts a-blast, behind you begins a glissade of kitchen plates.

The noise! There are no two ways about it, either you are Italian or Italian-built and don't hear it, or you are not and you do and it is unbearable. Scooters revving, motor horns, open exhausts, female lungs, a steam drill, canned music and nimble hammers pounding on sound steel – shuddering noises, fine noises, honest noises, noises for noise's sake, from the backyard, from next-door, from the cinema, from the café, from the street . . .

Italians, for all their happy gregariousness, seem to do things best individually. One houseboy and the house is kept scrubbed, polished, in beautiful order, the marketing is done, drinks served, delicious meals appear, the guests' luggage is gently taken down, disposed of in the car. All this with calm, the unobtrusive smile. Two boys: voices raised, dithering to and fro, a tug over each suitcase – off flies the handle – general agitation. Three boys: a crowd. What traveller has not been the centre of these tussles, at the station, the taxi-rank, leaving an hotel, trying to take a boat? It is wearing to be put into the position of the Solomonic baby several times a day.

Fifty million Italians do not make so much a democracy as Disraeli's Two Nations. Italy, too, or most of it, is prospering. The well-to-do are doing extremely well, the poor are much less poor and some of them beginning to be even decently well-off. But the dividing chasm is still there, tangibly and intangibly, in education, in civic and political responsibility – the poor are the wards, the others not the guardians but just privileged citizens – to a diminishing extent in dress, and most decisively in the outlook of the two sides themselves and in the outlook of the Church. Such division – among many other things – is limiting, it stunts evolution, growth. The haves are almost pushed into cynicism and frivolity; the poor stay blocked in their sphere: work, frugality, acceptance (or rebellion), ducking under the bureaucratic snares, the family, the day and what it brings, enjoyment, zest for life, getting on with it. Admirable much of it, but is it enough? And on top of it all there are the foreigners streaming in, and who are they, all rich of course, incomprehensible, alien in their virtues and their ways, another species; the Church insinuates that they are outside the pale – no stockings in church, sun-bathing, smoking women – again it does not help. So in the end modern Italy is really split in three, the rich, the poor and the tourists.

ROME. It is a name so potent, a spell so great. Rome, the most superb of the live hunting-grounds of magic, the seat of the gods and man, the capital of pleasure, a feast to the eye, to memory, to all the senses . . . Love renders mute. I cannot write of Rome; it is far beyond my powers. Anyhow, Rome is there to be plunged into, to be believed. You walk in Rome, you eat, you see, you sniff, if it comes at all it will come to you in that way. But here again, this is no longer true, we are up against the facts of modern life – can one still walk, can one still *move, breathe*? No longer in Rome: the cars and their fumes fill everywhere, stagnant, solid, or moving at mowing speed. Every crossing is a hazard, every outing an ordeal. The Piazza San Pietro is a car-park, Bernini's façade disfigured by a hundred excursion buses. The traffic in Rome has attained nightmare dimensions; it is not too much to say that this is a tragedy.

To the many of us whose love of Italy had been instilled early, the very thought of the incomparable beauty and riches of Italian art and the Italian countryside has been a solid possession, an inexhaustible promise of a perennial inheritance to come into, to explore more deeply with time and a mellowing mind; but already today physical existence in the larger towns of Italy is viable only for the tough and the young. What's to become of it all? If we are not going to blow up our planet, we are going to ruin it by our numbers and our wheels. Everywhere there is galloping up on us the same new story, before we have been able to grasp, before we have learnt how, or even decided to cope: over-population. Too many sheep in the pen. And with it, decline in the quality of living, frustration of spontaneity, universal dullness.

Let us turn to more manageable aspects, let us turn once more to the pleasures that are undiminished: one eats in Rome as well as one ever did. The half dozen or so places with the now international reputations are doing fine; if some of them have become a bit more furbished and a good bit more crowded and high-priced, the food is still first-rate, and for each of them there has sprung up round the corner, in the next street, across the river maybe, an old trattoria on the way up, getting a new name. It will be discovered, enjoyed, praised, written-up, crowded-into, re-decorated (here always the last step but one) and replaced. A healthy state. I dined out every night I could and each time I went home more than pleased. That is not the case with all travellers in Italy, and I think that questions of taste apart it's a matter of ordering. If the restaurants look much alike, the menus, too, read much the same. This means little. One should choose from what one sees exhibited so proudly on the table coming in – the dish of new shelled peas, the coiled fresh pasta, the trussed birds, stuffed peppers, salad bowls, wild strawberries – and according to what one feels like eating. There are some prawns, the waiter proposes them grilled, one is hungry, could one not have a risotto of seafood? Certainly, if one is willing to wait twenty minutes (while eating something else), and now is the time to say *how* one would like the risotto made. They expect it. Creamy? on the mild side? or with plenty of saffron and spice? The French would send you packing. Here, nearly everything can be ordered as you like it: boiled, fried, grilled, hot or cold, in butter, in oil, without fat, in batter; without sage, without Marsala, with garlic, with an egg . . . Nor is it *necessary* to begin a meal with spaghetti. I happen to be fond of nearly every form of pasta; I like it with bacon and red peppers, I like it with young green peas, with chopped ham and cream, with filets of fresh tomato, or *in bianco* just plain with butter and cheese. I like tagliatelle, taglioline, fettucine, cappellini, lasagne, farfalle, parpadelle, tonnellini. I like rice, I like gnocchi, polenta, cannelloni and pasticci, but if I did not, I could spend a month on end in Italy without having to touch pasta asciutta for any course. Well, what else *is* there?

There is ham, salami, smoked ham, melon, figs, fresh mozzarella or ricotta, anchovy, tunnyfish, artichokes hot or cold, finocchi, chickpeas in oil, salt cod, vitello tonnato, quail, soups, cream soup, clear soup, chicken broth done with any garnish, omelettes, flat stuffed omelettes, truffles in cheese, truffles in egg, small marrow, spinach crusted with parmesan, asparagus, peas with ham, little hot dishes of sweetbreads, or of eggplant and bubbling cheese, mushrooms, gamberi and scampi, frittura, anything you wish with a mayonnaise, and about three dozen varieties of fish.

When it comes to the main course, ask again, ask to see the meat, the new catch – it will be brought to you with pleasure – pick out your lobster, choose your cut. Never get discouraged by the menu; never eat at places that have menus written in English like this:

scalope bolognese style	* scalope pleasure style
scalope according	* meagre of scalope
arrosteds	* paste & bean
humids	* foot & bean
fritters	
green from season	

Some Highlights: White truffles grated at the table over a plate of very fine egg pasta (Rome, Turin). Pilaff of prawn and mussels (Venice). Pasta of a kind that puts it in a class apart (Bologna, Rome, Milan). *Gran Bollito*, boiled beef, veal, fowl, sausage and tongue (Piedmont, Rome). *Bistecca alla fiorentina* (Florence, Rome). Young vegetables and primeurs (Rome, Naples, Florence). Rare salad greens (Florence). Mozzarella, the dawn-made buffalo cheese dripping with its own milk (the south). Wild asparagus, apricots, melon, figs, peaches, grapes.

Some Stand-Bys and Good Things: Hams, smoked meats. Thick soups. The bean dishes of Tuscany. The larger sea-fish, *orata dentice*, *spigola*, *san pietro*, swordfish, fresh tunny, also soles, red mullet and some of the small fry. Veal kidneys, *fegato alla veneziana*. Boiled chicken, boiled beef. *Ossobuco*, *stufato*, spiced sausage. Most of the short-orders of veal, *saltimbocca*, *involtini*, *milanese*. Baked lamb (good sometimes); the fillets of turkey and chicken. Broiled Tuscan chicken. Melanzane, fagiolini, zucchini. *Fave* off the pod. All salads. The taste of the tomatoes. The olive oils. Ten cheeses. The pastry in the larger towns. Sicilian oranges.

Some Things to Avoid: Game birds as currently done – pre-roasted, over-cooked, smothered in sage and re-heated. *Pasta pronta* – nine times out of ten, soft-flour spaghetti kept warm, dished up with tomato and meat sauce. Pizza (nearly always). Most restaurant roasting. Rosemary, apt to protrude like too many pine-needles from an overwhelmed bit of pork. Thin insipid puddings like *zuppa inglese*. The open white wines dispensed in Rome. Pasteurized chianti, dead in the glass; wine in fancy bottles.

Two postscripts for dispelling gloom. To make certain of some swimming (in early May) we went south below Salerno, into the Mezzogiorno. After a short initial streak of foul weather, it got hot, it was summer. Drawn by the pleasures of discovery, we drove down well into Calabria. How easy it is now. When I was a child much of it was malaria country and I remember being hurried away from Paestum before sundown; and even a few years ago casual travel was not to be undertaken lightly because there was hardly anywhere to sleep. Now there is a network of Jolly Hotels and *Autostelle* – motels, run (well) by the Automobile Club of Italy. There is also a chain of the new Agip gas stations (the centipedal dog) which sport showers, coffee-bars and luncheon-counters, so that one is now most competently and cleanly lodged and looked after in the deep south. The beaches are unbelievable: wide, long, white and empty. There is fishing. The roads are good; the countryside is as beautiful as a dream, untouched, unspoilt; the people friendly, with a grave archaic grace, the open hand raised to greet the stranger.

The last lap, Florence. We had three days. While the sun was up we pressed in rush-hour crowds through the Uffizi galleries, the Pitti, the Bargello, across the Ponte Vecchio . . . At night we ate. There was a back-street place I knew in the old days. It had two bare tables in a sort of hallway to a smoke-filled kitchen into which one squeezed, first come first served. It was always hot, hellishly noisy and afterwards the stink of burnt meat lingered in one's clothes for a week. The customers were Florentine workmen and aristocracy, smart professional men and paunchy visiting Milanese. The benches were hard and narrow and not provided with backs, the service rough and none too ready, and at one time of the evening this broiling cage would be invaded by an itinerant band. One endured it because of the food. The food was superb. The best of its kind in Europe.

We arrived. The queue stretched half-way down the street: Italian sports cars, a Mercedes, American limousines. Italians in evening clothes and diamonds, Americans bristling with the less obvious exterior signs of wealth. Everybody stood and waited for about three-quarters of an hour. The cage was just the same; nothing had changed, the benches, the service, the din, the smoke from the charcoal fires. In due course we ate. We ate birds off a spit and a plate of Florentine grass, the whole white of a chicken in foaming butter out of a little battered aluminium pan such as I have never eaten and shall never eat elsewhere, we ate steak, wild asparagus, strawberries. The red wine was delicious. We paid as we went out – there were no menus –

the prices, too, were unchanged. It had never been for nothing, it was not so now, but for what we had been given we had been made a present.

The second night I tried to get to a place that had been described to me in Rome as the heir apparent to our No 1. It has no name. What it says over the door is simply TRATTORIA. As it happens the street, a streetlet, is un-named too. The directions I had been given sounded like an incantation: stand with your back to the fountain, face such a bridge, count twenty paces to the west . . . It worked. I found it.

A back-room attached to a kitchen, bare communal tables, benches, cool scowls for welcome, crowded to over-flowing, but no queue. No diamonds, no foreigners, no Giuliettas. The customers: Florentine aristocracy and workmen with a sprinkling of professional men. Good bread, olive oil, bowls of grated cheese, fresh-cut lemons and good young wine in profusion on the table. We ate cecci, baccalà, grilled chicken, beefsteak, garden asparagus, grana, raspberries. It was superb. We paid as we walked out; the bill was small.

The third night we set out for a place known to a local friend. It went by a nick-name. Same décor, same initial lack of cordiality (they all warm up when you've had something to eat). The customers: workmen, clerks, petty officials. We ate boiled beef and *fave*, we ate a savoury mince, a thick grilled fillet of veal with hot asparagus, green almonds, mascarpone and wood strawberries. Decent wine flowed. Nothing could have been better. As we left we paid and the sum was ludicrous. I put down the address, in a couple of years it will be spelt out for the asking by the head-porters of the Excelsior and the Grand – the third in line for the carriage trade. Long may they all flourish.

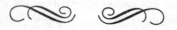

THE ANCHOR AND THE
BALLOON

A Diary in Switzerland
1953

SATURDAY, AUGUST 1st. Morning. Stepped off the
train, still trailing a little sand, by the door swung shut last
night on the platform at Cannes, funnelled through the passage
of the double customs – *Douane Française*, other colours, a
common language, a different design of caps, *Douane Suisse* –
followed the unhurried porter's trolley to the cloakroom down
the kiosked hall and walked, free for a space of hours between
a choice of trains, into the spacious sparkling luxurious town,
pouring with light, ablaze with water, snow-lit above the
summer blue: Quai des Saules, Pont du Rhône, Pont de l'Isle,
Quai des Bergues – the Lake of Geneva, wide-shored and open.
Sails: the Jardin Anglais, full of tidy people on the benches; and
there, the Jet d'Eau, slenderest fountain shaft, white comet of
water, self-flung into the sky.

Hôtel Métropole, well-kept in gilt and awnings; wide crossings intricately marked, elaborate signals. Place Bel-Air, rue de
la Corraterie. Large-fronted banks, slow passage of lustrous
motor-cars bearing Egyptian and Bolivian licence plates, very
wide shop windows displaying the single salmon on his block of
ice, the one bolt of silk; fruiterers' windows with liqueur whisky,
sherry, satin-ribboned corbeilles of tiered pineapple and grape;
windows lettered *couture* with nothing in them except a small cut-
glass bottle of Chanel scent, and the discreetly wire-veined
windows of L'Horlogerie-Bijouterie.

. . . Fifty steps inland and all is changed. An older smaller rooted world. The roofs are lower and the façades more simple, dazzle of lake and mountains are shut off: there are plane trees in the square, and a little shade, print-shops, flower-stalls, cafés; women walk by with bread; the Metropolitan Spa is a quarter in a provincial town.

. . . Up cork-screw streets into the Old Town; Saint-Pierre's, with the bishop's fine stabling below, a scramble over a hill top; then drawing level to another change – stillness, lines of patrician streets, municipal buildings with private façades, hints of gardens behind walls. In the yard of what may be the Town Hall a father is explaining in *incroyable* French the workings of a mediaeval piece of artillery and its neat pile of croquet balls to a small boy.

And so on and up, standing, drifting, pushing on, concentrated and aimless, in the manner of a traveller who has neither duties nor time-table, who wants to take it all in but knows that he will not sleep in the town, whose north is not even the hotel but the railway station. A not unrecent Swiss guidebook read, 'As we pause in the Bourg-du-Four to buy ducks' eggs . . .' Ducks' eggs! And who are those who pause and walk on, not with a picture card or postage stamp, but a live smooth egg in a fragile pale-green shell? I did not find the shop; perhaps its place in the quiescent, crooked square was taken by the shop of the Chinese merchant, Descendant and Successor, the sign proclaimed, of one L. Tschin-Ta-Ni, Fils Céleste, who set up in this very spot in 1779, and where then under the picture of a Dock-Road Chinaman, in a penumbra of canisters and an atmosphere of Sherlock Holmesian *sous-entendu* belied by transparent neatness, I had myself weighed an ounce of Gout des Caravanes by a Swiss tradesman with Mongolian eyes, seized by a strong sense of being present in some double exposure of time.

. . . By noon all movement has ebbed away. It is very hot. Summer quiet in the rue Calvin, in the rue du Puits, in the rue des Granges . . . Only small chink and clatter from area windows and the smell of melting cheese floating from doorways where cats lie already curled. Then down the Promenade la Treille, by the ramparts, into those open spaces, those rural gaps, each with its building in pompous, inflated, ephemeral official stucco.

'Excusez moi, Madame, c'est bien la Société des Nations?'

'Point, Madame. C'est un Musée d'Art.'

'Ah, et qu'est-ce qu'il y a dedans?'

'Des bureaux.'

Time up. Brief broiling journey in the trough of the afternoon. In our roomy carriage the blinds are down; the train only hums; it is dark, hot, static, like a farm-house parlour, yet one is alive to motion and progress through brilliance without. Rolle; Ouchey; Vevey; the train veers north: one last flash, stabbing bright, of Léman, Mont Blanc, the vineyards, grey stone châteaux and fat-leafed slopes of the Pays de Vaud. Now the green is lighter, the leaves less lush, the trees less high – sweet pasture country, softly moulded, orchards, fir-trees, cuckoo-clock houses, village spires: the cows have bells. Picture-book Switzerland.

I looked at it with reserve.

HUNDINGEN–WÜHTWILL–OBERWANGEN

. . . The light is softer now. Another long valley. And now we cross a bridge. It is the Aar. Look – how snug, how horseshoe-fitted in its river loop, lies the city of Berne, how small, how held! We stop and I walk into a hand-made, child-sized dream.

. . . No. This person in armour and the pink gloves on the fountain is a *bear*. And here, on another is a belted lion in azure, gold-laced boots and his cloak piped with scarlet, sword in paw, lifting a trusting muzzle to the plumed Good Duke; and on this emerald and crimson pillar sits a man in splendid wooden clothes playing bagpipes to a goose, and everything is spouting water and geraniums, and the clock-faces are painted too and as large as cart-wheels, and there are doves and hares and princes to strike out the hours, and *everything* is picked out in gold and scarlet, and there are thick-blooming flower pots everywhere, in all the windows, and the streets *are* arcades, all the streets, as far as eye can see and foot does carry, and here is a whole square spread with fruit, far into the evening – nectarines, apricots and melons and wild berries – and everybody strolls or sits or is selling honey-cake or scout-knives, and everybody is friendly to everybody, and what they speak sounds so extravagantly homely that it dwindles to harmless absurdity, and nothing, nowhere, is ugly or big or grubby or chic or new.

Then another fast Swiss train streaked towards Lucerne in a long twilight. Next day, early, I took a paddle steamer down the lake to a small resort.

LAKE LUCERNE, AUGUST 5th

. . . Mid-trunk on the pollarded chestnut trees in the garden by the lake where the schoolmaster and the comfortable lady on the dais are playing Grieg on an upright and a fiddle, and the summer guests and villagers are sitting under leaves and sky in an after-dinner haze while the waitresses stagger by with *Kirsch* and beer, and the lake is rippling and the night is clear, the music earnest and hypnotic and the little coloured bulbs glow mildly like strings of insect beads and time is gliding and enjoyment placid and diffuse, mid-trunk on the bark, below the buoyant crowns, there is a circle of bright metal clothes-hooks. From them dangle mackintoshes, leather jackets, summer wraps. And in this garden of middle-age and innocence the eye strays to this Swiss skeleton as disturbed as by the supplicants outside the sunny palace in the plaza.

At midnight when the coats are gone from their indigenous racks and the violin has been bedded in its well-worn case, we examine the trees. It is all right! The hooks are held by an invisible leather brace. The inside of the leather is padded. The bark is not even bruised. We look at each other – how ingenious, how useful, how harmless, how neat. And how housewifely. Like those French crockery-shops that call themselves *à l'Agréable et Utile*. But, but . . . 'You know I don't know what to think of that,' says Mr Smith. Nor, really, do I. Mr Smith was an hotel acquaintance.

. . . The staff are always smiling. 'With pleasure.' '*Zum*

Wohl.' '*Volontiers.*' '*Subito!*' '*Gern.*' 'At once.' 'Please?' 'No thank you – *le service est compris.*' '*Bitte.* Thank you. *Grazie. Merci.* Please.' Why?

We had spoken first outside the carved Kodak and news shop, waiting for the boat with the papers to come in, but their names I only learned later on from the register. Mr Smith *mit Gemahlin und Tochter.* I don't know how they like this, but that's the way it is. The entry plainly conveys what it means – Mr Smith with womenfolk. Herr Camenzind, the manager, strolls through the lounge in a black coat, silk tie and polished boots. Everybody calls him Monsieur le Directeur. His glasses have a thin gold rim and he has well-kept hands. His wife wears an apron and her identity among the service-daughters behind the cake and coffee counter is not generally revealed. Herr Camenzind imparts facts, figures and opinions to the Belgian businessman across the room. The very information I am anxious to acquire. Wages – Enough to live on? Well *yes.* Electrification – Pretty general . . . On the farms, for house-work . . . For working people? Everybody works . . . Oh, factory workers? Yes, naturally . . . Yes, nice homes . . . A few very large fortunes, not many . . . At Geneva mostly and Zurich . . . Why, invest it . . . At home? Yes. Hospitals, museums . . . Taxes? Pay them? Certainly . . . The old? The old have had time to put something by . . . There's things you can do in summer, and others you do in winter . . . My neighbour now, the one who has the Crown Inn, he's clerk of Weights and Measures, and Secretary to the Council – of course that's not paid – and he works at a saw-mill . . . You can't sit in a chair all the time. Oh, I'm a *hôtelier de métier* . . . Unemployment? We have to have people in from outside each year to help with the unskilled jobs . . . Start work early? No . . . the boys have to get their training, for what they want to be; one's got to think of the future. *All* the boys? On the whole . . . Find a job waiting? Why yes – that's what they're learning for.

Yes. Not really a rich country . . . Much of the land unproductive, got to import food, not many raw materials . . . Exports – precision instruments: very well; but who needs

precision instruments ad infinitum? or can always afford chocolate and cheese? We *have* our problems.

'Not being alone on the planet.'

Army at nineteen . . . training every year . . . For life . . .
During the war there wasn't an hour when everything wasn't
ready for blowing up the roads and tunnels and half the country
with them. Beggared us? Changed our lives for twenty, thirty,
fifty years.

'You have had the devil's own luck,' said the Belgian.

'Yes – luck. With the passes up we shouldn't have been much
use to anybody wanting to get through, pity you and the French
and the Dutch weren't so well placed.'

But to me Herr Camenzind only says, 'Yes, it's a fine day.
Yes, in winter it's not so fine. Colder, yes. Yes, the war. Hard,
yes.' Of course the women do not vote in the Confederation.*
Everybody seems just as pleased.

. . . Hopscotch on the paddle-steamers – those paddle-steamers
so like tall mock swans, so white and high, so slow, so calm, so
majestic: so crowded – across and back and aslant the lake
to the places one might have, but did not stay at. There are
thirty-six village resorts, not counting Queen Victoria's
Brunnen which is almost a town, on Lac Quatre-Cantons, the
Vierwaldstaettersee, the Lake of Lucerne. All are variations of
one pattern. Landing-stage and promenade on the shore; the
one stone building, the Big Hotel, nineteenth-century, heavily
verandahed, well to the front, flanked by confectioners, kiosks
and a spruce little post office flying the Swiss flag on a square of
lawn; behind the gabled inns, *Gasthaus zur Krone, zum Schwert,
zum Schwan*, and the *Pension Beaurivage*; the village street and
two general stores with soup advertisements in the windows,
more confectioners, a beef and sausage butcher's tiled and
chromiumed like a bath in *Vogue*, a cobbler, a master harness-
maker and two ironmongers, a dairy and a seamstress' sign; a
lane, an opening and the wooden white-washed church with

*They do now.

40

pitched roof and bulbous tower, behind the graveyard; then up and out, past the great propped plum-tree, over the foot-bridge and the stream, at once alone, up through meadows, through the stile, up through noon and sudden shade, up into sharper sun and finer air, up the gently rising mountainside.

When I had walked once, I walked every day. Three hours, five, nine. It was like a new grace. Coming out of the hotel in the morning with five francs in my pocket and a stick and starting up a slope, or seeing a boat bound down-lake and catching that and beginning from another valley. I could walk over the pass and down to Immensee and bathe in the Lake of Zug . . . I could get to Schwyz across the Scheidegg and back again through the fields . . . This was no mountaineering: I never went anywhere I could not lose myself, bumbling along absent-mindedly on rope-soled shoes. What did one take? Nature in Switzerland is not extreme, not in summer, not below six thousand feet; the freedom here is freedom also from the pioneer's domestic cares. There's many a discreet amenity – a hut, a shelter on the summit, an inn, where one could eat and sleep and have one's ankle set. A jersey then, and a torch, a knife, and a light satchel to hold them and some food; dry compact clean food only, hard black bread, hard cheese, and a long hard black smoked sausage, smooth like a thin cigar, and for pleasure an aluminium flask to fill en route with spring-water and wine. Paper and pencil. An apple one could count on finding on the way. I never took a book.

I met few people, except those whose business it was to be about – hay-makers in the distance: they were cutting the third hay, a short crop but thick and sweet with herbs and clover; men working the pulleys of a milk lift on an upper slope – but I was seldom out of sight of a cow. The cows of the Four Cantons are fawn-coloured, not large, with short horns and unalarmed dark eyes set beautifully in the creamy markings of their faces, and they potter about all day long *où le coeur leur en dise*, eating good grass, leading the best of cows' lives. To keep them from falling over the precipices, the Swiss with unflinching practicalness apply the sensible corrective touch to nature by stringing wires with a feeble electric charge across panorama and promontory. I often lost my way. Once I got soaked in a storm, went on and came to a house where they lent me a clean dry garment to sit in. The countryside as usual had been empty, but like Alice's pool the parlour filled at once with dripping people and their boots and dogs. The windows were shut tight against the rain and there we waited in a smell of wet leather, plum brandy and soup. When it cleared the front-door flung open, the men looked up on the threshold and stamped their feet before going out, there were shouts of *Adieu* and *Vergelts Gott*, and, before my things had come back from the oven, they were all absorbed again into the landscape. Once it was night before I reached a town; a fast electric train took me to the junction on the lake; there the last boat had gone but I found that I could hire without fuss a well-oiled bicycle at the station.

THE WEATHER of this long quiescent summer had set at last in full and rare perfection. The granted, still hot days were of a luminous blueness so light and fine, so present, that oneself moving in it felt melted into slow vitrescence. And sometimes from a height one was confronted by yet another blueness – a glimpse of bay below, a rock-set hyaline circlet, suspended lapis lazuli and air, flashing upward light as though a fabled grotto had opened to the sky. Sometimes, woods and silence occluded sparkle and the droning noon; sometimes all was space and form. Once I walked all day along a curving ridge that followed but seemed to design the outline of an open plain. Once I ate my lunch in a brook.

What was this magic? The beginning each day the same: the cold, slow, sluggish start with unthawed limbs and disjointed casting mind; the first hour the longest; the first stretch of climb a dull effort. Then came a warming, a change of rhythm, a switch to another strength, and one was in – swinging along at ease, fused in body and motion and mind, in the air, in the sun, the grass, breathing the green and brooks and hay, swinging in the sound of scythe and water, swinging along alone, happiness welling in the heart, happiness made known in a flight of unspoken words, walking, swinging, in a long moment of infinite content.

> Par les soirs bleus d'été j'irai dans les sentiers,
> Picoté par les blés, fouler l'herbe menu;
> Rêveur, j'en sentirai la fraîcheur à mes pieds,
> Je laisserai le vent baigner ma tête nue.
> Je ne parlerai pas, je ne penserai rien,
> Mais l'amour infini me montera dans l'âme;
> Et j'irai loin, bien loin, comme un bohémien,
> Par la Nature – heureux, comme avec une femme.

> (Arthur Rimbaud)

Then came some breaks but they maintained the mood.

. . . Zurich for the day. How nice the trains are, how clean. Such pleasure to lean out of the window, got down by twirling a light handle, and watch them put the milk and crates into the van. All done so neatly, on such a man-sized scale. Sometimes the guard takes off his coat and gives a hand. And all *smooth*, never breathless or wasteful: no waiting. I walked down the Bahnhofstrasse in midday heat under trees and awnings – a solid mile of Good Shops. Zurich is the largest town in Switzerland and one cannot say that this street is not urban – plate-glass, streams of people, traffic, stoniest Haussman fronts, and very ugly. Yet there is also a sense of spaciousness and enjoyed prosperity, and nobody looks quite pressed, and it is such a fine day; the trees give shade and the awnings look bright and cool; besides, nineteenth-century ugliness has lost much of its power these days. The things in the shops make one wish to set up house. This coffee-machine will work; this paint-job is going to last; this tool-box looks too good to miss. And now the street has come to an end – we stand on a quay by a bridge over a widening river before another lake alive with a hundred small white sails, row-boats bobbing for hire, and beyond the shores and streets and dwindling villas rises a hillside of orchards and, above, a double range of mountains ending, blue and white once more, in snow and sky, and again it is intense clear open summer, fanned by a little wind.

And there are two rivers running through the town and that means water-fronts and water gear, uneven houses with cellar-shops and protruding upper storeys, steps and alleys. And across the Limat there is a cobbled and timbered quarter, odds and lengths of streets, and squares leading any which-way, and old wine-rooms with the date painted carefully over the door. I ate shavings of dried smoked beef and drank wine in a shuttered wainscoted tap-room with a Swiss family tucking into a large noiseless lunch, a place one could hear the flies buzz. And then off and all over the town, in the heat, over bridges, checked in squares, chasing the best thermos flask there ever was from glittering sports-shop to sports-shop, now stopping to look at the new flats going up, now for a distrustful look at the milk-bar, now in and out of Zwingli's very late Gothic Minster, chilled and halted by finding it as Protestant churches always surprise me by being so *filled* with varnished pews; now standing to read the play-bill: Shakespeare, Anouilh, Schiller, Shaw; now in a book-shop, now in another, picking up a pocket Montaigne – such good print – for half a franc; then finding the *Kunsthaus* and in it, shockingly hung on a staircase in bad light, a long-sought Claude Monet, the *Déjeuner dans le Bois*, also other treasures: the Man with the Umbrella coming down a tunnel of leaves, Apollinaire with his striped cat at his arm done by Douanier Rousseau and two or three of those tiny Renoir land-scapes . . . Fuselis by the yard and walls of Picasso, and Expres-sionist Germans, powerful, twisted stuff, composed in an ugly mood; no Klee; what else? but time is up, they're closing. '*So* late,' the woman at the entrance had said: 'I'm going to mark your ticket so that you can come again tomorrow without paying.' I shall not be here tomorrow, but did not like to say so; now going out I looked at her again and thought of how much of this there must have been behind the Impressionists, and how little of it behind contemporary painting. And how splendid of the Swiss, how Voltairean, to collect and show it all.

Who goes to these galleries? Who subscribes to the repertory and opera, and hires the sail-boats and buys the cooking-stoves and good shoes? The inhabitants of Zurich of course. About a million of them now. And they work in factories and offices, use transport and live in residential suburbs on the lake-shore. For Zurich *is* a modern industrial town. But how mitigated! The factories do not smoke. There are no slums. Nothing is really far. The town offers something of the scope of urban pleasures of London, Paris and New York, with less effort, less unbalance and without the cost in health and nerves. In Zurich, one is aware of the lake at every point and the mountains can surely be seen from almost any window. It is not an ideal place, but it is still a good one, and in it no man or woman need live, no child grow up, outside the bounds of nature.

Then I went and sat in the Café Odéon, that old haven of Zurich where in cool dimness on worn leather in an atmosphere at once philistine and literary one can read the newspapers of six countries and sit browsing all day over a cup of coffee, and I thought of first causes and of wisdom and accident and planning, of the mess and the lateness, luck and folly, and with sadness of England and with impatience of America, and of the irrevocable duty of casting always, always, the bread of humanism upon the waters.

. . . Into Lucerne to hear Mozart played in the open air at night across a small cold pond. It was pitch dark and music and musicians came curiously distorted over the intervening water. The strings, now muted, now carried, floated thin; conductor and violins were reflected, enormously agitated, tail-coated cardboard frogs, head downward on the wavering surface. Was there an echo? The whole quite unreal; lovely; though perhaps too charged with romanticism. Mozart does not need this setting. Emerged trance-like and was glad to find, at eleven o'clock, the friendly animation of the town. Sat by the river and drank some wine, and watched the city swans.

Returned on the boat next morning, and found a new ease among the old guard. 'Ça sent la fin de saison,' said the head-waiter. Herr Camenzind is in the wine-room with the Padre and a bright industrialist from Lille. I am now admitted to these colloquies, at least as a listener.

'We *are* our government,' says Herr Camenzind.

The country is small enough, he says – four and a half million – to be a graspable community. The Cantons and the Boroughs are largely autonomous and run by the inhabitants; pretty nearly everybody knows what he's voting and how it's going to be carried out and by whom. As to the Federal Government, any measure, on thirty thousand signatures, is put to the general question.

'On paper?'

No, says Herr Camenzind, there's a Referendum every other week; and explains also the Initiative, a provision by which a man, any man, with the proper number of signatures can propose a bill to the Assembly.

'Guillaume Tell.'

Not at all, says Herr Camenzind. A recent Amendment. 1874.

'What's your President like?'

'Padre . . . ?' says Herr Camenzind.

'On the tip of my tongue,' says the Padre.

'Don't you know his name?' says the Frenchman.

'He's just been changed.'

'Ah.'

'He is every year.'

'God help you,' says the Frenchman.

'Not elections,' says the Padre. 'Council members take turns. Isn't that right?'

'That's right,' says Herr Camenzind.

. . . ASCENSION DAY. Off to Einsiedeln with great expectations. One will never see Dresden or Bamberg now; two weeks ago I hadn't as much as heard of this Baroque Swiss Abbey. It was fabulous.

First the ride in brilliant weather in the open car; over the ridge down to the Lauenburger See, up a mild pass and then through a light forest swiftly into another valley; the spires, slender gold, visible a long time in the sky and vanishing again as we draw level with a compact, animated eighteenth-century town; a long high street, winding, no issue in sight, then sudden embouchure: a vast square, flown with banners, waters playing, thronged, aloud with bands, and here it lies, the Abbey, wholly glorious in the sun, the sweep of it, in weathered stone, arcades and statuary, the wonderfully rounded centre swelling forward as though to meet the eye; one floats across, is wafted up the steps, borne towards the entrance, and now, in a press of people, clergy and a Cardinal from Rome, through clouds of incense, one is assailed by flying form, by gold, by white, by scarlet, by wings and swirls and intersecting cupolas and linking angels, felled in one stroke of wonder by prodigy and harmony and daring, swept by the ecstasy, the joy, the beauty – the jubilant innocence of the interior.

WHEN AT the end of a month my meteoric and impatient friend, Martha Gellhorn, arrived for three days, 'I could make it four,' from Yugoslavia on her way to London, Israel and Rome I was, as well as pleased, dismayed. I did not want to be prised from my lair of discovered joys. I wished indeed to share my store with Martha, but would she see it so? Martha, in a heroic mood, a thousand miles' forced drive straight from Ragusa, with the bronze of an untouched and beautiful country and a people brave as lions still upon her? Martha, who would as soon burn her boats as look at them two times? She seldom has to; and I need not have feared. Twenty-five minutes after she and her small neatly-loaded motor-car had crossed the border, she had seized all. 'My dear,' she said on the telephone (Martha rings up across countries), 'but how clean, how cheap, how honest; how innocent, how comical, how *kind*! Why didn't we come to live here?'

'M.,' said I, 'I have been up the Rigi.'

'Good,' said Martha. 'I want to see all these mountains, I want to see everything. Can we get to St Gall and the Engadine and to Bale, and do you think the Grisons? Can we be off at eight tomorrow? Have you been to many doctors? This *is* the place. And we must do all the passes, I did the Bernina and the Splügen this morning, I love them; and I want to see the Rhône glacier.'

'I went on foot.'

'*Listen*: where *is* Gersau? Kraut-Swiss, isn't it? Never mind – be with you at five. Lay on a room. I must get some sleep, and perhaps I'd better eat, I forget when I ate last. I want to gorge on all those delectable *Schübblis* and *Pasties* and *Wiener-lis* . . .'

'*Zwischenverpflegung.*'

'What's that?'

'In-between-meals taking-care-of.'

'Oh darling – *bliss*!'

She got there; and in the morning we were off on a swift light journey . . . Lucerne before the shops opened . . .

'A lake in every town,' said Martha, 'I do call that stylish.'

'It is rather a geological speciality of these parts.'

'Any sights?'

'We'll walk around and get them by osmosis.'

'I didn't know Mediaeval could be *white*-washed. A brilliant idea. Why is one told Lucerne is pompous?'

'Not this part.'

'And look at those children's fountains!'

'Wait,' said I, 'till you see Berne.'

'Now, that's the kind of luggage I like, unpretentious, sensible. We must get everything we possess repaired.'

'One can send one's bags through the post office.'

'Oh, look. Look . . .' Across the road two wax young ladies, one dressed in white tulle, one in pink, were obliging in a store window on an Erard grand. The music open on the stand was a Wolf song; a fire glowed in the grate. On a settee two suitably gowned matrons and a gentleman in a dinner-jacket were listening with gestures of fixed rapture. An old lady had folded her hands over the sewing in her lap and the master of this apartment had dropped his newspapers. The pink tulle was 87.50. 'How much is that in dollars?' said Martha. 'You know I believe one could marry their decorators.' She turned to the shop-assistant. 'I'm sure these are going to be the most divinely comfortable things I ever stepped in but you wouldn't have a pair that doesn't *show* it quite so much?'

'Madame wishes walking-shoes or social-shoes?' said the assistant.

'Walking, I suppose,' said Martha. 'But perhaps looking just a tiny bit social?'

'Perhaps Madame is thinking of a street-shoe?'

'Oh, I could hug them,' said Martha. 'Now I must look for a long time at these watches; we can't afford not to buy everything we see. Now, *why* aren't we exhausted?'

'We have it all to ourselves,' I said.

Streamers, strung from thatch to gable, read:

MOTORISTS, PLEASE STOP YOUR CARS OR DRIVE ROUND.
LEAVE THE INNER TOWN TO THE ENJOYMENT OF THE
PEDESTRIANS.

'Of *course*,' said Martha. 'Space.'

We had elevenses at the Bellevue & Balances on the strip of terrace by the river, flush with the water, where it is almost still and widens towards the lake; and we fed the swans.

'Grand Canal.'

'Better,' said Martha.

'Now, now,' I said.

'Let's shove,' said Martha.

We shoved. Along the Alpnacher See to Sarnen; to Sachseln, to Giswel, to Meiringen, up the Handegg and down into Brigue; to Visp, to Sierre, to Sion, to Martigny, past Aigle, past Chillon, through Montreux, through Vevey, through Lausanne, to Yverdon, to Neuchâtel, to Murten, to Fribourg, to Berne; we shoved over the Brünig and the Grimsel, into the South, along the Rhône, through the Valais, struck west into the Vaudois skirting Léman, and up into the Jura and the borders of France; we shoved through the Gruyère Valley and the Bernese Ober-land – *Glissez, mortels, n'appuyez pas* – through floating space and grim altitudes and mild pasture country, through cicada country and bare-baked hills, through lanes and orchards, through woods scented by stacks of fresh-sawed logs and through fields one would have liked to cover with a hand; we saw pine-dark rock never touched by sun and blanched terraced slopes, grey stone and tawny stone and honey-coloured walls; we saw barns and chalets, scrubbed village baroque and story-book castles and the elegant lines of residential Louis-Seize, and at the foot of the Simplon we saw sprung an ochre Italianate arch. We saw college towns and watch-making towns and market towns spruce as a new-groomed cat; we saw shrines at cross-roads and villagers on their ways, children toddling with their satchels, and cattle; we saw funerals and pulled in for the yellow motor-post sounding a hunting horn, and we saw barrels carted to the vintage and the changing shapes of the straw-stacks; we saw the water coming down the mountains and saw it run icicle-sharp through the hollowed tree-trunks by the wayside and spout from pretty basins in the squares; we saw lakes open as the sky and we saw the Lake of Thun with its curved Elysian shore rich with fig and vine. And always friendly, always light: our progress abetted, smiled at, waved on. When we were hungry, we ate; when we were tired, we slept; when we were in doubt, we asked. There was always wine, room, a word.

'Can this be twentieth-century travel?' said Martha.

At Sarnen we fell for a manor with chevroned shutters painted white and crimson. '*This* is the place,' said Martha. 'So pretty, so soothing; and think how one would work. Though what about *l'heure bleue*?'

'There's always a retired major with a collection of Monteverdi records,' said I.

'Would he *talk*?' said Martha.

At Sachseln we looked at Brother Klaus, the Hermit Saint of Unterwalden, embalmed in silver armour in the parish church, and wandered about the graveyard among rows of crosses of generations of Zinsalpers and Geishofers. *Hier ruht in Gott* . . . 'It must have been so bad for them,' said Martha.

'Not incest,' said I. 'Feudalism. Same seigneur.'

On the Brünig we talked ourselves up eight thousand feet – 'Do remind me some time that I'm driving,' said Martha – over a road rising gently through soft woods, and when we stopped on mid-pass it was winter. We ate ham, trout, rye bread and apples in a pitch-pine inn with a boiling stove and drank two kinds of white wine and spread our maps and books and spelt out the proverbs on the walls. Then the pass meant business – a stark unending road climbing, turn above looping turn, into an eminence and yet another eminence of sheer stone, stone on top of one, stone at arm's reach, stone rising; a vastness of stone stretching to grey horizons: and there we were, adhering to the bends with a kind of insane precision, swishing about the edges of the world inside a mechanical mouse.

'So good for one,' said Martha. 'You know; for the spirit.'

'I'm not Emily Brontë,' said I.

Martha blew out her nostrils. 'I love the mountains.'

'A nice hill,' said I. 'With two cypresses.'

'This makes art look small.'

'I like it small,' said I. 'And please may this stop.'

It went on. Space expanded; stone rose beyond sea of stone; the serpentine road unwound nine lives. 'I admit it is getting rather uncosy,' said Martha.

'I am quaking.'

'It does make one quake,' said Martha, delighted.

And then we saw the hotel on top. Not a refuge, not a hostel, an hotel-sized hotel. 'God bless their hopeful hearts,' said Martha. 'Whom do you think they had in mind for this pleasure-dome?'

'You and King Lear,' said I.

DOWN IN Brigue the air was mild. Petrol station and lavatory were clean enough but not *sparkling*.

'Not up to standard,' said Martha. 'Cisalpine.' And then we walked under the arcades of a most civilized palazzo.

At Sion we pulled up as they were saying compline in the darkening church, and sat for a while under the vaulting, the vestments gleaming in the fading light, the voices rising from the choir stalls. Orate pro nobis . . . This Romanesque church of Sion is beautiful, and so is the setting of the town in the vineyards and austere hills of the Valais, 'the rainless apricot country between Sion and Sierre'; and the town too has beauty, perhaps magic, but it is also – what? – a shade desolate? transitional? run thin? Crummy, Martha said, but no – strayed rather, of two climates, astride like the Rhône towns above Orange, disturbing with intimations. We drank Fendant de Sion, the live pale green wine of the country and that night I walked alone in the vineyards above the town and the ruined tower under a cloud-chased moon, stumbling and transported, grazed by twig and leaves, holding the grapes, crushing the berries sulphurous sweet into my mouth. And in the morning we slid off, glad to be gone, glad to be moving, into the scrub and polish and simplicity of Swiss Switzerland.

At Bex crouched a castle large and innocent with turrets and chromatic tiles. A small, long-faced, spectacled little boy informed us gravely in sing-song Swiss how to get to the Châ-teau.

'Safe again,' said Martha.

At noon Lake Léman and the Dents du Midi blazed before us.

'*Can* this be Chillon?' said Martha. 'It's become so small.'

At Lausanne we remembered nothing. A town, packed and ungelled: brick-dust, gaps, new buildings. I asked for the Hôtel Gibbon. But the Hôtel Gibbon is no more.

'*Vous avez toujours le Lord Byron près de la gare.*'

'French Swiss isn't the answer either,' said Martha.

But at Yverdon the sun lay on the square like butter; at Morat we saw another manor with striped armorial blinds; and Neuchâtel was all clean provincial handsomeness, long-warmed walls, purring in afternoon calm. We picked up some fruit and washed it in a fountain and sat by another, and ate and talked and strolled and looked into people's windows and wrote postcards.

'What a genius they have,' said Martha, 'for the small change of freedom.'

At Payerne something dropped out of the engine of the car, the man said it would be mended by a quarter to five, and it was.

'Why does it all feel like a balloon outing, when it's really so solid?' said Martha.

'The happy ground crew.'

AND ON the third day, in the morning, we got to Berne.

'I believe in it now,' I said.

And there it was, in the sun; a general market spread through the arcades; and there was the black, gloved Bear and there was the golden Lion, 'Look at his dagger', 'Look at his spurs', and water in all the fountains and flowers in all the windows (may life be like this) and there, rock-crystal green, swirling and seething, straight and wide, was the Aar, dashing itself through the town in an extravagance of foam and speed, and whisked past in it with their laughter the heads of bathing men and boys and women.

'Shall we . . . ? Can we . . . ? Shall we . . . ?'

We have just flung ourselves into the Aar. Four times. Such a glow. First I did not think I'd have the nerve, then did, then again, four times. Now we are laughing all over – sitting on the grass in the sun in wet bathing suits in the people's Free Bath. Chestnuts and lime-trees, clerks and typists in their luncheon hour, soldiers and girls and elderly people, a living *Grande Jatte*, playing draughts, playing ball, reading, eating hard-boiled eggs and sandwiches from the marquee, drinking things through a straw, resting from their glory . . . It is a happy way of bathing, the most exhilarating I know. First one strolls up the tow-path, two hundred yards, three hundred, half a mile – in the middle of the capital, at noon – then comes the long moment of almost blind decision, then the incredible icy suck and churn and stunned immediate action when one must strike at once from the hurling waters of the bank and gain the smooth-flowing sunny centre, then the rapid, breath-snatching downstream whirl in the clear racing water redolent of moss and snow and mountain mirth, flashed past shore, roofs, willows towards an alpine outline, and then it's time – the sluice approaches – to strike hard once more towards the bank and grasp a passing rail . . . one's missed the second, the third is whisking by and here's another: the last . . . feet thrash, knees graze, an arm shoots out – safe.

'Again?'
'Again.'

PORTRAIT SKETCH OF A COUNTRY

Denmark
1962

THEY SAT down at our table, this gentle couple, after a shy smile of inquiry. He wore a stiff dark suit made of good stout cloth, a waistcoat and a clean shirt with a low round collar. There was a wedding-ring on his stout slow well-scrubbed hands. She was a small woman, thin, just not frail, and she wore a white blouse trimmed with embroideries under a jacket of old-fashioned cut. On her hands, which were small and finely shaped, she wore a pair of transparent gloves made of some light lace, and these she did not take off, not even when she came to eat, morsel by morsel on the little fork, the slice of cake brought to her on the pretty china plate. They were country people, country-bred; and they had come to enjoy the wonders of this pleasure garden and the world. They were both utterly brushed and festive, but the most remarkable, the unforgettable thing about them was her face.

His face was placid and honest, the face of an honest fellow, with that look one finds in the North, in any North, on hard-working people of good stock, on peasants, on sailors, and also on labouring and contented beasts. Her face was goodness incarnate. We all have become used to the ease with which we can convey nastiness and horror; their opposites have no such ready currencies. I can only try to put down what in fact I saw. This woman's face, then, shone with pure sheer golden goodness, with gentleness and innocence and patience and a kind of grave alertness; it was an open face, water-clear, and one could watch the movement of the slow good thoughts across it. *She* – stout fellow though he was – was worth ten of him.

You knew that he might well be a bit of a fool over the mortgage, a bit of a brute when in drink or with the ox and plough, but she was there, she was always there to make it right. They scarcely spoke; she did not bustle or fuss or pour out his coffee, she just sat with him but you knew that she was looking after him all the time. They did not, but they sat as if they were holding hands; they sat in still awe, seeing what had charmed their parents and *their* parents and *their* parents for a hundred and twenty years now and what we, too, saw for the first time – the old, tall trees under the night-sky with their summer leaves made emerald young again by caverns and splashes of light, by Chinese lanterns glowing fat like tropical fruit, by luminous dragonflies large as seagulls, by quicksilver shafts of water; they saw the fountains, the pleasure-boats floating upon the artificial lakes, the ducks and live swans; they saw the Pagoda, the pavilions, the toy-soldiers' parade, the high swing of a trapeze; they heard, muffled, shrill, inviting from across water, from beyond trees, the strain of fiddles, the rise of fair-ground voices, the swish, the cracks, the sudden cry, the laughter; the drum-beat, clangs and crashes from booths and roundabouts and Russian railway, the call to the fireworks, the pantomime.

At last our couple rose. In her gloved hand she held the bill for their refreshment. She read it once, they read it twice; her lips formed a figure, his repeated it: their eyes met in wonder. She took out a purse and, incredulous but happy, they arranged a little pile of silver.

WRITERS (of genius) take some traits of their people as they find them and blow them up; the people take in that larger and explicit image of themselves and grow to live up to it. This process may go on for a good long time, through generations, but it does not last for ever. Fewer Spaniards look or act today like Don Quixote, and the Balzacian strain appears to be weakening among the younger French; very little (unselfconscious) Dickens is left in contemporary England. Daisy Miller is seen no more and Babbit himself is far from what he used to be. In the 1960s a good part of the people, the houses, the habits and the look of things in Denmark are still pure Hans Christian Andersen.

Andersen was a man well on in his thirties when the Tivoli Gardens opened in Copenhagen in 1843, twenty acres of trees, lawn and lake in the centre of the now largely modern town. This enclosure is still intact. The illusionist's summer-night world has little changed – the same décors (beautifully repainted), the same props and shapes, the same *Commedia dell'Arte*; serene and unrowdy the crowds mill and partake, the young and old, the simple, the civilized; but let there be no misunderstanding, if there is naïveté in the pleasures offered at Tivoli, there is no artlessness; there is a sound almost fundamentalist kind of showmanship and some uncommon technical skill – the fireworks are superb, the swings fly fast and high, the rifles at the ranges shoot loud and true, the slot-machines spit (and swallow) hard live money and the standard of the variety shows is as good as the best in the Americas and Europe. And as for the pretty little confections of anchovy and leaf and jelly and shrimp on creamy whorl, served in pretty coloured cups and dishes on a dozen flowered terraces by pretty ladies, these are not so much meat and drink as gracious living substantiated, gracious living not out of the magazine but out of the fairy tale.

This delicate and somewhat dreamlike night-life flourishes among a people otherwise solid, stolid salt and earth, a nation essentially of farmers, craftsmen, seamen: but then even the Andersen tales themselves are not all snow and thimbles but robust with such facts of Danish daily life as acres, horse-troughs, straw and winter fuel. It must seem that the good Danes have some particular talent for getting the best out of the basic and the complicated, the old ways and the up-to-date, the land and the machines. And a talent, also, for continuity, that so

disregarded human need, a talent for tempering and human-
izing change. The castle, the church tower, the manor house,
the cottages, barns and yards and fields look as if they had stood
here, been tilled that way, for a hundred and another hundred
years. Beside the porcelain stove, the beams, the inherited tables
and chairs, the sleek herd and the mare nursing her foal, you will
find harvesters, electric ranges, separators, churns, the latest
devices of agricultural and domestic know-how. The people on
these farms are (mildy) prosperous. They read. Fifteen books in
fact, if you go to the statistics, per head for every one book in the
United States, but a great many books less than Finland where
the nights are even longer and the electricity is cheap. They eat
much and well, veal and cream and butter and butter-milk,
fresh and smoked pork, smoked and fresh fish, slabs off great
round dairy cheeses, potatoes, eggs, pickled beets and sound
black bread. The Danes work hard – but not back-breakingly
hard; the work is not ill-rewarded or degrading; it is work of
care, and those who do it belong to the land and the land (or 95 %
of it) belongs to them.

Indeed half the Danes live in or off the country. Half the
Danes means two and a quarter million, they are luckily for
them not overpopulated (yet); of the rest one quarter are compressed in Copenhagen, and the others live in small towns.
Dapper small towns with market-squares and water-fronts and
flowers in the casements, arcades, patrician houses and a Folk
Museum, every one of them prettier than the other and not
two of them quite alike. Of course the country itself is a small
country, how small one only realizes on learning that it is in fact
the size of half of Scotland; a Scotland, at that, fragmented into
one chunk of peninsula (Jutland), one fair-sized and two smaller
islands, and some five hundred tiny islands, one hundred of
them inhabited. From any point of Denmark no one is ever out
of easy reach of the sea: a beach, a jetty, a ferry or a sailing-
boat. And these thousand coast-lines, these bays, these rings of
sea, are complemented by inner circles of still water, marshy
lakes flat-set into the land, and village ponds under the willow-
trees, round as a hole, round as the cartwheel that props the

stork's nest on the thatched roof-top.

The weather changes with the sea-winds and the winds change twice a day. The overall climate is cool, grey, blustery, rain-sprayed, a climate that may just do for winter, autumn, spring, but cannot quite make summer, at least not every year. The Danes, with their worship of the sun and their joy in out-door pleasures, do not have the climate they deserve. Yet who knows, if they had been reared in some tropical latitude, by some warmer shore, they might perhaps not have attained that very deservingness. And when it *is* fine in Denmark, when for an evening or some morning hours the sky is clear with that light Nordic blue, a-sail with cumulus clouds white as a ship, as swift as down, the fineness has a gossamer quality, an essence of calm and rareness. It is the weather of childhood, some ideal child-hood fixed in an Impressionist vision of spade and bucket on beach and the long grass of the dunes.

The Danish countryside, too, exercises a soothing charm. Tilled to the nines, not quite flat, uncluttered – there is always a long view to the horizon – green, flaxen and red with pasture, ripe barley, cornflower, sunflower and poppy, the scene of centuries of man and nature going hand in hand, it fills the eye and mind with measured calm and peace.

To get about, on wheels, afloat, on foot, is unfrustrating, easy. The ferry steamers and the fast clean electric trains run like clockwork and running ply the willing travellers with food, *snaps* and beer. Stationary sustenance is provided on *terra firma* by country inns which go by the engaging name of *Kro*. The roads and side-roads are good and, apart from the six-lane Copenhagen–Esbjerg highway which crosses the country (and the seas), innocent of traffic. Copenhagen is another matter. There, the traffic is not only dense but (Denmark is not without its psychological riddles) ruthlessly fast, as fast as the most headlong Italian driving though without the Italian dash and driving skill. This death-race is intricately regimented by a spider's network of white lines and guiding lights quite sensibly worked out, provided you live long enough to learn the ropes.

The learning must be voluntary, there are very little traffic

police about, or indeed any visible police at all. In three weeks of
Copenhagen we never saw a policeman on patrol by either day
or night, and as capitals go Copenhagen is well on the noctam-
bulistic side. Anyone who so wishes may drink in a public place
all night; sensibly and tolerantly the government does not inter-
fere, when one bar or café has to close there will be another about
to open, quite legally, down the block. Likewise it is always
possible in Copenhagen to find some place to eat hot food round
the clock, respectably and at the normal price. Incidentally it is
Sweden that has all these restrictions on the buying and consumption of drink, it is Sweden that has the alcohol problem. And
Denmark is *not* the Scandinavian country with that high suicide
rate. Denmark is a part of Scandinavia; so is Canada a part of
America. Danes, Swedes and Finns and Norwegians are
Scandinavians in the way that Americans and English are
Anglo-Saxons, and Brazilians and Bolivians are South Americans. Denmark once owned Norway and ruled Sweden. Norwegians up to a hundred years ago spoke Danish. Now
Denmark and Norway and Sweden are neighbours and good
neighbours. They share some of their outlook and their policies.
There are affinities. Looked at from the outside, and even from
the inside, they have a good deal in common, and a good deal
that they have not. Readers may recall Miss Katherine Ann
Porter's Swede, Arne Hansen, in *Ship of Fools*. Herr Hansen,
admittedly a knotty character, flies off the handle when persons
he is introduced to take him for a Dane and when corrected wave
aside the difference. Swedes are not Danes, and Danes are not
Swedes and not Norwegians, and they would have you know it.

ONE OF the unique things about Denmark, and one that it is
not easy to convey, is that this rural, this bourgeois, this deeply
democratic country without class handicaps, without great
fortunes, without poor, this solid welfare state where a social-
democratic party has been in office with few interruptions for
about forty years, does not only possess an aristocracy and live
with it harmoniously, but has itself in many ways an aristo-

cratic air. Look at the architecture. The very cottages have line and grace, and those small-scale seventeenth- and eighteenth-century manor houses (inhabited) that are everywhere have an elegance, a fantasy, a style to them, that takes one's breath away: they are ravishing. They are also unexpected – dazzling white picked out with slate-grey, they are entirely unlike anything one could meet elsewhere in those temperate parts, in Holland, Austria or Germany; if there is any reminiscent link it is oddly enough with the domestic baroque of Northern Portugal, those delicious nunneries and *quintas* of the Beira and the Minho. Perhaps not so oddly, the Portuguese like the Danes were once a sea-faring, predatory and adventurous nation – and how far, how far apart! have they travelled since.

Architecturally Denmark also has its ample quota, lovingly preserved, of the more conventional sterner stuff – craggy dragon castles and vast ornate renaissance boxes spectacularly sited on sea-board or park-land, the homes nowadays often of schools or the old. And then original again, another unique delight, pink-washed mediaeval village churches, Aslev, Højerup, Morgenstrup – one could almost invent the names – painted inside and exquisite in form.

Architecture without pain, art looked at in undiluted pleasure, enjoyment without anxiety, compunction, heart-ache: there is no beggar-woman in the church door, no ragged child or sore animal in the square. The water is safe and the wallet inside the pocket. There will be no missed plane connection. We are in a country where the curable ills are taken care of. We are in a country where the mechanics of living from transport to domestic heating (alack poor Britain!) function imaginatively and well, where it goes without saying that the sick are looked after and secure and the young well educated and well trained, where ingenuity is used to heal delinquents and to mitigate at least the physical dependence of old age, where there is work for all and some individual leisure, and men and women have not been entirely alienated yet from their natural environment, where there is care for freedom and where the country as a whole has renounced the drive to power and prestige beyond its borders and where the will to peace is not eroded by doctrine, national self-love and unmanageable fears: where people are kindly, honest, helpful, sane, reliable, resourceful and cool-headed, where stranger – shyly – smiles to stranger.

Tak is the word for thank you and the Danes thank one another all the time, when they hand or accept an object, when they put fork to food, when they rise from table, when someone has said thank you – *tak*, *tak tak*, *mange tak*, *tak for mad*, *tak tak*. And caught in that virtuous circle the foreign visitor, too, soon goes about clacking like an amiable turkey-cock.

WAR AND the threat of war begin when all is not well at home. Countries that solve their own problems are no problem to others. How did it all come about, how did the Danes get that way? Why are they what they are? Was the country particularly favoured? Did they try to keep the peace in the past? Did they practise religious tolerance? The answers are no. Is it then all hit or miss? A people holding a territory poor rather than rich, with a history as long, mixed and disturbed as the next country's – are these the facts that must be fed into the computer, and what might the computer's answer be? Portugal? Switzerland? Prussia?

The most cursory catalogue of Danish antecedents bristles with the violence, confusion and vicissitudes commonplace in European histories. The computer would have been told about Viking terrorist raids (the Vikings of course being the fore-fathers of the Danes), successful invasion of England, the line of rough-hewn kings: Haarik; Harold Blueteeth, who forced his subjects into Christianity and subjugated Norway; Gorm the Old, who had a slogan for his conquests: 'Denmark's Repair'; Sven Forkbeard. Been told about expansion in the twelfth century; dynastic disputes; absolute monarchy; a chain of regicides; invasion of Germany; nobles' risings; conquests and re-conquests culminating in Valdemar the Great and Danish Ascendancy, hegemony in the Baltic, rule over the whole of Scandinavia, Estonia, Holstein, Greenland, Iceland. Strife;

decline; division; Reformation and religious wars; the Blood-bath of Stockholm; the Counts' War; participation, inevitable and debilitating, in the Thirty Years' War. And so it went. By the end of the eighteenth century there was a wind of change, relief from oppressive taxation, improvements in justice, some liberty of the press. By the nineteenth, Denmark's troubles came thick and fast: in 1801 a British fleet (Nelson) bombarded Copenhagen, a few years later the Danish fleet itself was destroyed; Norway and Sweden gone; a rough deal at the Congress of Vienna. Fifty years later, American and Australian influx of cheap wheat was pricing Danish grain out of the European markets, and Bismarck embarked on the first of his planned wars, and won. The Prussians – so much stronger – took Holstein, South Schleswig and a hunge chunk of Danish Denmark, North Schleswig. It was a devastating defeat. Denmark was left nothing but itself: a country the size of less than (at that point) half of Scotland, a country with no metals, no iron, copper, tin, no oil, no coal; no colonies, no overseas possessions (except for the Virgin Islands which only went to the USA in 1916). A devastating, a traumatic defeat, and the Danes might well have fallen into a Treaty of Versailles mentality. Mysteriously, they did not. Instead they re-directed their aims and will; they did turn inward. They changed their agriculture from grain to dairy products, they set up co-operatives, gave their attention to social and economic advance, chose a neutral policy, developed an altogether new kind of adult schooling. It was a chain-reaction, but the links gradually forged themselves into a virtuous circuit. It has turned out well.

Why – we are back again at our original question – were the *Danes* able to use a particular chance, one they could then hardly have seen as such, in a beneficient way? Did national character determine their choice, or did the choice stabilize that character? Perhaps, for want of a better answer, all one can say is that Denmark at one point entered a phase of historical luck. *Tak.* Long may it last.

NOTES ON A JOURNEY
IN PORTUGAL

1958

PORTUGAL BEGINS AT Portugal. For days we had been progressing across the immense and empty landscapes of Castile and Leon under a driving rain, quaking and shivering inside a small slow motor car, a couple of pygmies creeping over the face of the earth. Under that planing sky, the land stretches, treeless, unconcerned, to the far and low horizon; now and then throws up a cluster of flat clay huts. At the Spanish frontier post – adobe to adobe – there was no one on duty; I had to go back some way, still in the rain, to find two soldiers, thin as crows under their black lacquered hats, to stamp our exit; three hundred yards further along, the Portuguese customs sat squat and mute in a trim white house, sparkling rings on their fingers.

Stares, but no questions; slow, blank scanning, a foretaste of the general Portuguese reluctance to terminate a transaction, to let go of any piece of paper-work; then a flickered half-smile, the lifting of a barrier brightly painted like a lozenge at a fair, and we were in a river valley shining with new leaves – there was magnolia and oleander, fig and eucalyptus, water chestnut and spring maize, hay-stacks pressed like sugar-cones hung from the boughs and along the roadside the young birch trees were garlanded with vines. Lyre-horned oxen, under painted yokes, advanced hoof before slow hoof; women moved by with forests on their heads. Against the cork oaks leaned shepherds stiff in rain-coats made of straw. Rococo shrines, white picked out in grey, stood upon the hillsides, water gushed from tritons' shells and at the end of many a flowering orchard there could be had a glimpse of the pediment of a small manor house. It was Cimarosa, the *Sette-Cento*, a setting to some bucolic masque – we had entered one of the most innocently beautiful regions of this earth, we had entered into an Arcadian dream.

It never fails this first sense of pleasure, light as feathers, of the land entry into Portugal. Whether one comes into the Minho through Galicia or into the Tras-os-Montes from Leon, whether one arrives in the East by the Salamanca road or from Spanish Estremadura in the Alentejo, there is always that entire and abrupt – and never wholly explicable – passage from the harsh sublimity of Spain to the slow-moving lyrical beauty of the well-ordered, handmade, water-freshened countrysides of Lusitania. And there is also of course the arrival by sea, the first look at Lisbon from across the Tagus. One cannot go wrong with one's first step.

Ten minutes later we were in Chaves. Even the rain had stopped; the sky was gentle blue. (By sheer chance; it rains, alas, a great deal more in Northern Portugal than in those plains of Spain.) All Portuguese towns are pretty; some are very pretty; a few are exquisite. Chaves is charming and dotty and unexpected. The houses, all the houses, are painted green or pink or blue or tiled, with delicate balconies and of some faintly outlandish eighteenth-century shape. The corners of the roofs turn up in a pagoda tilt. There are arcades. Everything stands sparkling clean in the light sun. The chief trade appears to be the sale of very large poly-chromatic trunks. The whole effect is that of a pastiche whiff of the Far East with something of the spruceness and well-being of a small town in Switzerland.

On the Spanish side it had been too early for luncheon; here it was too late. In actual time it was now a little after two o'clock. Everything was *fixado*, shut, closed down, fixed – a most favoured word. The gaiety and lightness seem to be confined to nature and to stone and stucco, it is not reflected in the people's clothes or faces. Male peasants wear inky tatters, the men in cafés wear inky business suits; the women are beasts of burden in field and street, and otherwise not seen. We retired into the car to think. Instantly we were surrounded. Portuguese stares are blank and black, immoveable like flies on butcher's meat. You turn, you whisk, you say something: they are still in front of you. The disturbing thing is that there is no curiosity. The faces do not see. No flicker of interest or communication animates them. Speech effects no break-through. Ham, the good smoked mountain ham of the region, is *presunto* (prshoont), bread is *pão* (pong). The general recipe for pronunciation is to forget everything one has ever heard or learnt of Spanish and Italian, to lop off final vowels and as many others as laziness suggests, drawl out the remaining ones, change any consonant into one easier to say, replace all s's with a double shsh, aim at a nasal twang (a blend of Cockney with Meridional French will do), sing the whole like Welsh, explode it to sound like Polish, and do not forget a hint of Dutch. Begin with the name of the capital: *Leeshsh-bowah*. The trouble is that the Portuguese will not even try to listen to your efforts; they don't believe a foreigner capable of managing a single sentence. And there they are right of course. They themselves – outside the Lisbon–Cintra–Estoril circuit and the big hotels – firmly speak Portuguese and Portuguese alone.

A DAWDLING afternoon drive got us to Vila Real. Vila Real has two streets that end by their (baroque) façades joining in an arrow-head – a startling architectural turn, dexterous and graceful, one finds again in two or three other places. Here we were at a crossroads. A choice had to be made. One could be at Oporto before nightfall – on the threshold of the port wine country, one need only go up the Douro . . . from there perhaps try getting up into the high wild parts, the serras of the Tras-os-Montes, to Mirandela, to Vinhais, perhaps reach for far Bragança . . . There is so much to see, so many places

– names – one is drawn to, and what one sees is so fresh, so different, so ravishing, that one wants to linger and enjoy. We did not want to leave the fertile North, the Elysian pastures, the land of light and fanciful, white-trimmed domestic baroque. For days we went about in circles.

We went to Vila Mateus, the most fantastic of eighteenth-century country houses, the like of which could only be seen in Portugal, and in Portugal only once; we went over the Serra do Marão and came down from the heights and out of the pine-woods and had luncheon in the sun at Amarante by the river looking at the tiled cupolas and the bridge with the obelisks; we crossed the Tamego and here, in the province of the Minho, the Arcadian dream thickens, the vines grow higher upon the trees, oranges are ripe, melon and roses flower beside the gentle corn-fields, slow the wheel turns by the well – so idyllic is the country-side that, in the words of Sacheverell Sitwell, 'the action of passing through it induces a mood akin to that of being in a trance'. We went through Guimaraes and saw the coloured palaces and streets; we came to Braga with the twenty churches and saw the golden organs, and slept in moon-lit quiet and cool – in an excellent hotel – in the sacred garden at the top of another architectural extravagance, the ornamental staircase, pilgrim shrines and fountains of Bom Jesus.

Vila Verde, Ponte da Barca, Ponte de Lima, charmingly spread along a riverside, Barcelos, Valença, Viana do Castelo – quintas and convents, façades bats-winged and sea-scrolled, manoelino doorways, azulejos, painted ceilings, barley-sugar columns, formal gardens, markets in the squares, octagonal chapels no bigger than a sentry box and crumbling monasteries vast as railway stations, flowers in the ruins and statues in the fields . . .

Everywhere the wine is pleasant and very cheap. I have a fondness for the *vinhos verdes*, the slightly (naturally) fizzy wines of the Minho: the white which is very dry (*too* acid, sometimes) for apéritif; the red, which is reminiscent of some young undoctored Tuscans, with simple food. I recommend, too the red wines of Colares and of Dão (Dong) and a crystalline pink wine made at Vila Mateus. If one is looking for vintage port one will be disappointed; what is sold in restaurants and shops is sound enough commercial stuff. Great port is drunk chiefly at the English shippers' and growers' tables, where the hospitality to travelling strangers is Dickensian, Oriental, something no longer met with elsewhere in these diminished days. Food is agreeable, plentiful, fresh and unaspiring. This goes for the country in general; at Lisbon and Oporto restaurants the standard is either lower or higher. Olive oil and fish are always excellent, and the bread is often. Beware of large round loaves that look like dark country-bread: that is *brua*, maize bread and as heavy as wet cement. Butcher's shops are best left unvisited by what the French screen warnings call *Les personnes sensibles*.

AFTER A stay in satrap comfort at a port-wine quinta and some lonely days in the extreme wilds of the Tras-os-Montes, we found ourselves once more at Vila Real from where we started weeks ago, on our way at last to the more known regions, to the lions of the traveller's Portugal. Two-thirds of the country lay still in front of us – the towns of Guarda, three thousand feet in the air; Lamego with its peaches and baroque; the double staircase, chess-board statuary and nine landings of Nos Senhora dos Remédios fantastically covering a whole hillside; Viseu incomparably elegant; Oporto; Coimbra with its under-graduates in black tail-coats at noon and the magnificent library; Obidos, alas much man-handled and restored; Evora classical within mediaeval walls shimmering in the heat of the Alentejo; Estremoz and Elvas, the white towns of Estremadura, brilliant with Arab domes; the unique abbeys: Alcobaça, a Cistercian shell; the lovely manoelino fantasies of Batalha and the stupendous Convent of Christ at Tomar; São Jéronimos at Lisbon, the Tagus, the Alfama quarter, Black Horse Square, the golden coaches and the tower of Bélem; the dank woods and hermitages of Cintra so dear to our forbears; the gardens and pink palace of Queluz, a Lusitanian Trianon; the sea – never far! – the white fishing ports with their curious craft, their glaring cubic huts and smells of tunny and sardine: Nazaré (self-conscious now and tourist proud); Setúbal; Sesimbra; Olhão in the Algarve . . .

MAIN ROADS are not bad and, except for some busloads of pilgrims, unencumbered. Side-roads can be frightful. Native driving is individual; like Edwardian chickens, the species has not yet bred the survival qualities required by a motorized society. Good hotels are very good; not so good ones, tolerable; the rest are either what are called *dormidas* (mixed dormitories and no drains) and quite unbelievable, or do not exist. The *pousadas*, the Government inns, often set on a cliff or a hair-pin bend at the dizzy edge of some panoramic wilderness, are near perfection of comfort, quiet and general pleasantness. They are exquisitely clean and not at all expensive . One can eat and drink and take one's time in Portugal without having to think much about money. Bills are honest, easy to read and without those vexing taxes and surcharges that one finds so often in Italy and always in Spain. Hotel room prices are posted on the bedroom doors, and stuck to. Bargaining, even if one could attain to it, is blessedly unnecessary, although that is not what one's Anglo-Portuguese friends will tell one. According to them, their beautifully arranged domestic lives – five servants is a modest minimum – are spent in a perpetual robbers' den, a view that seems to be shared by the Portuguese well-to-do judging from the way in which they keep themselves and their goods under lock and key – at nightfall the countryside resounds with the bolting of shutters and the barring of gates. One may assume that they are spoilt and no longer aware of the contemporary world and its ways. During a long stay – complete with house-keeping, servant coping (*one* servant), car repairs – we found the Portuguese people, who work very hard and very long for abominably little, touchingly honest. The modern Portuguese are in fact a mystery. Travellers have complained about them bitterly for centuries – ruffians, robbers, brawlers, filthy, lazy. Now they are browsing, placid, kindly, patient, slow. Laundry is being washed morning, noon and night; a second-class hotel or a Lisbon boarding house is ten times cleaner than its equivalent in France or England. There is no quarrelling in the streets, hardly any crimes of violence in towns or country. Bull-fights take place in an atmosphere of a garden fête that takes rather long to get going and nobody is ever killed or hurt. Aside from the inveterate staring they are kind to strangers and take endless trouble. If you ask in a shop for something that isn't there, half the staff and all the customers will walk out with you and down the street to find you what you want. This does not succeed because when a Portuguese accompanies a foreigner he automatically becomes a foreigner too in the ears of his compatriots, and they can no longer hear him.

Foreigner: 'Tmat'sh?'
Portuguese shop-keeper: 'Euhhh – ?'
Portuguese accompanying foreigner: 'Tmat'sh?'
Poutuguese shop-keeper: 'Euhhh – ?'
Second Portuguese accompanying foreigner: 'Tmat'sh?'
Portuguese shop-keeper: 'Euhhh – ?'
Portuguese child accompanying foreigner seizes some tomatoes from a basket.

After this they all flock out again and into the next shop to find · another item. Painstaking, patient, kind, placid, slow. Above all, very, very, very slow.

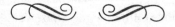

A JOURNEY IN
YUGOSLAVIA

1965

FIRST HOURS

NEW GROUND, these days, is rare. On this clear May morning we have left Trieste, that sparkling, opulent, friendly, noisy Western port; the glittering sea-road winds steeply towards the Yugoslavian border. I am driving slowly: pleasure, curiosity, are tinged with apprehension – I am about to cross into a Socialist Federal Republic, into what must be, however mitigatedly or loosely, a curtained country. A string of Italian cars warily pull up behind me and I feel obliged to put on speed. Travellers' tales about the roads had made me decide to keep my own car at home and to rely instead on a huskier, and expendable, hired one. When the rented Fiat was delivered in Florence I had been disconcerted to find that it was snowy white, like the proverbial sacrificial lamb, and appearing to be, though fast and willing enough, a rather nervous creature. As we set out on the Via de' Tornabuoni intent on getting on the right bridge for the autostrada, I became aware that other cars were keeping a quite unusual distance. Not one tried to cut us at corners, not one raced us to the traffic-lights; we were given precedence at every turn. This puzzling circumspection, so contrary to the nature of Italian motorists, continued on the open road. If I waved one on, he would hang back. We stopped to get some lunch at a gas station – broiled chopped steak, spring vegetables, iced pink wine, chilled apricots, black espresso coffee –

one of those new mass roadside eateries which the genius of the country (it *is* no less than that) had endowed through the sheer cleanliness of the surroundings and the brilliant freshness of the food with a character of exquisite luxury. It was here that I gave another sharp look at the alien Fiat; so did an attendant. 'You *are*,' he said, 'from Naples?' And before I could say oh-dear-me-no, I tumbled to the mark of Cain or talisman which had bewitched our journey. It was the letters NA on the registration plates. NA for Napoli. For some good reason of their own no doubt, the firm of car-lenders had seen fit to provide their hireling with this dashing identity. Neapolitans on the road are dreaded for their skilled fiendishness and nerve; theirs, in a land of pretty nippy drivers, is a reputation for lawless dare-devilry. So here with the NA large and clear for all to see was a Neapolitan car, manned what's more by that improbability – legend also has Neapolitan wives and daughters harem-bound at home – that superlative of terrors, a Neapolitan woman driver. Handsome is who handsome does. Reckless is who reckless seems. Inevitably, I tried to live up, at moments, to my suggested second driving nature.

And now we have passed Fernetti, the Italian frontier post, a wave-on – as has now become the good European custom – rather than a full stop. *Buon giorno, buon viaggio*. A few hundred yards of no-man's-land. Another barrier, new flags: a sweep of stripes, blue/white/red and the Red Star large in the centre. Fernetti has become Fernetič. We stop. I switch off the engine. I repeat to myself the words of the official hand-out (*all* hand-outs in a state-controlled economy are official; the government as it were underwrites the ads), 'The customs procedure for foreign travellers when entering or leaving Yugoslavia has been reduced to a minimum.' I step out, a light fixed smile upon my face. An official approaches. Our passports are looked at, seriously. (Car papers, not at all. Liability insurance, rather alarmingly, is not compulsory.)

'What have you to declare?'

I open the boot. The man peers, but does not touch; he seems reluctant to take an initiative, reluctant to let go. He is not surly, he is not friendly, he is hesitant and intent. Intent not to slip up. And at once I am on familiar ground. This might be Portugal, Central America . . . It might indeed be the vanished Habsburg Empire on whose physical ground we are standing. It is a sad perennial pattern: the more overweening, the more unchecked the top, the more rigid and at sea the lower echelons, the under-educated, underpaid, under*trusted* functionaries of the sacro-sanct bureaucracy. These anxious, stubborn men are held to cleave to the letter, and the letter here is transparently double-faced. Smooth passage for the tourists; inflexibility about sections 214 to 315b. I decide to help and declare my typewriter. At once there is grist to the mill. I am told to enter an office; here other men of the same stamp – stamped by the same condi-tions – are at their task. Forms are made out.

'Number of the machine?'

'I don't know that it has one,' I answer and am aware that this is not the right tone. The men do not insist. Their task is extra-personal; they have not been encouraged to show either arrogance or servility (which might perhaps have come more natural to them for something of the Habsburg administration must still be in their bones). I sign. My passport is endorsed. There is no duty to pay. The sole object of the exercise is to keep me from selling the wretched instrument during my stay in the country or from giving it away. If I should lose it (unlikely) or it gets stolen (unlikely too, one hopes) I might find myself in hot water. Presently it's all over; I am back in the car. The barrier is raised. It has not taken long after all. The hand-out's first promise was honoured. Our journey has begun: we are off. We are in. We are free.

The road is wooded, less wide; motor traffic has dwindled and there is a peaceful trail of horse-drawn carts. The names on mile-stones and posts read Škocjan, Tržič, Kranj, Vrhnika, though the alphabet up here in the North has not changed. The leaves on the trees are the same early summer green and in the dis-tant blue we still see the delicate outlines of the Julian Alps. Deliberately, we dawdle. At the cross-roads a beflagged booth proclaims itself a MJENJAČNICA – WECHSELSTUBE –

CAMBIO – BUREAU DE CHANGE. I return from this money-changer's with my note-case stuffed with dirty dinar notes.

'How pleasant it is to have money, heigh-ho!'

It is noon by now and the day is perfect. Our aim is Ljubljana: a town of a hundred and fifty thousand, the capital of the state of Slovenia. In a new country I find it not a bad plan to begin in a place of middle size and save the coasts and the great sights, time willing, for later. But now it is too early and too fine and the town is already near. We decide to outflank it, to turn North, to follow the valley of the Sava and drive towards those mountains. The result is some hours of blissful drifting through a pre-alpine landscape. And before sunset we reach a lake. It is Bled, ringed by massed Alps light as cloud, light as blancmange, though close now, snow-topped, slate-blue and white: below a still dark water cradled in the setting of a Central-European children's tale. Tall dark trees descend to the shore, the craggy castle perches on the back-drop cliff, there is a tufted island, jumping fish, small row-boats jog their moorings. Happily we walk along the lake-front, spinning flat pebbles upon the glass-green surface.

LJUBLJANA

AT DUSK the outskirts are packed with trudging people, pedal bicycles, cars; the buildings are a-flutter with long banners, the national colours, the state colours, the red party flag. Workers trekking home? a general holiday? Ignorance makes stupid. At last we draw up on Tito Avenue near the hotel. These, we had learnt, are government-graded from A to D; there are at present about thirty A hotels in the country, and Ljubljana has two of them. We chose the older one, the *Slon*, the Hotel Elephant. Once more best smile forward I enter the lobby, which is packed, and make my way to the reception desk. A friendly young man assures me in good English that a room – with bath – is to be had. We have to hand in our passports before a key is surrendered, though mercifully are not required to do any paperwork ourselves. When I mention luggage, the young man says that just now he is overwhelmed (which is visibly true) but will try to give us a hand when he can. We start to cope on our own and the hard part of it is not the weight of suitcases but the density of people through which they have to be wedged. Unavoidably we brush against other belongings, bump into sides and legs. Nobody pays attention: they do not appear to see or feel. Presently our receptionist, assistant manager, hall porter turns up to help, and the emphasis *is* on help, on helping out, not service. The institution of the bell-hop appears to be unknown.

At last we are in; alone in that traveller's daily goal, the hotel bedroom. The door is shut. I turn taps, switch lights, open wardrobes – everything is reasonably clean, functions reasonably well (one cold tap trickles, one sheet is mended), there is decent if slightly shabby comfort. In most Western countries the hotel would pass muster as good B minus.

Almost at once I go out again into the streets, intent on immersing myself in the stream of evening life. The shops are about to close but food can still be bought and drink, and the coffee-houses are alight and the book-stands. It *is* a national holiday, a day celebrating liberation, but it was also a working day: there are lava tides of people both receding homewards and seeping in, sluggish and determined, a dark compact mass oozing over the pavements, stagnating at corners, filling up the squares. Their overall aspect is one of sallowness, burdens and poor clothes – raincoats and exiguous suits in muddy colours, mustard, gritty grey, off-brown. It is the all-pervading drabness of one's image of the streets of Moscow, and it is this congelation of people – to be encountered over and over again – that blots out all other first impressions. It is not a crowd as we know it, a crowd of occasions, New Year's Eve, Trafalgar Square, a crowd in elation or panic, it is the incidental crowd of a permanent rush-hour – too many people in too little space – cohesive only in a material sense, composed of particles obtuse to one another, struggling towards single ends. Immersed in it, I experience a sensation of hopelesness.

DINNER AT THE hotel restaurant: a cosy Germanic cellar, soon rent, alas, by loud thumpy music. Piano and one violin, live. No hat is taken round; the musicians, like the cook, are state-employed. One of the waiters speaks some German, another a little Italian; neither is enough to interpret the dishes. Never mind. I had taken care to provide myself with some thirty words of Serbo-Croat (Srpskohrvatski), things like Good morning and Please and How much and Thank you. I had also rooted out and put to memory a pocket-size gastronomic vocabulary, the names for meat, shell-fish, vegetables, how to say iced, hot, grilled, boiled. It is no great feat, and yet those Slav nouns, however cavalierly you leave out the inflections, are not house-hold words. *Maslac* does not trundle off the tongue as easily as *burro* does for butter, nor *odrezak govede* as glibly as *bifteck* for beefsteak. Now, hunting through a complete menu I was getting baffled, practice as so often making a hash out of theory; with a busy waiter at my elbow and the cutlery quivering with a gipsy waltz, I could not quite identify a single word. At length the sauce-stained polyglot menu was produced. I have never found these to be very accurate or literate, but here some bold if unspeculative mind had solved the problem of translating (into five languages) with neat consistency. Krumpira Soup–Soope de Krumpira–Zuppa di Krumpira–Krumpir Suppe this accomplished document began and went on to tempt the customer with Cutlets Serbian Style, à la Serbe, alla Serba, nach Serbischer, Art, Bosnia Style, Slovenia Style, Istria Style and so on with blithe economy down the list. Knowing I had lost that round, I ordered one Bosnian and one Dalmatian style. What came – after a goodish wait – were large platefuls of meat and very little else, one of them undoubtedly pork, the other a miscellany under pepper and tomato sauce. Quietly we swallowed the lot: we shall never know which had been which.

(Only days later, having left Slovenia, did I realize that Federated Yugoslavia is in fact still multi-lingual. The dice on that first evening had been loaded against me: in the manner of someone trying Italian in a Mexican restaurant, I had been pitting rudimentary Serbo-Croat against good Slovenian.)

Later on at night the crowd on the pavements has thinned, though it is still a crowd, and the cafés are jammed. There are young people about – this is a university town – girls on their own in groups or pairs, looking purposeful and animated. The boys sport jeans (large KO-BOJS stitched across back-pockets) and have fine sulky eyes; they look virile and glum, handsome in a lean dark way. The middle-aged look less Slav and more Central European, soft-hipped men and square-built women, with here and there a painfully worn, thin one; and the few old people in that crowd look a different breed again. They are peasants of another age, groping along the pavements, strangers strayed into the city on some errand.

Our night walk leads to the river. We stand on a bridge. Here there is peace, old houses reflected in still water and the glamour night bestows even on quite modest architecture.

MORNING CONFIRMS that Ljubljana is a pretty town at heart. That corner where the river curves *is* charming; there are some passable baroque buildings, an exuberant fountain with an obelisk, a few pink- or apricot-washed façades. There is also the castle, a Franciscan church, a subtropical garden and an opera house – much in use – left from the Habsburg days. Add to these, flower-boxes in windows and a view of Alps – Ljubljana may well appeal to those who are fond of Austria, except that those might prefer to take their Austria neat. Pretty at heart; but the heart of the capital of Slovenia is a shrunken core in a shoddy contemporary spread. It is what is left of an old town on a strategic cross-roads that has undergone its share of history. What Augustus founded, Attila razed. After Romans and Barbarians, Slavs, Austrians, Napoleonic armies and Austrians back again. Each pulled down, each built. 1919 brought national independence, 1941 Nazi Germany; 1945 independence once more, this time with a communist regime. And under those auspices the 1950s and 60s brought the Modern Age in its most graceless form.

Only the Turks, who for so long occupied the other parts of present Yugoslavia, never took Slovenia. It does not bear the scars of what are called the Turkish Centuries. Hence today the consciously emancipated, the Occidental air of Ljubljana where the women study mathematics and girls are allowed out alone at night in public places.

EN ROUTE

WE HAVE left behind the mountain valleys of Slovenia and are progressing through a wide rich plain. Young wheat, tobacco, corn; fruit-trees. We are bound for Zagreb on the Sava (on the principle that one ought to spend a few days in at least one of the big cities). Zagreb is the second largest, only some hundred thousand below Belgrade, and reported to be the show-window of the Republic, abundantly stocked with consumer goods and *Kultur*. The road is the central highway that runs southward through the country from Austria to Greece. The 85 miles between Ljubljana and Zagreb are officially classed as a motorway. In fact, it is a wide road, barred to animal-drawn vehicles, accommodating, but not divided into, four lanes and without separation from oncoming traffic. The surface, for miles on end, is excellent. A pretty fair effort one might say for a country whose technical and financial resources are not exactly unlimited. If it were not for the pot-holes. These appear at irregular intervals deep and sudden on this declaredly fast road. Sometimes there is a warning sign, as often there is not. You can feel in your spine what would happen if the car slammed into a hole at seventy-five an hour; what one does is to skirt the hole by a wild last-second swerve, praying that the devil will not get the hindmost.

Fortunately, the traffic is on the thin side. The proportion of foreign tourists' cars is very high. Cars run by Yugoslavs are either very large or very small, polished Mercedes – often bearing the red number plate denoting a high official – or tin cans.

We have made two stops. I must mention them because they pointed up what I would learn to recognize as the two main themes that confront the traveller in Yugoslavia, themes that run parallel at times and often intertwine – the country's great natural and architectural inheritance and its present way of life. The first stop was at the snack bar at a filling station. We picked our way through a barrage of trucks and light motor-cycles. Inside it was packed with men. The air was hot and smelt of cigarette smoke, stale clothes, spilt beer and sour milk. The floor was thick with stubs, food parings and other waste products; the counters were wet and cluttered with smudged glasses and used plates. Behind them a man and youth in stained overalls valiantly strove to cope. They were not speeded on by their equipment. Soft cheese had to be balanced on a pair of copper scales against a set of fiddly little weights; the thumb that had handled the dinar notes was pressed into the spam-type sausage while the other hand was busy with the slicing knife. The customers ate and drank. What mattered – one felt – was their being able to earn enough to do just that.

The other stop was off the road on the green banks of the river Krka. There was an idyllic little island tethered by a wooden bridge, and on the island an old manor house in a shady scented garden, turned into an hotel. Roses were in flower, there was quietness; waterfowl swam past. It was, in fact, enchanting – as restful and pretty an half hour as anyone would like to remember on his travels. By the roadside there were waiting some official and some foreign cars.

ZAGREB

THE CENTRE of this city which was once under the Hungarian wing of the Dual Monarchy is all vast squares, wide avenues of heavy gray buildings lined with dusty trees, and rectangular public parks filled with troops of shirted youths being led off to some meeting or excursion; something of the Balkan climate, of harsh winters and steaming summer rains appears to have seeped into the paving stones. The Palace Hotel is a, not very cheerful, relic – plush and gilt need keeping up – of pre-1914 splendours. The main staircase seems to have been narrowed though there are still palms on the landings; the rooms are still high-ceilinged, the beds vast, the tubs deep, but the tasseled cord no longer pulls the faded curtains, the casings of quilt and pillow are coarse and patched, and in the bath there is a smell of drains. (Let me add that there is an alternative grade-A hotel in Zagreb, a brand-new leviathan by the railway station with car park, air-conditioned cells and Western service.) From the bill-board in our lobby one can see that there is plenty going on. A soirée of folk dancing, a symphony concert, a repertory opera programme, an exhibition of contemporary sculpture and the play tomorrow is going to be *Who Is Afraid Of Virginij Vulf?*

At the post office (the hotel porter, not untypically these days, knows the postage required for a letter to the U.S.A. but not to England, and at any rate his stock seems to have run out of stamps of any useful denomination) there are long queues in front of every window. I spend a salutary twenty minutes standing in one of them. Salutary, because it seldom comes amiss to experience at first hand how the other half lives. The post-mistresses look learned and are certainly efficient and quick. The snail's-pace is caused by the quantity of their clients, who for the most part do not look as if they corresponded often or with ease or were accustomed to tying up cash in anything but the instantly consumable, and by the minute volume of their business – one man, one letter, one stamp.

Yet education is one of the regime's most proclaimed concerns, and in the cities one does see many well-lit and invitingly arranged bookshops. There is apparently a large market for translated fiction. The bulk of it is classics: English, French, American. Contemporary writers like Sartre and the existentialists, who were illegal a few years ago, are now admissible but publishing houses and faculties are still hampered by very limited allowances of foreign currency to pay for translation rights. So you may find an entire show-case devoted not to *Peyton Place* or *The Naked Lunch* but to Džek London, Mark Tven (Tom Sojer), easily spotted under their light Serbo-Croat disguise and, rather harder to unmask, Džejn Ostin and Fenimor Kuper (*Postdnje Mohikanac* by the latter is a clue.)

The shops are full. Of goods and people. The goods are of poor quality and there is little or no choice, everything being allotted from some state manufactory or canning plant. Prices are high; that is, a shoddy pair of shoes costs about as much as a good pair in the West and, as people earn a great deal less, the real cost, say, of an overcoat or an electric stove would seem to be quite shocking.

We found a touch of opulence in the sight of men at breakfast in the boulevard cafés. They start off with a jigger of slivovitz, that tough plum brandy, and light a Turkish cigarette – everybody smokes like chimneys – then appear coffee, smoked ham and eggs. The eggs come bubbling in a little copper pan, hot, irresistible, and freshly made. We took to them and found that north or south, town, village or resort, grade A or C, this was the dish that never failed.

We went for a Sunday walk up the hill into the old quarter of Zagreb. There are churches, vistas, traces of fine buildings and row on row of low houses in various stages of decay, peeling plaster, damp patches, broken shutters, paintless casements . . . These human habitations bear the signs of overcrowding, dirt, discouragement, a state of being where the purchase of a pot of paint is beyond moral and material means. A man's spare suit is hanging from a nail on an outside wall. In a doorway a woman with bespattered ankles, bare feet in slippers, is beating her small boy with a switch; the boy has been handling his toy football clumsily. The quarter is as picturesque – under a gray sky – as the back streets of Naples have been said to be, and it turns one's stomach.

Further down a cookshop sells for a few coins a creamy-crusty concoction of macaroni and white cheese hot off the stove, called *burek*. There are no tables, only a shelf that runs shoulder-high along bare walls. A young man comes in, not ill-favoured in appearance; he takes his plate of *burek*, puts it on the shelf and, head down, hands dangling, begins to eat with his mouth, face in plate. One can see that he is entirely practised. When his plate is clean, he leaves the shop. Not a word was spoken, not a glance exchanged.

We walk back, down into the official town, along the avenues drained by Sunday quiet. All is empty, remote and still as if one had sunk beneath the surface of life into a vast, gray crater.

THE SIXTEEN LAKES OF PLITVICE

SIXTEEN LAKES – a range of lakes flowing, tumbling, cascading one into the other – and a hundred and one waterfalls! It was by luck and the word of a friend that we went there. The guide-books' synthetic gush is sprayed impartially upon the mediocre and the sublime. It might have been a public show of one of nature's larger stunts, an hour of shepherded gaping with one's fellow sheep; it is, the water-play at Plitvice, an enchantment, a scene of solitude, of infinite and slow and varied wonder.

All went well from the beginning. A few hours' drive; an excellent road – the lakes are enclosed in a National Park in a mountainous region of dense forests; arrival towards evening; the sound of water, the first breath of the deep cold tree-fed air. The ample hotel is on the edge of the Park; the snug, spruce, well-designed rooms smell of fresh-cut pine. Dinner. Sleep. Breakfast, some easy clothes, a map, a ticket and one is through the gate left free, all day if one so desires, to stroll mile after mile through a water-landscape that is at once primaeval and still changing, a glorious and fantastic configuration created by century on century of interaction of water, stone and vegetation. The upper lakes are broad and placid, deep-shored, set among old trees, maple, flowering ash, hornbeam, mountain elm; the

middle lakes are swifter flowing and of many shapes, and on
the lowest levels they are compressed to frothy, turbulent inlets
that have cut themselves – with what tremendous force – into
a narrow canyon. Everywhere there is plant-life, shrubs, wild
flowers, rare mosses, ferns, on the banks, under water, on the
rock-face, subtropical, alpine, hydrophilous; but the dominant,
the all-pervading element is water, live water in every phase
– water on the move, on the roll, foaming, whirling, swishing
water, rapid water toppling over cliffs in suicidal dash; still
water, majestic water, horizons of water; tinkling water
splashing in elegant quicksilver rays, hissing water spouting
from stone and earth, thunderous vertical water roaring sky-
ward in strong jets, folds of creamy water descending in soft
cascades.

There are pools, there are brooks, there are streams; grottoes
and caves abound. There are miniature, Chinese-sized water-
gardens; in one clearing there stands a perfect semi-circle: here
the falls have reproduced in water the architectural shape of a
Greek theatre. And as one wanders immersed in the profusion,
now stunned by roar and speed, now becalmed beside some
peaceful pond, captivated by yet another flourish of light and
leaf and spray, one is walking also through a landscape that is a
natural prototype, one that the masters of the baroque did never
see, but must have dreamt, and to the wonder of which they gave
shape, less innocently, on another scale, in the fountains and
façades of Rome; and so that here, in the limestone mountain
ranges of deepest Croatia, one can recall the related raptures of
Trevi, Quattro-Fontane and Navona.

We allowed ourselves to stay three days.

DALMATIAN COAST:
RIJEKA – ZADAR – ŠIBENIK – TROGIR – SPLIT

BACK TO earth, down to earth; not unpleasantly so in this easy-
going, not unprosperous sea-port. There is often a tinge of civic

freedom to be found in large shipping towns whatever the colour of the dictatorship. Rijeka, moreover, once known as Fiume (remember d'Annunzio and his private capture of the port in defiance of President Wilson and the Allied Powers?) had belonged to Italy as late as 1948 and something irrepressible seems to have remained. The crowds in the drab clothes are here but they look less Slav, less monolithic, they are crowds that stand and stare *all'italiano*. There are plenty of ships in the harbour, a brisk smell of salt and sea, good-looking food in the markets; the town hall is ochre-washed and gay with a huge round clock-face, the small pink churches in the back-alleys are charming and the price of the standard cigarettes changes from street to street.

Rijeka is a starting point. It is here that the classic traveller's route down the Dalmatian coast begins; here that the tourists – in the new skyscraper hotel with the view over weathered roofs and sea – sort out themselves and their baggage before taking ship for Dubrovnik or a dozen islands, or the road south as far as it will lead.

We took the road. A few miles of shrubby trees and suddenly one is out under the sun and hard dazzling mountains, bone-bare, bone-white crags, jagged, piled high into the sky; and on the other side the quiet blue sea, view upon view of smooth deep bays and islands, always islands, stretching low in a slight mist tawny and light as the bloom on a peach. All day we drove, drenched in that beauty. At noon we ate ham, fruit and bread on a promontory; a peasant woman clothed in black lay full length under three blades of shade; the mountains shimmered, the sea below was glassy still. At sunset we reached the Zadar peninsula. The most wonderful drive, we said, we had ever experienced.

There are things to be seen in Zadar, the ex-capital of Dalmatia – Roman gates, ramparts, an early Christian church – but the town is spread out thin, without a defined centre, and so rather invertebrate; and I found it drab again, deprived and sad with that whiff of sleeping underdog melancholy to be found in poor places ruled autocratically. For the transient, however, there is easy escape: a couple of miles out of town to the beach and pine-woods of Borik, to an agreeable hotel in a garden giving straight on to the sea, with good food and clean, uncomfortable rooms. While we were there the jasmin was in flower and the garden at night was filled with sweet scents and the song of nightingales.

The coast immediately below Zadar is tufted green with small rounded bosky mountains; further south it becomes fertile with figs, olives, vines. Less astonishing than the blanched mountainscape of the day before, it is still beautiful. All at once the road ends. Ends. There has been no forewarning (except fine print on the map). We are at the edge of a wide bay among a phalanx of impatient cars. There is no choice now except to take a ferry; to queue, to be precise, for this compulsory service. We wait; we pay up; we grumble. Midway across, we forget: for there is rising before us the sight of an old town of mellow stone, fan-shaped, a hemicycle spread-eagled upon a rock-wall high above the sea. The vision grows: it is Šibenik, founded and fortified nine hundred years ago, the veteran of a score of wars between Venetians and Turks, of prosperous, powerful past and placid present. We land: the promise of the approach is not belied, the inside is as lovely as the shell, compact, almost secret – narrow, shaded streets, steep and vaulted, a Venetian piazza, sculptured lions . . .

It is too early in the day to spend more than a loitering hour; this town is only the first encountered of the string of Adriatic ports of high beauty on this magic coast. Less than thirty miles further south there is unique Trogir, the Tragurion of the Greeks, perhaps the most flawless of them all, a walled town on an island reached by bridge. Here, everything from the rare Croatian-Romanesque basilica in the sun-soaked square to the city gates is harmonious and untouched. Nothing is new, nothing jars.

Another drive – the sea is translucent green now, afloat with small, tortoise-mound islands, the mountain slopes have turned stone again, lavender-grey stone, but cultivated (by what crushing patient labour) into stone fields, immense ones, of sparse symmetrical vines – and already we are in Split, in Spalatum

(I find it hard to use the contemporary Slav diminutive for a place so filled with Roman echo). The first thing one is struck by is the animation: on the quays, in cafés, under awnings, movement is spilling over the pavements; Spalatum is no museum-piece, it is an active port, a live city alive with its own business of which the sightseers are only a part; a city, also, that encloses within vast inner walls another live city, the nine and a half acres of classical ruins, later juxtaposed with Romanesque churches and Venetian gothic, that had once been conceived as the abode of one man, built for the life and death of the Emperor Diocletian. That palace and mausoleum were begun in AD 295 and when they were ready Diocletian – Gaius Aurelius Valerius – himself a native of Dalmatia, abdicated the Roman Empire at the age of only sixty-one and retired. With him, there were housed within the palace walls a court of attendants, guests, guards and slaves amounting to 2,000 souls. At the Emperor's death this place of unmanageable size became public property and was accommodated now as an army camp, now as a market place of refuge from invasions; gradually the rooms and banqueting halls were broken up and parcelled into private dwelling-places, new architecture was piled on old, Christian churches raised on pagan ground. Nowadays, as one enters this core, this inner city, in the evening, as one should, at the hour of blue dusk, one finds oneself inside a hive of slit streets and small piazzas, a-lit with bars and stalls, bee-loud with chatter, clotted with milling people. The Venetian façades have delicately arched windows and twining balconies trailing vines, all is a gracious commixture: pillars rise from fountains and birds nest on the pillars, columns are topped by roofs and the roofs by bushes – it is an easy pleasure to stroll here. A sudden turn and one's breath is caught: here under a rectangle of intense night-blue sky, empty and dark, stands a colonnade – we are in the peristyle, the inner temple above Diocletian's tomb, the core within the core. A black sphinx crouches, there are two lions; the place gives off an impression of immense stillness, of imperishable being at the end of the tunnel of time. It is not large, the peristyle in Spalatum, no larger than a casual corner of the Forum: one stands, seized at the throat by emotion, the sense of having come near the heart of classical antiquity.

ADRIATIC ISLANDS – DUBROVNIK

A STORM kept us land-bound in Spalatum before we were able to take ship. The least said about these vessels the better. They are not big; they are not very clean at the beginning of a voyage, at the end they are indescribable. The passengers are packed like sardines, only, as someone said, that sardines are neater. Officers, stewards, crew, salaried officials to a man and unsusceptible to tipping, are impervious to the discomfort of their charges. Bands of schoolchildren and adolescents – who may travel free in any class they choose – swarm over saloons and decks. Their comportment would make American children look inhibited. They are oblivious of living human flesh: the floor, a deck-chair, the breathing form inside it, are all the same to them; a defence mechanism, we decided, developed by the perpetually over-crowded. If you are four or six to a room and can never be by yourself, you must come to treat your brother and the aunt as so much furniture or go crackers. They plump their knapsacks on anyone's knees, dig elbows into elderly bosoms, eject sweets from mouths on to anyone's clothes. A youth sat down on my feet, guitar and all, another propped his tin of tunnyfish, open and oil-dripping, on my lap and set to eat, while a girl reclining against my side spat sunflower seeds – all done as unselfconsciously as a dog would crunch a lamb-chop on the carpet in the living-room. One realizes that here no educational counter-measures are likely to be taken by parents, school or public press. The parents cannot alter the living conditions, the schools do not incline towards indoctrinating bourgeois manners, gracious-living columns do not (yet) exist in the magazines. What one wonders about is the future. Will it be a graceless stark new world? or might there be a revival either of humane or formal manners? We may know more when, or if, prosperity has at last arrived in Yugoslavia. The islands are worth the journeys: Korčula – birthplace of Marco Polo, a hedgehog-shaped round town encircled by orchards and beaches – Bräč, Hvar and a hundred small others, the climates are sheltered, the sea marvellous to swim in, there is diving, fishing; birds, wild fowl, endlessly varied vegetation, walled towns; pleasing harbours abound . . . Like the mainland, the Adriatic archipelago is quite fabulously endowed with scenery and architecture.

Further south there is yet another charming small resort, called Miljet, and still further – by frightful road – two walled towns, Budva and Sveti Stefan, and above all Kotor, the mediaeval port at the mouth of a deep-cut bay where cathedral spires rise against the tremendous Montenegrin mountains.

THE ISTRIAN PENINSULA: PULA – POREČ – PORTOROZ – RUMINATIONS – PIRAN – LAST HOURS

TIME WAS running out. Having begun the journey as we had in Ljubljana we had missed a stretch of the coast, the Istrian Peninsula, of long Venetian occupation. Perhaps it is a mistake to leave it to the last, to see it spoilt and sated as we were, for it is good travelling country. The roads are never far from the clear sea; one passes alternately lush vegetation, salt flats, charming villages, vineyards, olive groves, oyster bays. The towns look gay, graced as they are with their campanile, with loggias, pilasters, lacy arched windows – oh yes, the Venetians have been that way – and it is always easy to find a good simple place to eat. For the sightseer there are many casual treasures and there is Pula, a somewhat rusting port, with a pleasing Roman temple and Augustus' amphitheatre staring white, massive, impressive from the outside, rather falling apart within; and there is the very very fine sixth-century basilica at Poreč with its glowing Byzantine mosaics.

At Portoroz, port of roses, another storm overtook us, the sea went wild, and we spent a day of rain and frustration in the largest hotel's largest room while the wind was shattering the glass in the window-panes. I lay in a vast sunken bath of very hot sea-water, thalasso-therapy, and ruminated on our journey. What had been best? What had been bad? And what else? What else did we see? Where else did we go?

There had been the days, strenuous ones, in the Moslem parts (a million Yugoslavs belong to that faith), the drive through Bosnia-Herzegovina into Serbia to Sarajevo. Herds of goat and pig; women in Turkish trousers of flowered stuff but faded and caked with mud (it rains hard and often in those parts), toiling under burdens by the roadside, in the fields (no studious Portias they, like their Ljubljana sisters); Banja Luka and a first glimpse of mosque and minaret; the Turkish cemeteries, curiously moving, lying abandoned, overgrown with weeds, their grey headstones mounted by sculptured turbans, weather-worn, snail-smooth; the drive through the rocky, gorge-cleft Vrba valley, and the Bosnian fortress town Jaice standing on a cliff above two river-falls. The monster-road, the non-road, the forty miles of holes and stone and mud which shook every screw and bone and had to be ground through in second and first gear, which made one pray at every jolt and wish that one had hired not a car but a brace of jeeps (one for spare), but to which our white eggshell of a Fiat (which I had been treating with the anxious care one always bestows on the neighbour's child rather than one's own) stood up gallantly. The increasing evidence as one went south of century-encrusted poverty and sloth; the mean box-shaped houses without a lick of paint; the silent, watchful children; the lean-ribbed cows, the chicken tethered by a string; the scarceness of the petrol pumps; the stop where a sheepdog was so ravenous that he seized and wolfed down a whole loaf of dry bread in one single snatch; the up-to-date hotel where the chambermaids – ageless drudges – went barefoot and the tablecloths, absorbing egg-stains, grease-stains, soup-stains, ash, remained unchanged from breakfast till night; the disarming friendliness of the hard-worked men and women on the solitary roads always mustering a wave, a smile to salute the stranger splashing comfortably by. Sarajevo of haunting memory, where one finds that a street is named for that earlier Lee Harvey Oswald, Gavrilo Princip, and a plaque put up to mark the spot from which he fired the two pistol shots that murdered the Archduke Ferdinand ('The shots that killed seven million men'); Sarajevo, a teeming hotchpotch of Balkan and Oriental, mosque and business streets, *souks* and slums, and an atmosphere of contrivance, limitations, restlessness – nothing ever, perhaps, quite safe, quite clean, quite straight – that produces its own kind of galvanized vitality, but makes me cry for Switzerland. Mostar, still deeper south, more stagnantly Oriental, with the wonderful old Turkish bridge of one great arch.

What else? A sprint into Montenegro, land of incredible mountains and the brave. The hair-raising ascent of Mount Lovcen – by huge touring bus driven with steadfast skill and care by a middle-aged Croatian family man; I have seldom seen such driving – view opening on stupendous view turn after corkscrew turn; noon hours in quiescent Cetinje, the old capital; a visit to the Royal Palace turned museum – an armoury, a billiard table, 'This was the King's dining-room – Do not step on the carpet', cabinets with photographs of moustachioed nineteenth-century gentlemen hung with small-arms or stuffed into frockcoats bristling with decorations; the somnolent square where males of a recognizably similar stamp slouched a-spitting . . . And what else? The skull-and-bone scare-signs warning against reckless driving, the huge posters depicting green-tinged skeletons gripping the steering wheel as the car hurtles over the precipice in flames. The contrast everywhere between the old architecture of the country and the new which was nearly always without merit, garish, shoddy, daubed with loud but dismal colours, chocolate brown and magenta being frequent favourites. The megalomania of the official sculpture, the monuments to liberation, industry and war, so reminiscent of what Mussolini used to perpetrate.

Food. Even in out of the way places you will get a fairly well-cooked meal, sounder and more plentiful than you could expect in similar localities in France or England. There *are* shortages and the variety is often small. The chief lack is fresh fruit and vegetables. Distribution and preservation are at about the stage they were in the West a hundred years ago: you can get only such vegetables as are in season and are grown nearby; so in winter and some places you get none at all. Yugoslavia goes one further because even if there are broadbeans, lamb's lettuce and cherries on the market stalls, the A and B hotel restaurants will seldom alter their menu of state-canned peas and salads of pickled beet and cabbage. We got by in these by ordering lemon with our tea, chopped onion with grilled meat and the excellent stewed fruit that is always on. Starches, curiously for such a Middle European-inspired cuisine, are parsimoniously doled out, a few sticks of potatoes, a scooplet of rice, and expensive. A minute helping of limp spaghetti costs as much as a full-sized pork chop. The mainstay *is* meat. Veal and pork, some beef. Steaks are not bad, though below Anglo-Saxon conception. Chicken, when it is to be had, comes grilled and is as good as any I have eaten, if not better. The same goes for fish. Scampi, mullet, fresh tuna, bass, straight out of the sea, hot off the grill, of beautiful flavour and firmness are served in harbours and side-streets.

The cooking blends from the Austrian into the Balkan. Veal on the bone in the north, veal stuck on skewers in the south; but far the best food is to be found in the Italianate parts. Privately owned, family-run pensions and restaurants have recently become allowed. Quality in the grand official places varies. At Plitvice it was fair; at Split outstandingly good. Indeed in small places inland and in regions of poor supply, the restaurants of A and B hotels are your best bet; whereas on the coast or in the cities I would always rather go to the native grilleries and taverns.

Yoghurt is served everywhere, in large jars, and is partic-ularly good. Tea is stained water, coffee a misery. In Slovenia they use espressos and a few real coffee beans, elsewhere it is coffee stretched with roast barley and malt, wretchedly flavourless and thin. There is more body – and coffee – to the sudsy syrupy Turkish brew that comes in those copper pots, but it isn't everybody's taste and certainly not for breakfast. One must do as the provident Germans do who carry their own tins of instant.

Wine is cheap and drinkable. I would not put it higher. Cigarettes, Turkish and some Virginia approximations, are very cheap, loosely rolled, not strong and, I am told, not satisfactory to the heavy smoker. Beer is poor stuff, and everywhere there is slivovitz, that fiery plum brandy, which is quite wholesome and costs only pennies. In the cities and at Dubrovnik there are special shops where foreigners paying hard currency may buy Scotch whisky, American cigarettes and other articles not available to the inhabitants.

Language. In spite of Slovenian and Macedonian, Serbo-Croat is the official language of the country. The few words of it one is able to acquire during a journey will be of some slight help in sorting out Entrance from Exit, Right from Left, Open from Shut, and they will please the Yugoslavs. Unlike other nationals, who prefer to show off a foreign language and will not thank you for massacring their own, they display a childish pride at your uttering two syllables of their speech. For your real needs, you will find some German, Italian, English or French (in that order of frequency) spoken nearly everywhere. *Spoken*; not necessarily understood. People may talk to you in English with deceptive fluency without really catching on to your answer, or your question. This is never admitted and may cause disappointment and confusion. So do not be too certain that because the nice girl at the desk has said Yes when you asked to have your washing back before the boat on Monday that you will get the washing.

And the Yugoslavs, how do they judge their own condition? Do they feel hopeful? resigned? content? Do they feel trapped? Do they feel free? It is hard to answer. For one thing, their terminology of freedom is not ours. For centuries these people were great fighters for freedom; they fought and they fought – to drive out Barbarians, Turks, Venetians, Austrians, Italians,

Nazis; they fought each other. What they fought for was an idea of national freedom; they did not fight for *individual* freedom, for *civic* freedom; democracy has never been a living concept in the Balkans. Now they have driven out the invaders, their intense sense of nationalism is satisfied. One must remember their inheritance of misrule and oppression, also the fact that most of the Slav people who now constitute Yugoslavia were hostile to one another during most of their history. Now they are united; there is internal peace – certainly a desirable and desperately difficult achievement. And the price is Tito Communism. It is not possible for a short-term visitor to say what they may feel to have lost, may feel to have gained; whether, for instance, the lack of the freedom of political choice has any reality for them. *We* know that the Yugoslav regime is far less totalitarian and more Westernized than Moscow Communism (and may become more so), but do the Yugoslavs themselves look at it in terms of East and West? One does hear some criticism – among the highly educated – some scepticism about far-flung economic plans, is told of discontent among the peasantry who have had the very dirty end of the stick: attempted collectivization but no social security, no health insurance, no old-age pensions. (Yugoslavia is far from being a welfare state and people will hardly believe what you can tell them about postwar England.) But discontent and criticism appear to be on the fringe of general acceptance and much pride in the state of things: the young know nothing else, the middle-aged remember the war and occupation, some of the old have seen better days, some worse.

As for the foreign tourists, they do have their freedom. They may go where they wish. There are no compulsory guides, no factory tours, no proscribed areas. If you happen to pass what may be a military installation, there will be merely a pictorial sign asking you to keep out and not to take photographs. No one waves a gun. You are not bullied (except when you cross against the light as a pedestrian). You can eat and drink at most hours; wear what you like. The beaches are blessedly unprudish. Unlike Spain, there is little police in evidence. You do not feel, and I think are in fact not, followed or spied upon. This applies to the foreigner going about his holiday, changing his money at the official places. I do not know what might happen if he tried to poke his nose in a bit more. People do talk to foreigners, and some will talk freely, but they lower their voices when doing so and first look over their shoulder.

THE SKY cleared that evening in Portoroz. It was our last night. We went out to eat some fish. Next morning we departed. I had left Piran, the most Venetian of the Istrian cities, to the end. As we turned the bay, the whole port came into view, in the clear Adriatic light, the front of painted houses at the edge of the water and their reflections, like a sea-mirage, red, umber, rose-pink and blue; a lovely farewell.

An hour later we were through the border, my typewriter checked out, the dinars turned in: fifteen English shillings' worth, the exact lawful amount. On the Italian side we declared our Turkish cigarettes, two hundred each. 'Two hundred packets?' the guard said and grinned. In Trieste I stopped and bought *The Times* and the *Herald Tribune*, the first English newspapers in many weeks. In the hotel I left a stack of letters at the desk to be mailed, ordered and drank a capuccino, then shot up in the lift. I was happy, very happy to be back; and glad to have been away. One day, if the gods be willing, I shall want to go again, go again for the freshness and the utter change; for the translucent sea, the round towns, the proud architecture; for the mountains, the incomparable scenery; go for the sense of wonder and renewal at the sixteen lakes, go for the islands, go for the sight of Spalatum, Trogir and Piran.

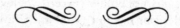

VENICE IN WINTER

1967

WINTER IN VENICE. Arrival. The moment of doubt: will it be there, will it have subsisted this grandest, this strangest, most fabulous of white elephants of the past? Can that magic still work on the inhabitant of an increasingly different world? The handing into the *motoscafo*, the bestowal of luggage – signori! – moments of Italian action that can be fraught with strife or pass with luxurious smoothness: the gliding away, ensconced in soft rugs, only the face stung by cold and air; the moment of transition: the curve in the waterway: seeing. Façades, reflections, bridges, perspectives, animation – the great back-cloth and the swarming movement: a hundred water-craft cavorting in front of palazzi on palazzi, water-gnawed, extravagant, melancholy, voluptuous, glowing in decay. Here it is, then, laid bare as it were, bare of the dazzle, the panache, the golden banners of high summer, bare to the bone, the perennial, the mysterious beauty of Venice.

After the sleigh-ride, after the overwhelming: refuge. Inside a polished walnut, the elegant small hotel. Warmth. Welcome. The major luxuries of travel are a sense of security, freedom from friction – order, comfort, calm. The Italians, in the right mood, when not swung into an opposite direction, have a genius for providing them.

Ten minutes later the urge to set out again, the longing for more. On foot now. This is the city where locomotion itself is pleasure, is ease – a choice between gliding and strolling. Nothing is far because an essence is always here, before one, wherever one happens to be and round the corner as well. One has only got to look up; to look.

These walks! Round the corner and the next one, and the next. Here, there is no wasteland, no dull stretches, no intrusions, no ugliness: the bank is as splendidly housed as the bakeshop. And the variety is unending. One can walk for hours, seemingly lost, never quite lost, and not cease to come upon the undiscovered, the rediscovered, the new – come from the sumptuous shop-lined street into a dramatic square, plunge under an archway, follow the boy with the trolley of tangerines, emerge into a triangular piazetta, cross the bridge, pass the colonnaded church, over the next bridge, up more steps, through a long street where cabinet-makers are chipping at their trade, take the sharp turning, find sunlight, a market, an asymmetrical piazza blown by winds, a vast looming church, take another bridge and a street of bright, prosperous foodshops, dive into a passage, shoulders touching walls, come out onto a minute widening by a canal. One stands alone. The water lap-laps against the sides of a small pink-washed palazzo. The barley-sugar columns framing the windows are exquisite; washing is hanging out. There is one tree.

The very street-signs lure one on. Fondamento, Campo, Largo, Riva, Piscina, Calle, Calleone, dedicated to deity, to saints and ages, heraldic animals and past sensational events. Who can forbear to enter the Sottoportico del' Uccelletto, to follow the Riva degli Due Assassini, the Street of the Almonds, the Narrow Street of the Young Bears?

Seemingly lost; never quite lost. There is the occasional arrow pointing a direction – San Marco. Rialto. Ferrovia. There are, always obliging, never themselves at a loss, the Venetians. The question is simply framed, one names a landmark: Accademia? Piazza? Albergo? 'Cross the bridge!' they cry, '*Fa il punte!*' They pronounce *ponte* thus. There follows some eloquent and effective gesture. Another passer-by stops in his tracks and takes it up: he is headed, he signs, precisely in that direction; he beckons, ambles on, you follow his swift progress with his burden, a tall pair of gilt candle-sticks, a tray of sweet-meats, a string of fiaschi, for the Venetians are forever trundling food and drink and chattels from one point of their maze to another. Upon their heads in huge flat baskets or boat-shaped wooden bowls, or propelled on those special trolleys mounted on low wheels and stilts that are able to negotiate steps. '*Gambe!*' they shout, 'Mind your legs!' as they come charging down an alley-way five feet wide with their cargo of ship-irons or wine. Recently some of the younger porters have changed their warning-cry to a simple-minded, 'Hello!'

Winter belongs to the Venetians, the inhabitants of the large and teeming city have come back into their own. The air is filled with the ring of their voices, with those curious local cadences, both harsh and lilting, singing out greetings and good wishes. For it is the long slow festive season that stretches though practically the whole of December on to Twelfth Night and the teeming city, one now realizes, is really a small town – *Dottore, buon giorno – Buon giorno, Padre – Serafina, ciao – Tante cose – Auguri, auguri* . . .

At every turning women stop to meet, men raise their hats to one another. There are few visible tourists, no hordes milling in Piazza San Marco; this does not mean that the streets are empty at all hours; the rhythm of native Venetian life is as regular as the tides. At noon and again at sunset people pour *en masse* into streets and squares to stand and talk, drink coffee, eat cakes and ices before drifting home or into the trattorie for more solid meals; low-tide comes by eleven at night and during the long post-prandial hours of the afternoon when all at once there will be space and a great stillness – it is now that the magic is at its most potent and one can hear the sounds of water, the small sounds the gondolas make straining at their moorings and the sound of foot-fall upon the slender bridge.

It is the spectators' city, the place of ecstatic wanderings, it is also the place of perpetual covetousness. One covets what one sees – the silks, the leather, the ornaments, the hundred handsome things made by hand, displayed with such love and art. The seductiveness of those shop-windows, the intimacy. And the food: surely nowhere else in the world is food made to look as beautiful as it does in Venice. There is the colour and extravagant variety of all that sea-life that comes out of the Adriatic, there is the dewy, new-born freshness of the roots and leaves grown on the mainland, the Veneto di Terra Firma, there are the simple, the biblical shapes of bread and cheeses – the very colours and shapes of the fruit and loaves and fishes that have been used for centuries by Venetian artists, by Carpaccio, Bellini, Tintoretto, Veronese, in their allegories and painted feasts.

To see it in its subtle glory one must see the food of Venice as it arrives at day-break at the quays of the Rialto markets, the *pescheria* and the *erberia*, and watch the cargo-gondolas being unloaded in that first blue and hazy Adriatic light. One will never forget that sudden transcendent quality of ordinary things, the glow of the fruit in its own leaves, the purple and green of artichokes with bushy tails, the delicacy of the sea-creatures, silver, lilac – pale and coral red.

From the barges to the vendors' stalls. Vegetables are built into banks, fish laid out in patterns on marble slabs, and with what skill and care, what instinctive taste – that pyramid over there of saffron and scarlet peppers, that spray of spinach assembled leaf by curly leaf, that sea-spider flanked by rosy prawns and scrolls of sole – with what patience, what devotion! In the cold, the stone cold of this December dawn, bare hands are plunged ungrudgingly again and again into the dripping baskets to create these ephemeral still-lifes. And for whose eyes? The shop-keepers' and the green-grocers' and the restaurant-keepers' who come morning after morning to buy their day's supply – surely we have here one of the purest examples of art for art's sake? Perhaps there is in the people of Venice still something of the human spirit that conceived of the *tour de force* of building a city in the sea and then far from contenting itself with a primitive dwelling or a Spartan fortress went on to create a place of incomparable fantasy and splendour.

A splendour that has endured, as have its people. For how many centuries more? How many ocean-tides, how many winters? Let us go there while we may.

II
RIGHT & WRONG

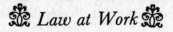 *Law at Work*

'Justice without mercy is
cruelty, mercy without justice
goes to waste.'

Thomas Aquinas

A LOOK AT JUDGES AT WORK

England
1965

BELOW THE DAIS, on the steps of the throne as it were, stands a tiny elderly woman, blank pointed face turned upwards, straining towards the robed presence.

'You don't want me to tell about the key, your Honour?'

Above, the resplendent crimson figure hardly stirs. Now comes the clear, cool voice. 'The key is wholly extraneous to the case, madam.'

She blinks at him over steel-rimmed spectacles. 'But I've got it. Don't you want to see it?' She is that bane of lawyers, litigant without counsel; she is a plaintiff appearing for herself. She rummages in a cardboard suitcase, finds. 'The key [coaxing] to Emily's wardrobe, your Honour. Where she kept the will.'

'*Be quiet!* You won't do your case any good by bringing in matters which I disallowed.' The tone is as harsh as the words. That suit has now dragged into the second day. The voice betrays exasperation, infuriated boredom.

The litigant lifts a peaked, uncomprehending face. 'Do you want me to go on with the letter then? The solicitor's letter?' She is impervious, inward-looking, self-absorbed, obsessed. The Judge on High is manifest to all in court, he is the focal point of all the eyes, the apex, Jove in the driver's seat. *She* sees his Lordship no more than his Lordship sees her.

She is contesting her late sister's will. They made it together, on a will-form. When one died the other found that the will was not held to mean what she believed it was meant to mean. She did not take the solicitor's No for an answer. The will, somehow, somewhere, between the funeral and the lawyer's office, must have been tampered with; by a nephew, by a third sister's husband, by a clerk. Today she is here. In court, at her own expense, fighting the windmills.

Has she a case? Or is she, like so many of the independent litigants who haunt the law-courts, pursuing a fantasy? That is what Judge X has been trying to unravel, if not with patience, with persistent fairness, for the last two days. Both – the learned judge and the woman – are largely here because of what they are. Along his road, the call to the Bar, the call to the Bench, there was the possession of a functioning mind, the ability to recognize and evaluate facts, the capacity and will to think impersonally and generally, to accept the accepted, to stand by and honour the rules. The world of law has its limitations but it is not a small world. *She* came by way of under-education, a spinster's life, the will-form bought in the High Street, the refusal to take advice, to learn, to listen, to look at a set of facts from any point but her own, the constrictions of a suspicious temperament confirmed by misfortune. From the opposite ends of the scale, the trained professional and the ungifted amateur are bent on their pursuit – to coin a presentation of events; she to run from reality with one single-minded fact as she wants to see it, he to assemble an ordered whole, an ideal reality, where there are no gaps and no loose ends, where C and B inevitably flow from A.

The litigant confronts the defendants, relations, stubborn, embarrassed men whose answers to her accusations (she is unable, expectedly, to frame a question) do not add one shred. The judge tries to assist her. '*Do* stop talking for a moment. Listen to me.' The result remains the same. Two people support her, a hairdresser and his wife who witnessed the original will and now hint shiftily that the signatures on the contested copy do not look quite like their own. An expert called by the defendants quickly demolishes that. It also turns out that the litigant had promised the couple £500 for 'their trouble'.

'You can now address me on the whole case,' says the judge.

She produces a ruled copy-book and begins to read. 'I did not start this case for money nor for gain. It has cost me £1,400 and my health. . . ' It is her moment. The self-represented layman has all the rights of counsel, and the judge allows her rope.

When it becomes quite evident that no argument will develop, he reminds her, 'You must try to prove your case to me, madam. You haven't begun to.'

She looks up over her spectacles and says dismissively, 'It is not my sister's will – it's *altered* – I don't want to see it again.' She resumes her reading. 'Your Honour, I did not bring this case for money . . .'

The unhappy judge lets her ramble on for the best part of an hour. Then it is his moment. Delivery of judgment: a succinct and easy narrative. 'A home-made will drawn up in 1963 and, as home-made wills so often do, has caused a surprising crop of litigation . . .' Stray dates and figures click into place. The net value of the estate . . . A reference to various tests . . . to the hairdresser: '. . . as unprepossessing a witness as one might encounter in the box; he went as far – under considerable inducement – as he was able to without committing the criminal offence of perjury'. There is no room for doubt; soon comes the clincher. 'It is lamentable that this action was ever brought. *The plaintiff's action is dismissed.*'

She had been drinking it in with an expression of smug eagerness. Now she rises again. 'And you will give me my costs, please?'

'I cannot give you costs . . . I have just awarded them to the defendants.'

A look of awful understanding dawns on her poor face, 'You are *not* passing my copy, your Honour?'

TO COMPRESS, to shape, to label the erratic sequences of life – where does responsibility lie in that broken marriage? Did that brawl end in wilful murder or in misadventure? Was that slip a fraud or an honest error? Who was negligent, who was malicious, who was careless? – is the perennial function of the judges. And of counsel. (For all his immense prestige, an English judge like an American judge, and unlike a European, acts as a conductor rather than a performer through the first parts of a trial or a case.) The courts are run by team-work, close co-operation of *professionals*. The daily prime material, the unprocessed human element is kept in check by stringent rules of procedure and by sheer expertise. The pros are here every day and thoroughly at home; *they* – delinquents, co-respondents, bankrupts, accident victims, innocents, petitioning wives, injured workmen, monomaniacs, liars, self-seekers, evicted tenants, dangerous motorists and good citizens – are nearly always miserable, apprehensive and very much at sea. The great thing is to keep them quiet. They are managed by reducing them as long as possible to silence. Lawyers talk; the prisoner in the dock is mute; the jurymen in their box stay mute (till the last word); the layman's turn comes only in the witness-box. It is here that the unpredictable, the incoherent, the mumbled muddle will come in, but the lawyer's front knows how to cope with that, it is only when the rogue litigant crashes in, doing as counsel does without counsel's skill, that the whole thing looks like breaking down and time and tempers are worn out. So, on that same afternoon Mr Justice X can be heard trying a defended divorce action (both parties represented) with patience, courtesy and tact, qualities for which indeed his reputation in his court stands high.

ACROSS THE corridor – Probate, Divorce & Admiralty Division – there may currently be witnessed a display of professional urbanity on a scale uncommon in these days. It is Mr Justice Scarman hearing another contested will case, one of such ramifications that it may well become the Jarndyce v. Jarndyce of our century. Let us call it *Gould, deceased and another v. Gould and ors. pt. hd.* For ors. read others, who here are ten defendants most of them at loggerheads with one another; pt. hd. is part heard and means that the case has been, and no doubt will be, going on for a good stretch of time.

The court looks crammed with men in wigs and black gowns, row upon row of counsel, a galaxy of QCs with their juniors behind them; ledges, tables, the floor, are covered with papers, scattered papers, stacked papers, bundles of papers loosely tied, toppling, reaching to the ceiling. To maintain both – counsel and documents – the case is said to be devouring £5,000 a working day.

The judge having fallen ill there has already been a week's adjournment. Now the usher bellows (always like a drill sergeant), 'Silence! Be upstanding in court.' And in ambles the lanky – gracefully lanky – figure of a youthful judge. Leading counsel for the chief plaintiff rises. 'May I express my learned friends' and my own delight in seeing your Lordship restored to this court?'

The judge's face breaks into a sweet, a boyish smile. 'I am very glad to be back in your company.' It is a most unusual face: enormous eyes deep-set between high cheek-bones and a jutting skull, a pale face, a hollow face with skin stretched taut, and yet the mouth is full and there show dimples in the sunken cheeks; it is an ascetic's face lit by charm, given the lie by a cherub's smile.

Immediately the case grinds on as if it had never stopped. A Harley Street man is in the box. He is asked to define terms such a *lucid, pliable, confused*. He does and nobody seems the wiser. Could he not define the late Mr Gould's mental capacity (at the time of course when he was making the fourth codicil) in layman's terms?

Specialist: 'It is such a long time since I've been a layman.'

Chain of laughter.

Did he make a certain test? Why not? 'Well, I don't necessarily do, unless there's a lot at stake.'

The Judge: 'You can take it, *quite* a lot was at stake.'

Jimmy Gould came to England as a boy before the war. He was partly Jewish and a refugee. His father was dead and the family had owned large industrial holdings in Germany. When the Hitler regime was over, the German Government offered a choice of compensation to Jimmy and to one Gould cousin, either £500,000 a piece in cash or their rightful share in the actual holdings. The stock of German industry then did not stand high. The cousin took the half million pounds and Jimmy would have done the same had it not been for the strong advice of an older man, an intimate friend, a solicitor, whom we may call Mr Franklin. So Jimmy chose his share and in a not very long time became a very rich young man indeed. He also appears to have been a displaced one. He had become a British subject and attached to London; he had studied in America for some years and became attached to that continent; business interests and his – possessive – mother who had remained there brought him back to Germany for long periods and he found again some good in that country. Great possessions entail great responsibilities. Jimmy took his seriously. He looked after his numerous relations and connections and brooded over ways of providing for them equitably. He served on the boards of his many companies, but was often over-ruled by older men. He tried to build up a venture of his own; it failed. He became engaged to a girl who had stood by him, then was persuaded to break off the engagement. He married another. The marriage was not happy and his wife left him shortly before his death. He was also very fond of a cousin, a young actress who lived in New York who was divorced herself and rather unhappy. Mr Franklin remained his friend, his advisor and companion.

Jimmy furnished or built houses in many countries and he kept a number in the Toronto telephone book. He travelled constantly. From London to Frankfurt, to Milan, Philadelphia, St Moritz, to the Lido, to Baden-Baden; and from all these places and to all these people he wrote streams of bilingual letters, now collected in those bundles in the court. He made a long and careful will leaving scaled percentages to mother, ex-wife, fiancée, cousins, nieces, friends. There was a decent bequest for Mr Franklin and a larger one for charity. In 1961 Jimmy Gould became ill. He was operated on and survived for rather more than one year. During that twilight period he made frequent alterations to his will by codicil, decreasing or increasing some bequests and making a new, not insubstantial one, to a doctor who was attending him and who allegedly had typed the relevant codicil himself. In 1962 Jimmy Gould, that rather tragic young man, died. His estate was estimated at six million pounds and nearly all his heirs went for each other's throat.

In a case of this sort, in a case of this length, there fall upon the judge two paramount tasks. One of course is to arrive at a just true end. There is no jury. Decision, judgment will be his and his alone (subject to the Court of Appeal). Was there undue influence, who behaved with propriety, who is to get the lion's share? to get something? to get nothing? to get all? It is the judge who will have to hand out ruin, exoneration: the money. To do this he will require iron concentration and a nimble memory to hack himself a path through a forest of facts. He will also have to resist the judge's common temptation of making up his mind before the whole of the evidence is in. His second task is to create and maintain, during the days and weeks to come, a tolerable working atmosphere. He must be able to reduce clashes between counsel without seeming to suppress them, unruffle a witness, rescue a point from being buried in a mass of detail, and above all he must keep the case moving. Few things are so demoralizing in court as the sense that the case can never end. It is up to the judge to trim a cross examination that has begun to move in circles, or to stop a dead line of inquiry. A good judge sets his own pace in court, and if he can do so with an air of amiable give and take, so much the better.

Sooner or later he will have to say, as Mr Justice Scarman did say, 'We know Jimmy's position in his mother's house [they've all come to drop the Mr Gould; the dead man's personality is extraordinarily present in that court], it isn't something in dispute, it's common ground. I don't think we need go into it again.'

'Your Lordship is quite right,' says the QC.

Or, 'Mr M., I don't think we need trouble with that question – the case will stand or fall by the reliable evidence of witnesses and not by witnesses' *opinions*.'

'A thoroughly professional judge,' says the press reporter, one of those wise ones who appear to nest in the Law Courts in the Strand.

At times there is need to ease tension. The judge puts in a word, not to hear his own voice, but just for that.

> *Counsel* [to a so far most competent legal witness]: 'When were you married yourself?'
> *Witness* [thinking hard]: 'Er . . . ah . . . in 1946.'
> *Counsel*: 'Seems always a difficult date to recall.'
> *The Judge*: 'For the male species.'

It may not sound like much outside of court, here it is agreeable, like being able to sneeze or stretch a leg.

Mr Justice Scarman is a young judge (called in 1961 at the age of forty-five). There have been judges at least as young, but there is something striking about this man with the austere head and the schoolboy smile, an irresistible combination of youthful charm with a mature and balanced mind. The atmosphere in his court is bonhomous, one might almost call it affectionate, but it is also intelligent and common-sensical. Strolling into *Gould, deceased and another* after a Queen's Bench, say, or a Chancery court is like walking into a very masculine and rather worldly club. Mr Justice Scarman is perhaps a new kind of judge; it is impossible to imagine him bullying anyone. Yet, he is held in respect: there is no doubt that authority flows from him. At one point he found it necessary to make a brief speech. 'What is at stake here is much more than money. It is the reputation of at least two professional men. Let us be as open about this as we can.' It was said quietly, without the slightest trace of pomposity. It was said from the bench, it might have been said from an armchair. The audience were a score of seasoned practitioners of the law. A pin could have been heard.

MR JUSTICE LLOYD-JONES has been described about the Temple as an intellectual and an absolute dear. He, too, sits in the PD & A Division, which means divorce and divorce and wills and more divorce with an occasional ship thrown in. There are times when contesting heirs appear positively chivalrous compared to those about to take the lid off their marriage. The aim seems to be to make everything show up more shabby that it could possibly have been.

'He didn't send me a present on my birthday.'
Counsel for the Petitioner: 'Is it not a fact that your husband, who was hard up at the time, sent you a card?'
'It came by the second post the day after my birthday.'
Counsel for the Respondent: 'Will you tell his Lordship what your husband did when you went to parties?'
'He never talked to me.'

The judge, whom the wig makes look a bit like an eighteenth-century outdoor squire, says, 'Mr G., I shouldn't interrupt you, but are you saying that this was one of the matters that undermined the marriage?'
'It might be said to have undermined her confidence.'
The Judge: 'We are trying to find out what went wrong with the marriage, a mystery not cleared up by these *cheese-paring* points.'
Yet, case in, case out, the cheese-paring and the distorting points crop up. 'The husband came in from work and found no meal.' 'My Lord, I am instructed that she left him a pie.' 'It was only a bought pie.' 'The allegation is that you hit her in the bath with a wash flannel.' 'Only to keep her from talking.' 'No sexual intercourse took place since 1958?' 'Well, it just stopped.' 'I said to him, I don't like your methods, dear, it's *perverted*. He said it was only horseplay.' 'He bought himself a magnifying glass, it cost 37/6 – for his hobby.' 'She wouldn't feed the dog . . . She went off with the sheets, she went off with the key, the stamp collection . . . a suitcase . . .' It is trotted out to prove technical cruelty, to kick back at the past and the

person once seen in another light, to justify one's own conduct and oneself. Today Mr Justice Lloyd-Jones has come to the moment where he has to ask the rather pretty plump wife in the box, 'Will you now tell me the circumstances that led you to commit adultery?'

She is totally unable to do this. Only a few days before she had written an affectionate letter to the husband. The post mark is examined, the letter is read aloud. 'And does my darling still love me as much as I love my darling? X X X.'

The co-respondent had been a friend of the husband's and had stayed on previous occasions with the couple. There were then, says counsel, no allegations of improper relationship.

The Judge: 'One talks of improper relationship in various senses – it covers a multitude of relationships.'

The wife is still standing at a loss. A curious thing happened, she says, just at the time, her wedding-ring came off in the wash.

'Rings do come off in the wash,' says the judge. '*Who* took the first step?'

'I don't know. We were fooling about.'

The Judge: 'Who started the fooling about?'

'I don't know.' Then, as if something had occurred to her.

'Oh, it wasn't him. If anyone, it was myself.'

Another letter to the husband had quickly followed. 'I am in love with Ted. I've gone away with him. Will you give me a divorce.' The husband ('I was completely and absolutely knocked over. I couldn't eat, my mouth was dry . . .') took a headlong railway journey across country, found the couple, begged the wife to return.

Witnesses had come and gone, giving evidence as to the married couple's normal, decent life before her fall. The wife's cookery has been praised, her spotless home, her thrift, her loving wifely ways. Now the co-respondent is on the stand and put through the hoops.

Counsel [for the husband]: 'Is she a good cook?'
Co-respondent [happily]: 'Oh, yes.'
Counsel: 'A good housekeeper?'

Co-respondent [who does not see it coming]: 'Yes, indeed.'
Counsel: 'A nice girl?'
Co-respondent: 'Hmm.'
Counsel: 'A woman beyond price?'
Co-respondent looks a little startled.
The husband is asking £1,500 damages.

The other side tries to establish some form of condonation. When the husband, driven by the news, had arrived, he had sat down, they say, and drunk coffee with the adulterous couple.

The judge quickly steps on this. He says kindly to the husband, 'I gather you had rather an exhausting journey behind you?' and to counsel, 'What has all this nonsense about coffee and breakfast got to do with it?' He then inquires about finances and is informed that the co-respondent has no assets other than the clothes he stands in. He is earning a small yearly salary with little immediate prospects of increase, and the rent of his cottage is going up.

The Judge: 'I am very much obliged to you for your assistance to the court – a very frank assistance.' The clerk below the dais now gets out of his seat, stands up on tip-toe and whispers to the judge who says courteously, 'Will you please excuse me for one moment?' Later: 'It's got to be a lump sum [as if puzzling it out for himself], I couldn't make an instalment order . . .'

Counsel for the Petitioner: 'In my submission, considering all the circumstances of the case, the sum of £1,500 would not be excessive.'

The Judge: 'If it causes the co-respondent to go bankrupt? It would be idle not to have that in mind.'
Counsel: 'My Lord, with respect, the husband is entitled . . .'
Mr Justice Lloyd-Jones [sadly, wisely]: 'I am only trying to introduce that note of relevancy.'

(The outcome: a decree nisi and £750 damages to the petitioner.)

HIS HONOUR JUDGE AARVOLD, the Recorder of London, has been a judge at the Old Bailey, the Central Criminal Court, for eleven years. It is a grim place, as places must be which are given over to dealing with criminal offences and with those who per-petrate them. Some people have been tried there in this and the last century who were genuinely and entirely innocent; yet on the whole, if a man has been committed to stand his trial at the Central Criminal Court it means that there is a fairly strong case against him and the chances, not of his getting off, but of his total innocence are low.

The day, as often, begins with applications. A man – open-mouthed and none too prepossessing – stands in the big dock, a uniformed warder at his heel. He is in custody on a charge of larceny, and applying for bail.

The Judge: 'Any police objections?'

Two previous convictions, the new offence committed just after release from prison.

The Judge [not addressing anyone in particular]: 'Not a case in which I think it appropriate to grant bail.'

A young barrister in a clean white wig ups and says that the accused man's wife is expecting a baby.

Eleven years spent in these courts toughen a man. The judge now looks across at the dock. 'One of the gravest punishments for crime is of course the trouble caused to families. I shall not grant you bail.'

'Put up K . . .' the usher cries and a frail little boy of seven-teen bounces up in the dock and the real case – lasting three days – begins. The boy pleads Not Guilty to several charges of Shooting with Intent. The prosecution opens with a shocking tale about this little creature wandering about London with a hired gun ('This geezer lets me have the Biretta till Monday for a couple of pounds and forty fags'), screwing empty flats, holding up sweet-shop tills and boys in cafés for their fancy clothes ('Take that leather off or I'll shoot you'). Some took it off, another got shot in the leg, another in the stomach. When he was arrested the boy is supposed to have said to the police, 'Has someone grassed on me? I'll kill him. You can't hang me now even if you did find me guilty. I'm not going on any fucking parade so that any crooked John can pick me out.' But he did. And he was picked out. He said, 'You are earning your fucking money today, it looks as if it was on me.' (And now the classic that crops up in so many statements made to the police.) 'All right: I did the lot.' Prosecution witnesses are called. A boy who was shot. A police inspector. The case tightens. A gunsmith. Judge Aarvold is being very good with him.

The judge is beginning to show his mettle. A workmanlike judge, not a talker, knowing his stuff inside out, not over tender. Yet wholly equable, unlikely to cry for the moon. He is a big man who was a rugger blue, plays golf and tennis. The face is round and full, and of healthy complexion. He once said in a speech, "There might be a lot to be said for corporal punishment of the juvenile, but one cannot put the clock back.'

The defence's turn. Their case is that the boy shot, but did not shoot to harm. He aimed into the air, he shot to miss, was able to do so being a good shot, having played since childhood with guns. On the two occasions when there *had* been harm, the boy had not been there. He had alibis. Moreover during the period of the hold-ups he had been under drugs. 'A few of the boys were on the pills – purple hearts – dexedrine – they made me feel *good*. I was blocked.'

K., a sickly slip of a boy, a kind of baby brother to Pinky in *Brighton Rock*, gives evidence. He is respectful, scared and wretchedly inarticulate. Only during one exchange does he show something like life.

'Have you disclosed the name of the person who rented you the gun?'
'Pardon?'
'Have you told anyone his name?'
'No.'
'Why not?'
'I'd get done.'
'Do you *really* think so?'
'I know so.'

The first alibi looks threadbare. K. had been down at Liverpool Street Station with a mate that Monday night.

'What for?'

'We were 'anging about.' The boy's voice hardly carries. No one bothers to do something about the microphone.

'From 7.30 to 10 p.m.?'

'We had a coffee . . .'

'What was the attraction of Liverpool Street Station?'

'Birds.'

The alibi for the second shooting is a serious matter. A real puzzler. (The jury later disagreed on it.) The boy says he was spending the Saturday night and Sunday at his mum and dad's home in another town. 'What did you have for breakfast?' 'I don't remember.' 'What did you do?' 'The usual things.' 'What were the usual things?' 'Going for a drive . . . putting on a record . . .' 'What did you have for dinner?' 'The usual Sunday dinner.' 'What was dinner?' 'I don't remember.' It isn't necessarily because he is lying; the answers fit well with a general lack-lustre inattentiveness. Parents and two neighbours, all evidently most respectable people, give evidence that the boy was in fact home for the week-end. How do they remember which week-end? The judge tries his best to establish a measure of certainty. Counsel is about to ask what happened on Saturday 17th –

'Now, Mr S., you must not lead about the dates.'

Counsel: 'My Lord, I do not see how I can put the question in any other way. On which Saturday –'

'Please, Mr S., *please*.'

Counsel: 'I don't know how to pinpoint without – [in anguish] if your Lordship will help me out?'

'You as experienced counsel –'

At this moment the witness herself supplied the date.

Later on the judge, trying once more to clinch the matter, asked the mother, 'Anything special happened that Sunday?'

'No . . . We had dinner . . . I washed up.'

Judge: 'Did you not talk to your son about the job you had just written to him about?'

'Oh, that. Yes, I did. I didn't know you wanted to know about that, sir, I mean my Lord.' Which seemed to leave the matter again where it had stood before.

When both sides had finished, the judge summed up. (It is here that the English and American judge part ways. The American judge states the law in his, often brief, charge to the jury and that is all. The English judge states the law and then sums up; that is, he goes very fully, often at great length, over all the evidence on both sides of the case. He generally tries not to, but may and does express an opinion, but the jury are not bound to follow it. Whether they will or not depends of course on a perplexity of factors hard to assess and varying with the nature and the personalities involved in each case.) In the course of a fair, businesslike summing-up, Judge Aarvold coined a phrase, quoting a youth who had said that K. was nothing without a gun, he spoke of the 'arrogant assertion of gun authority'.

ANOTHER OLD BAILEY COURT, another judge. A guest judge this time drafted, as a number of them are each month, from Queen's Bench in the Strand for a turn: Mr Justice Melford-Stevenson. Well-known from his KC and QC days when he led for the Crown in the Kenyatta appeal and was the Attorney General's junior in the John Bodkin Adams case. On the bench, he has a reputation for wit; also sharpness. Today he is dealing with a pretty unsavoury list. One man is telling a rigmarole about having been asked to go and do away with a solicitor.

> *The Judge*: '*What*?'
> *The Clerk* [diligently]: 'Not so fast for his Lordship's pen.'
> The man repeats his story.
> *The Judge*: 'The name of the gentleman you were invited to kill escapes you?'
> 'It was only in the course of conversation, sir.'
> *The Judge* [dead-pan]: 'I was aware of that.'

He has a shapely, rather quizzical face that is sometimes
crossed by a look of tight displeasure. The mouth is thin. He
wears the wig and red and ermine well. Presently he has to take a
plea of Guilty. A Jamaican in the dock who has messed about
with a little girl. An elderly barrister speaks up in mitigation.
'He says he was pleased the matter came to light.'

The judge is listening as if to something that the cat's brought
in.

Barrister: 'Hope springs eternal in defence counsel's breast.'
The judge closes his eyes.
Barrister [struggling on]: 'He has become engaged with his
father's consent.'
The Judge [again all there]: 'What on earth has that got to do
with it?'
Barrister [quite unmanned]: 'The father knows –'
The Judge [brutally impatient]: 'Knows *what*?'
Barrister: 'That he is engaged . . .'

The judge does what is called reserving sentence. 'I'll deal
with it tomorrow,' he says without a glance at the dock.

The long case of the week is a shocker. A cool young man, a
driver out of work; a day labourer and a merchant seaman are in
the dock. (One of them is a runaway from Borstal; the judge
knows this, the jury does not.) Heaped over a chair is a sordid
exposure of worn clothes, a soiled shirt, sweaters, a duffle-coat.
The prosecution say that the cool young man went to a homo-
sexual's flat in Paddington one night, cooked a chicken for his
host, drank some wine and later on let in his mates. They struck
down the owner of the flat and tied him up, and went to ransack
the place. They found no money, so they kicked and beat the
man. They did not take away much, a cigarette lighter, an open
bottle of gin, some coins from the gas meter they broke; but the
man was dead. They took his teeth out and put him upon the
bed. There was much blood.

A witness says that the cool young man told him, in the prison
hospital, that he had burnt all his clothes and bought an identical
set from the same shop. This the cool young man denies.

The Judge: 'Not so fast. *Wait.*'

Young Man: 'It was a joke.'

Counsel [in cross-examination, driving very hard]: 'Why did you tell this story.'

Young Man: 'I dunno . . . I was fed up. [*Sotto voce*] A copper's nark –'

The Judge: 'Listen! *Why did you tell this story?*'

Young Man: 'I was pulling his leg.'

There is the question why he went to the flat.

Counsel: 'Homosexuals are notoriously easy to rob?'

Young Man: 'I wouldn't know.'

Counsel: 'Homosexuals are particularly defenceless?'

No answer.

Counsel: 'Homosexuals are attracted to young men?'

Young Man: 'Well . . . to some.'

The Judge: 'The answer to this question is Yes.'

The defence stories, presented by a trio of most able barristers, are that the cool young man wasn't there at all: he had left the flat and was home and in bed before the other two came in; the seaman was there but had some drink and dozed off in another room. The third man went to the bathroom, had a pass made at him and went berserk: it was manslaughter in self-defence.

Counsel: 'He had a horror of homosexuals. He told a witness that he had been indecently attacked as a small boy.'

The Judge interrupts: 'He told the witness that he *would say* that he had been attacked as a boy.' The jury takes the point.

Counsel enlarges upon the explosive element in the situation: one innocent man, one or perhaps two guilty – would they not have told on one another if their stories were not true?

Before summing up the judge apologizes to the jury. 'You will find that I will have to repeat much of what you have already heard . . . facts that you will no doubt have by heart . . . But repeat them I must.'

The regret is genuine. The exposition that follows is beautifully concise. The verdict is murder and the sentence for the three is death.

To RETURN from the unmitigated harshness of the Old Bailey is like coming out at the southern end of an alpine tunnel; for all their daily heartbreak there is an element of mellowness about the Law Courts in the Strand.

'£650 a year if you include clothes and extras. And that's not Eton.'

'Gone up again –?'

'*Well, well, well.*'

'What about the other children?'

'Mother suggests to decide it all later on.'

'You can't leave it – you have to put the boy down.'

Three Lord Justices of Appeal in full accoutrements are sitting in a row. The fate of a son of divorced parents has been thrown before the courts. The judge in the lower court has made an order to send the boy, as the father wishes, to a certain preparatory school. The mother is appealing. She would like to keep the boy at home and anyhow the school is far beyond his expectations.

The presiding Lord Justice says, 'It's a place with the aura of great riches about it.'

Lord to the Left: 'Who wants the tune must be prepared to pay the piper.'

Counsel puts in that there had been originally some provisions.

Lord to the Left: 'Always the same story: when people divorce they find out that it costs more to run two homes than one.'

Another school, says counsel, would have been ready to take him, but now term is about to begin . . .

Suddenly there comes a great mournful trumpeting wail from the lord to the right. '*Nobody has thought about the boy's future at all!*' It is a most idiosyncratic voice, powerful and at the same time pernickety, a private voice, utterly unself-conscious, and it is Lord Justice Harman's. 'We have been arguing and arguing for months and no one has been thinking about the boy's future *at all*. It's quite disgraceful.'

The mother, who is sitting inconspicuously in the back of the court, mentions – through counsel – a church school which remits fees for singing in the choir.

'Only the time his voice lasts.'

Lord Willmer, the presiding judge, asks, 'What's his voice like?'

Counsel whispers to the mother. 'Rather good, my Lord.'

'The fees in that place are £90.'

'If you didn't sing.'

Lord Harman, who has recovered, says, 'I see a shine of reason.' Then as a new thought strikes him, 'What about kitting out the boy?'

Lord Harman is a towering big man, looking more like a soldier than a lawyer. In fact, he is a scholar.

Their Lordships decide to adjourn the case. As counsel are shuffling up their bundles, Lord Harman is still worrying about something else. 'Who is the school to be responsible to?' he mutters. 'Who does matron get on to when the boy is ill or falls down the stairs . . . ?'

Next comes our old bugbear the single woman plaintiff.

'I gave the caravan to the agent to let it for me, to let it for me in the summer, he would give me the rent. He let it for many more weeks than he let on to me so he said he would give me £370 for Troubadour in part exchange for Sun-Parlour. Sun-parlour is my holiday van.'

Lord Harman: '*Really*.'

'He didn't pay the insurance company, I gave him seven pounds ten for that but he kept it. When he sent the man in the spring to fetch her he would pay only £345.'

Lord Harman (to himself): 'I don't understand this at all.'

'It was his own fault when the man came to fetch her in the bad weather. The registrar in the County Court said she had deteriorated but it was his pigheadedness really with the man's muddy boots tramping all over her. Troubadour was spotless.'

Lord Willmer: 'I confess I am very confused.'

'He said he had money on hand for me in October. £84–10–0.'

Lord Winn: 'Yes – ?'

'That was the account. He gave me a cheque.'

Lord Winn: 'Please don't believe I am badgering you – only I want to try to understand.'

'He should have paid me my payment. £25 is a small fortune for me.'

Lord Harman: 'Sorry, I can't follow.'

'It was because he said there was an odour, the liquid from the Elsan had spilt, the lino was stained, that's what he said to the registrar.'

Lord Harman (apparently seeing a shine of reason): 'Madam, *did* you accept a payment in settlement?'

'It was not my settlement.'

Lord Harman: 'Did you *accept* £84–10–0?'

'Well, I had to.'

Lord Harman (exploding): 'Why?'

'I didn't know a soul . . . I had been ill.'

Lord Willmer: '£84–10–0 for Troubadour?'

'Oh, no, My Lord, that was for Bluebird.'

Lord Winn: 'It is absolutely essential that we label these A, B and C.'

ASSIZE AT THE County Town. The sun is shining and Her Majesty's robed judges arrive along the High Street in procession. The town seems en fête for them, traffic stops, the Daimlers glitter, on the steps of County Hall a guard of honour is waiting.

Inside, there is an ease and friendliness not found in London courts. Warders, constables and public are on nodding terms. The jury in the box looks more alert, they are talking to each other with some animation. The usher, in a human voice, says,

'Rise, please.' Mr Justice Elwes walks on. One is captivated at first sight. His figure is elegant; his fine, handsome face looks both intelligent and kind.

A woebegone youth is sitting in the dock. He is quietly crying. The case had reached a closing stage the afternoon before, the judge begins at once in a low persuasive voice. 'It has nothing to do with me, members of the jury [he taps his breasts with a light finger], nothing to do with me, the judge has not got to tell the jury how they ought to find . . . Nor have you to pay any attention to any opinion I myself may have formed . . . You must exercise a measure of intellectual discipline yourselves. If you look at this boy, allowed to drive this large vehicle, this very heavy furniture van, for long hours, alone, without a mate, at night, this eighteen-year-old boy, at the beginning of his life, by one forgetful moment, in a head-on collision, causing the death of two innocent people . . . If you have sympathy with him, I do not disagree with you.'

But now he must come to the law. The law of Dangerous Driving is that it is no defence to say, I was tired and my concentration slackened. 'It matters not in law whether he was reckless, careless, momentarily inattentive after a hard day [the judge, speaking, uses his very fine, his beautiful hands, snapping long fingers], or if he was incompetent . . .'

Now the facts. A straight road. Good visibility. It had stopped raining. No crest; no mechanical defect; no emergency. The van just drifted across the road, crossed the white line, crashed. The defence say that there may have been a sudden glare, that someone in the oncoming queue flashed his headlights, that the boy was dazzled. A driver *might* have switched on full lights, *might* be reluctant to admit this in the circumstances. However, the jury would recall that witnesses who drove behind the van were certain that at all times the oncoming lights were dipped. 'Members of the jury, you must be fair . . . with a sensible, useful fairness . . .'

A working day at Assizes is a full day. As the jury goes out, the youth is replaced in the dock by a clean-shaven youngish man in a blue serge suit who looks like a police officer. He is a police officer. Today he is in the very unenviable position of having to answer charges of dishonesty. This man, this member of a local force, who is married, has two children, is said to be in no financial difficulties ('all his hire-purchase commitments well in hand'), has appropriated over the last two years lost property handed in to the police. Namely, according to the indictment, 'A black leather purse containing £3 in Bank of England notes, 1s. 1d. in cash, a packet of razor blades and a half-penny stamp.' Such theft necessarily involves some knowledgeable tampering with forms. Namely, 'Forging a Lost Property Sheet belonging to the X Borough Police, purporting to show that he handed back a black leather purse to the loser, one Mary W., who had signed a receipt for the same.' There are further charges of similar thefts – purses, wage packets – and false entries. The total sum involved comes to £23–5–7. The accused looks a man with his head well screwed on.

Before we get much further, the driving case jury returns. The police officer is bundled out, the youth bundled in. The verdict is Guilty.

'You have come to the only possible verdict,' says the judge, then, quickly, 'I think I can help. I want to give all the help I can to that clean-living boy . . . They are short of wage-earners in that family. I wish I *could* make out a probation order – as he needs looking after for a bit – but I cannot do that *and* disqualify him from driving.'

The officer in charge stands ready to step into the box to give information about the boy's character and circumstances. The judge waves him off. 'I don't think that will be necessary here.' Indeed, he already has it on his finger-tips. Now he speaks to the boy. 'I shall disqualify you for the next three years – I believe you will be the only man in England convicted of this offence who gets away without a fine. Well, a decent young man that you are, I hope you will allow people to help you to get another job, earning a good wage, perhaps a better wage than your last one?' To the tip-staff, 'Let him go now.' To his clerk, 'Perhaps one could arrange for the probation officer of the region to keep an eye on him, see that he gets a proper start?

He shouldn't be left alone now. If the officer would be kind enough to come here, I should be very glad to see him at any time.'

The police constable's case resumes. The whole thing was uncovered when some loser appeared one day to claim his property and found that it had been handed to someone else who had left a signature and an address. The address proved to be non-existent; so did a number of others on the books. Suspicion fell on every officer who had had access to the lost-property cupboards and the forms. (When the office routine as described by the prosecution is challenged on some points by the defence the judge intervenes, 'We want evidence not as to what the rules are, not as to what people *ought to do*, but what people *did do*.') Handwriting tests and interviews with a police inspector followed. Suspicion settled on the defendant when it was found that all the signatures appeared to be in his own, disguised, hand. This inspector now gives evidence.

'When confronted with the fictitious entries –'

The Judge (interrupting): '*Questioned* entries, would be better than *fictitious*.'

Inspector: 'He said to me [and now we have a policeman's words quoted by a policeman] "The Ws and Ys are similar but they are not the same, and if they were similar I wouldn't tell you even if I thought they were." '

The defendant elects to go into the witness-box. Mr Justice Elwes – Oratory School, Christ Church, Member Standing Committee of the Jockey Club, Recreations (*Who's Who*): Music, Letters, the Visual Arts – leans over and looks at him intently. 'Your evidence is so very important – especially for you – so will you please speak up?'

The policeman's case is simple. At every instance a man or woman came to him and claimed found property. He handed it over. They, not he, supplied the fake addresses, signed the names. Furthermore, on one material day he was never alone but working all day long at a small table next to his sergeant in the office.

Defence Counsel: 'I must ask you this. Did you steal that money?'

Defendant: 'I did not.'

Counsel: 'Have you ever stolen any money or made a false entry?'

Defendant: 'I most certainly did not.'

Counsel for the Prosecution [in cross-examination]: 'You had the opportunity?'

Defendant: 'Yes, but I didn't do it.'

Counsel: 'The opportunity for all six charges?'

Defendant: 'Yes, I could have done it, but I did not.'

He makes a good impression. Yet his evidence is totally uncorroborated. It is his word against everything else. The handwriting expert (who had been working with anonymous samples from every member of that force) is very definite. (Defendant: 'I can't prove him wrong. But I know he is wrong.')

Counsel: '*Is it mere coincidence* that six different people gave *you* false addresses?'

Defendant: 'I can only accept what people tell me.'

'Why should genuine people give you false addresses?'

Defendant: 'Well, there are people who do not like them registered by the police.'

'How can a fake loser accurately describe a lost purse? The contents?'

Defendant: 'There are ways. He might be a neighbour.'

'You say you were never alone, a sergeant was at your elbow? Who was he?'

Defendant: 'Sergeant P.'

'Is he alive? Is he still a member of the Force? *He is not here?*'

So it still is only the defendant's word. The judge, in a rather elaborate, strictly technical summing-up, leaves it squarely to the jury. Their verdict is Guilty and the convicted man – of hitherto blameless character – is sentenced to twelve months. The enigma of a life spoilt for £23–5–7 remains unrevealed.

The next case concerns a woman of forty and a farm labourer of twenty-three, and the facts make the whole court look very glum. He has pleaded Guilty to Indecently Assaulting a girl eleven years old, she to Encouraging Indecent Assault on a girl eleven years old, namely, her daughter. The woman looks bedraggled, the man looks an oaf.

The girl, counsel explains, is an invalid who spends most of her time in hospital. She is obliged to wear leg braces. On occasional visits home she had to share a bed with two sisters. The mother put her in the man's bed. He said, 'I asked Mum if it would be all right as we want to get married. Mum said it would be all right. "Don't touch her before she goes back to that hospital, they'll find out." I kissed and cuddled her, but I didn't do anything dirty.'

Counsel: 'My Lord, I understand that this man is very naive indeed. There are some rather unusually distressing features in this case. It all began when he first came to live with that family and was seduced by the elder sister, Dorothy, who is seventeen. He then started to have sexual relations with the mother, in fact he has been living quite openly with her.'

The Judge (quietly): 'The husband? With the husband in the house?'

Counsel: 'With the husband in the house, my Lord. There are also two brothers, in custody at present. There is a charge of buggery.'

The Judge (even more quietly): 'I think a probation order . . . The first thing seems to get this man away from that family . . .'

The word 'prison' is not spoken: the court staff look at one another with surprised long faces.

At the end of the day, another dejected youth is put up. He had pleaded Guilty the afternoon before to attempting to obtain a sedative by violence. He wanted to do away with himself. There is medical evidence of acute depression. The judge had reserved sentence.

He now says, 'We want to deal with the physical causes of your depression – that can be done, you know. What is said about you is encouraging: you need help, your intelligence is well over average. Now you need treatment, hospital treatment, you must understand that. A maximum of twelve months, but I don't believe for a moment that they will keep you there for anything like the whole time.

'I could not deal with this last night – for some purely administrative reasons – you *would* see that?'

For the first time the boy raises his head. He looks across the immense gulf that separates the judge from the dock. 'Yes,' he says. 'Thank you, my Lord.'

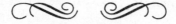

THE TRIAL OF *LADY CHATTERLEY'S LOVER*

Regina v. Penguin Books Ltd
1960

Lawyers have been known to wrest from reluctant juries
triumphant verdicts of acquittal for their clients even when
those clients were clearly and unmistakably innocent.

– OSCAR WILDE

How beastly the bourgeois is especially the male of the
   species . . .
Let him meet a new emotion, let him be faced with
   another man's need.
Let him come home to a bit of moral difficulty.
Let life face him with a new demand on his
   understanding
And then watch him go soggy, like a wet meringue.
Watch him turn into a mess, either a fool or a bully.
Just watch the display of him, confronted with a new
   demand on his intelligence,
A new life-demand.

– D.H. LAWRENCE

The CROWN v. Penguin Books Limited Before Mr
Justice Byrne And A Jury At The Central Criminal Court
London October 20 – November 2, 1960.

LET THERE be no mistake: this was a criminal prosecution. It was entirely unlike the action on the same book
between Grove Press Inc. and the Postmaster General that was

heard before a judge in the United States District Court in 1959. Publication of an obscene article is a criminal offence in Britain, and before the new Act of Parliament was passed in July, 1959, there was no defence against it – other than a factual denial of having published; the author had no right to be heard in defence of his own book, nor had publishers, booksellers, critics or members of the general or specialized public. The penalty could be a prison sentence, and there was no maximum limit as to the number of years. The book did not have to be judged as a whole. The practice was to give juries passages marked by the prosecution or the police on which they had to decide whether the book was obscene or not, and that was that.

The new Act was designed to protect bona fide literature, and it took five years of devoted effort to get it passed. It tightened the powers against pornography, Judge Woolsey's dirt-for-dirt's-sake. It did not put through all that the reformers could have wished, but the best, in the circumstances, they could get. The most important new provisions of the Act are that the book must now be judged as a whole; that literary merit is a justification; and that the defence may call expert evidence.

Almost exactly one year afterward, two things happened. 1960 was the year of the seventy-fifth anniversary of D.H. Lawrence's birth and the thirtieth anniversary of his death; it was also the year of Penguin Books' twenty-fifth jubilee. They decided to round off their edition of Lawrence's works by publishing the unexpurgated version of *Lady Chatterley's Lover*. The authorities decided to prosecute. Penguin voluntarily delayed distribution and, not wishing to involve a bookseller, provided evidence of publication by handing over some copies to a police inspector by arrangement, and so offered themselves up as subjects of a test case.

The reaction of one section of the public was that this was plain incredible; had not the new Act been created to protect precisely this kind of book by this kind of author? They began to read or reread *Lady Chatterley's Lover* (the American edition was circulating in the country) and, reading, became aware that indeed a grave injustice was about to be committed. It seemed a monstrous irony that the authorities – who surely must have *some* duty to the public – should have acted against one of the very few writers of our time who bitterly protested against prostitution and perversion. Scores of eminent people wrote to Penguin, offering their testimony, and so began the mounting of the first full-scale literary trial in our legal history.

THE AUTHORITIES prepared by sending down to the Old Bailey Mr Justice Byrne – since retired – considered by the profession one of the best criminal judges in England (he tried Lord Haw-Haw), an Irishman and seemingly a man with little taste for fiction. The prosecution was entrusted to Mr Mervyn Griffith-Jones, Second Senior Counsel to the Crown at the Central Criminal Court, Eton, Cambridge, Coldstream Guards, and a veteran of many previous obscenity cases. What one could see of his face in court was framed by the wig: high cheekbones, a florid colour, a strong jaw and a thin mouth – the head of a conventionally handsome man. He neither stooped nor lounged.

The trial, like every major trial for a century, took place in Number 1 Court at the Old Bailey. (And as if to nudge, as it were, the historical undertones, Oscar Wilde's son, Mr Vyvyan Holland, was present the first day.) Number 1 is the largest courtroom in the building, which does not mean that it is not fairly cramped and small. It uncomfortably holds two hundred people, most of whom are unable to see *and* hear justice being done. The acoustics are wretched. The huge dock, solidly planted in the centre, successfully shuts off vision and sound.

The first move was the calling of the jury. Now, in the case of United States *v.* One Book Called *Ulysses*, the parties waived their right to a trial by jury, and Judge Woolsey commented on this as 'highly appropriate in a case involving books . . . a jury trial would have been extremely unsatisfactory, in fact an almost impossible way to deal with it . . .' And, as it is ironical to remember in the light of what did happen, the defence in the present case is said to have shared that view; given the choice, counsel would have chosen trial by a judge. But in English law there is no actual choice; the magistrate must make the final decision; in the case of Penguin it was trial by jury.

An English jury is a permanent unknown quantity, a number of men and women chosen at random and finally by lot, about whom nothing is known, or allowed to be known, by anyone concerned. They are – for ever – so many names and faces. (There is an unwritten law that a jury cannot be spoken to afterwards, and even if somebody did try to speak to them – as some of the press did in this case – the jury would not answer, and if it did answer nobody would dare to print it.) The fine art of weeding out a jury, as is done in the United States, is no longer practised in England. The defence has still the right to object to up to seven jurors without giving a reason, the peremptory challenge as it is called. But it is an obsolescent right, very rarely used nowadays.

Here it *was* used. Counsel made some slight sign and the Clerk said to the man who had just been marched into the jury box, 'Will you step down, please,' and the man did. He left the box. We all looked at him. Why? He had been the fourth or fifth man called; the box went on filling up; the twelfth and last juror was already halfway through his oath when there was another last-instant rejection. Amen said, and it would have been too late. That last man had been making a hash of trying to read his printed formula.

Now, the woman who was drawn in the last man's stead, and who was to become the twelfth acting juror in this trial, was a most educated-looking woman, with an alive and responsive face, and she may well have been the kingpin in the decision of that jury. Of course we shall never know . . .

Mr Griffith-Jones, opening for the Crown, addressed them. His evidence, he said, would be this book: *Lady Chatterley's Lover*. Penguin proposed to publish it at the price of 3/6, and indeed had printed 200,000 copies of it for sale. His voice was thin, clear and slow, and at this stage neutral, level. He explained the law as it stood now.

' "An article shall be deemed obscene if its effect, taken as a whole, is such as to tend to deprave and corrupt persons who are likely, having regard to all relevant circumstances, to read the matter contained in it.'' ' There was, however, another Section of the Act which said that it was not an offence to publish ' ''If it is proved that the article is for the public good, on the ground that it is in the interest of science, literature, art or learning or other objects of general concern.'' '

The jury would have to give one verdict, but they would really have two questions to decide. One, whether the book was obscene; two, if so, whether its publication was justified as being for the public good. 'If you find the book is not obscene, that is an end of this matter and you must acquit. But if you find that it *is* obscene, then you have to go on to consider – is it proved that publication is in the interest of literature, art and so forth . . .

'A point you have to consider is how freely the book is going to be distributed. Is it a book published at £5 a copy as a historical volume, or is it a book widely distributed at a price the merest infant can afford?

'When you have read this book, you may think that it sets upon a pedestal promiscuous and adulterous intercourse, commends sensuality almost as a virtue, and encourages and advocates vulgarity of thought and language.'

Mr Griffith-Jones went on more emotionally: 'You may think one of the ways you can test this book is to ask yourself the question: would you approve of your own son and daughter – because girls can read as well as boys – reading this book? Is it a book you would have lying in your own house? Is it a book you would wish your wife or your servant to read?

'Members of the jury, you may think that the book is a picture of little else than vicious indulgence in sex and sensuality. I wish to concede that D.H. Lawrence is a world-recognized writer; I also concede, though not to such a great extent, that there may be some literary merit in this book, not to put it any higher.

'The book is about a young woman whose husband was wounded in the First World War so that he was paralysed from the waist downwards and unable to have sexual intercourse. I invite you to say that in effect the book is a description of how that woman, deprived of sex from her husband, satisfied her sexual desires – a sex-starved girl and how she satisfied that starvation with a particularly sensual man who happened to be her husband's gamekeeper.'

In a voice quivering with thin-lipped scorn, Mr Griffith-Jones went on:

'There are thirteen passages of sexual intercourse in this book. The curtain is never drawn. One follows them not only into the bedroom, but into bed, and one remains with them there. The only variation between all thirteen occasions is the time and the place where it happens. So one starts in my lady's boudoir; one goes to a hut in the forest with a blanket laid down on the floor. We see them doing it again in the undergrowth, in the forest amongst the shrubbery, and again in the undergrowth in the pouring rain, both of them stark naked and dripping with raindrops. One sees them in the keeper's cottage: first in the evening on the hearthrug; then we have to wait until dawn to see them doing it again in bed. Finally we move the site to Bloomsbury, and we have it all over again in a Bloomsbury boardinghouse.

'That is the variation – the time and the place where it happens with the emphasis always on the *pleasure*, the *satisfaction*, the *sensuality* . . .

'Sex, members of the jury, is dragged in at every opportunity, even the girl's father, a Royal Academician, introduces a description of his legs and loins. The book says little about the character of any of these people; they are little more than bodies which continuously have sexual intercourse with one another. The plot, you may find, is little more than padding, until we reach the hut again, the cottage or the undergrowth in the forest . . .'

The jury sat through this blank-faced as juries are apt to sit. Then came the shock tactics: the passage in the prosecution speech which is by now well-known, the four-letter-word count.

'The word "fuck",' said Mr Griffith-Jones, 'appears thirty times. The word "cunt" fourteen times. The word "balls" thirteen times; "shit" six times; "arse" and "piss" three times apiece.'

This was flung across the court with deliberate brutality. And we were shocked. Not because of the words – the words, paradoxically enough, are common-place in an English court of law; we are much less mealy-mouthed in that than many of the Continental courts – but shocked by the staggering insensitiveness of this approach, the bookkeeper's approach, the line of attack. So this was to be the quality of the stand against a work by D.H. Lawrence.

An American writer, who was next to me, said, 'Why this is going to be the upper-middle-class English version of our Tennessee Monkey Trial.'

The prosecution speech ended by pointing out that Penguin stated it had taken thirty years for it to be possible to publish the unmutilated version of *Lady Chatterley's Lover* in this country. 'You, members of the jury,' Mr Griffith-Jones said in a tone both ominous and smug, 'will have to say whether it *has* taken thirty years, or whether it will take still longer.'

Then the prosecution called their one and only witness, a policeman. Yes, he said, he had been given a dozen copies of the book in the Penguin offices. (This was formal evidence of publication.)

The chief witness, the book itself, was still unread; and before reading it the jury had to hear the opening speech by the defence. Penguin had briefed a dazzling team of counsel. The leader was Mr Gerald Gardiner QC,* one of the great silks of the London Bar, making one of the largest, perhaps the largest, income that it is possible to make there these days. Mr Gardiner is a Quaker, a law reformer and a man recognized for his high principles. His court style is unemotional, cool, undramatic; he's the man who appeals to reason. His juniors were Mr Jeremy Hutchinson and Mr Richard Du Cann, two distinguished barristers in their own right. Mr Hutchinson was himself brought up within an inner circle of the English world of letters, his father and mother having been patrons of the arts and friends of the writers of their time, George Moore, the

*The future Lord Chancellor.

Woolfs, Aldous Huxley, D.H. Lawrence . . .

This is how Gerald Gardiner began. He spoke gently, one might say compassionately. 'You have been told that this book is full of descriptions of sexual intercourse – and so it is. That it is full of four-letter words – and so there are.

'You may ask yourself at once: how comes it that reputable publishers, apparently after considerable thought and quite deliberately, are publishing an appalling book of the nature which has been described to us? . . . Penguin Books began in 1935 under a man called Lane, a man who thought that people like himself who were not very rich should be able to buy books. They started with a novel and some detective stories, then came classics and translations of masterpieces of literature, all costing sixpence. Twenty-five years later they had sold 250,000,000 books; they had published the whole of Shakespeare, most of Shaw; they had published fourteen books by D.H. Lawrence, and now they intended to publish the rest, including *Lady Chatterley's Lover*. This book has had unfortunately a history . . .'
It was written in 1928; it had not been possible to publish it at that time. 'There are many books circulating in London now which nobody would have thought ought to have been printed even twenty years ago.' There had been expurgated editions of *Lady Chatterley*, and there would have been nothing to stop Penguin years ago from publishing one, but they had always refused to publish a mutilated book. The expurgated edition was not the book Lawrence wrote. One could have expurgated editions of *Hamlet* and of the *Canterbury Tales*, but they would not be the books Shakespeare or Chaucer wrote.

The dock in this trial, said Mr Gardiner, was empty. The Crown had decided to prosecute Penguin merely as a company, and not the individual directors responsible. 'But there is nothing to stop them from what they frequently have done before. Possibly the prosecution thought that a jury might come to a verdict of Guilty rather more readily if the dock were empty than if they had someone sitting there.'

He then read dictionary definitions of To Deprave and To Corrupt. ' "To make morally bad; to pervert; to deteriorate;

to make rotten; to infect, taint; to render unsound, to debase, to defile . . ." ' Strong words, and, as Mr Gardiner at once pointed out, 'So for a book to be obscene within the meaning of the law, it must obviously effect a change of character, a leading on of the reader to do something wrong which he would not otherwise have done.

'When you have read the book you will see certain things which the author was aiming at . . . Mr Griffith-Jones has suggested that this was a book which contained thirteen descriptions of physical intercourse, and the only variation between them was the time and place. I would suggest that you will find exactly the opposite. Here is a book about England of the Twenties . . . Lawrence's message is that the society of his day was sick, the result of the machine age and the importance which everybody attached to money, and to the extent to which mind had been stressed at the expense of the body, and that what we ought to do was to re-establish the personal relationships. And one of the greatest things, the author thought, was the relationship of a man and a woman in love, and their physical union formed an essential part of a relation which was normal and wholesome and not something to be ashamed of, but something to be discussed openly and frankly . . . Now if a man is going to write a book of that kind, and deal with the physical relation between the sexes, it is necessary to describe what he means.

'I submit that the descriptions of physical union were necessary for what Lawrence was trying to say.

'It is quite true that the book includes what are called four-letter words, and it is quite plain that what the author intended was to drag these words out of the rather shameful connotation which they had achieved since Victorian times. The attitude of shame with which large numbers of people have always viewed sex in any form has reduced us to the position where it is not at all easy for fathers and mothers to find words to describe to their children the physical union. The author thought that if he used what had been part of our spoken speech for about six hundred years, he could purify it . . . Whether he succeeded or not in his attempt to purify these words by dragging them into the light of day, there is nothing in the words themselves which can deprave or corrupt. If these words can deprave or corrupt, then ninety-five percent of the Army, Navy and Air Force are past redemption.

'Whole parts of the book may (and I do not doubt will) shock you; but there is nothing in the book which will in fact do anybody any harm. No one would suggest that the Director of Public Prosecutions would become depraved by reading the book, nor counsel, nor witnesses; no one would suggest that the judge and jury would become corrupted; it is always someone else, it is never ourselves!'

When Mr Gardiner had done, it was already afternoon, and the Judge said that the question now was how the reading was to be arranged. Mr Gardiner stepped forward, and so did Mr Griffith-Jones, and the following exchange took place.

Mr Gardiner: 'I understand the usual practice has been for the jury to take the book home.'

The Judge: 'I don't think I'm in agreement with that.'

The Judge looked an elderly gentleman, with a polite, dry voice; a wizened bit of face looked out from the full wig. Upright, he gave the impression old judges sometimes give, of a husk, light as kindling, under the scarlet robes.

Mr Gardiner: 'The jury rooms are jolly uncomfortable. There are hard wooden chairs, and anything more unnatural than twelve men and women sitting on hard chairs around a table reading cheek by jowl in one another's presence is hard to imagine.'

The Judge tilted his head.

Mr Gardiner stood hunched up and tall. His face looked flexible, yet expressionless, and quite gray.

Mr Griffith-Jones: 'I have no wish to cause the jury any discomfort, but, in my submission, for them to read the book in the jury room is the proper way.'

Mr Gardiner: 'When you read, what you read is private to the author and you. Besides some people read more slowly than others –'

The Judge (quietly): 'In my experience, books are read in

court.' Here the Clerk put his head above the dais. Confabulations. 'The Clerk does not agree that the jury rooms are uncomfortable.' Pause. 'I have never been in a jury room myself.'

Mr Gardiner: 'The average rate of reading is about two hundred words a minute . . . What would happen when one member of the jury has finished reading and others have not?'

The Judge (to the jury box): 'I am very sorry, I don't want to put you to any kind of discomfort, but if you were to take this book home you might have distractions.'

So the jury was directed to present themselves next morning, and the case was adjourned.

WHEN THE case resumed one week later on Day Two, as they call it, the place was filled with men and women who looked each more like themselves than it is customary for any multitude to do: the expert witnesses. Rumours as to who was going to appear had been circulating for some months. In the press, names were piled on speculative names. In fact, the actual list was unknown, and, what's more, remained so until the last witness has showed up on the last day. The solicitors responsible for organizing the defence had kept it absolutely quiet. One popular paper spread the startling news that a fleet of London taxis was standing by to convey the poets of England from where they might lurk to the Old Bailey. As it turned out, the actual selections were much more subtle, much more effective and much more *terre à terre*.

The day began with Mr Griffith-Jones asking for the witnesses to be out of court during each other's testimony. Mr Gardiner objected that this was not the custom as far as experts were concerned. Mr Justice Byrne ruled that if there was no agreement on this point by the two sides, the custom was for the witnesses to stay out. A number of men and women thereupon withdrew.

How does one give evidence as to literary merit in a court

of law? We were soon to hear. The first witness called was Mr Graham Hough, the literary critic and D.H. Lawrence specialist, Lecturer in English and Fellow of Christ's College, Cambridge.

Mr Gardiner: 'When did you first read the unexpurgated edition of *Lady Chatterley's Lover*?'

Mr Hough: 'In about 1940.' (This question was put to everyone, and all, whatever their upbringing or generation, had at one time or another read an underground copy.)

Mr Gardiner: 'Will you tell us something about Lawrence's place in English literature?'

Mr Hough: 'He is generally recognized as being one of the most important novelists of this century. I should put him with Hardy and with Conrad and George Eliot. I do not think that is seriously disputed.'

'How many books have been written about D.H.L.?'

'About eight hundred published.'

'How do you rank *Lady Chatterley*?'

'I don't think it's the best of Lawrence's novels, but not the least good either. About fifth place. He wrote nine.'

'Will you tell us what is the theme or meaning of this book?'

'. . . An attempt to give a sympathetic understanding to a very painful, intricate human situation. The book is in fact concerned with the relationships between men and women, with their sexual relations, and with the nature of marriage – all matters of great importance to us all.'

Mr Gardiner: 'It has been claimed that sex is dragged in at every opportunity and the plot is little more than padding.'

'I totally disagree. If true, this would be an attack on the integrity and honesty of the author. But it is quite false. In the first place, it is a matter of simple numerical proportion – the sexual passages occupy no more than about thirty pages of the whole book, a book of some three hundred pages. No man in his senses is going to write a book of three hundred pages as mere padding . . . And then the literary merit of the non-sexual passages is very high.'

Mr Gardiner: 'It has been suggested that the book puts upon

a pedestal promiscuous and adulterous intercourse.'

Mr Hough: 'Promiscuity hardly comes into it. It is very much condemned by Lawrence. It is true that at the centre of the book there is an adulterous situation – that is true of a great deal of the literature of Europe.'

'It has been said that the only variation in the scenes of intercourse is in the places they take place. Do you agree?'

'No, I don't! They show the development of Connie Chatterley's awareness of her nature. They are not repetitive. They are different and necessary to the author's purpose.'

Mr Gardiner: 'How far are the descriptions of intercourse relevant or necessary?'

'They are extremely necessary. Lawrence was trying to show sexual relationships more clearly than is usually done in fiction. Lawrence was making a bold experiment.'

'A what?' said the Judge.

'A bold experiment.'

'A bold experiment,' repeated the Judge as he wrote it down.

Mr Gardiner: 'How far are the four-letter words relevant or necessary?'

Mr Hough: 'May I answer that by explaining why they are in? In Lawrence's view, there is no proper language to talk about sexual matters. They are either discussed in clinical terms, which deprive them of all emotional content, or they are described in words that are usually thought to be coarse or obscene. He wished to find a language in which sex could be discussed plainly and not irreverently, and to do this he tried to redeem the normally obscene words by using them in a context that is entirely serious. I don't myself think that this is successful, but that is what he was trying to do. In trying to treat sex in this way, Lawrence had few precedents before him. He had to try to find a way through.'

Mr Gardiner: 'Do you spend a great deal of your time teaching young people?'

Mr Hough: 'I do.'

'And have you a daughter of eighteen and a son of twelve?'

'I have.'

So far, so good. Mr Hough had given his answers with thoughtful care. The jury had been sitting through their course in literary criticism with non-committal attention. Now came the first cross-examination.

Mr Griffith-Jones: 'Do you know a lady called Esther Forbes?'

Mr Hough: 'No. I'm afraid not.'

'Do you know a lady called Katherine Anne Porter?'

'A writer of short stories. American . . . Very distinguished.'

'Are you familiar with a magazine called *Encounter*?'

'*Encounter*? Yes, I am.'

'Is *Encounter* a serious publication?'

Mr Hough: 'Reasonably so.' (Laughter, instantly suppressed, in one section of the court; stony faces in the rest.)

Mr Griffith-Jones: 'Would you agree with this American lady writing in *Encounter* that this novel is "a dreary, sad performance, with some passages of unintentionally hilarious low comedy", and "written with much inflamed apostolic solemnity"?'

Mr Hough: 'I think that is an eccentric opinion.'

Mr G.-J. (quickly): 'Because you do not agree with it? Do you agree with this view of Lady Chatterley, ". . . she is merely a moral imbecile . . . she is stupid"?'

'Connie is not stupid; she is an emancipated young woman of the period, friendly, warmhearted, patient –'

'What do you mean warmhearted – *filled with sex*?'

'No – this is not what *I* mean.'

Mr G.-J.: 'Miss Porter says the book is "a blood-chilling anatomy of the activities of the rutting season between two rather dull persons". Do you think that is a view one is entitled to hold?'

Mr Hough: 'Oh, anyone is entitled to hold any view. This one disposes of the argument that the book excites the sexual passions.'

(Again there is a slight ripple of laughter. Did the jury stir uneasily at academic levity?)

Mr G.-J.: 'Is this book "the feeble daydream of a dying man sitting under the umbrella pines indulging his sexual fantasies"?' (He puts the magazine down and looks at the witness.) *'Is this novel the feeble daydream of a dying man?'*

Mr Hough (very coldly): 'Lawrence died two years after publication.'

Mr Griffith-Jones dropped it, and started on another tack. 'Should a good book by a good writer repeat things again and again? This is a tiresome habit, is it not?'

'I don't agree with that. It is a technique frequently employed . . . There is a great deal of repetition in the Bible –'

'Never mind the Bible. We are concerned with *this* book. Listen to this [reading]: "Connie went slowly home . . . Another self was alive in her, burning and molten and soft in her womb and bowels and with this self she adored him. She adored him till her knees were weak as she walked. In her womb and bowels she was flowing and alive now and vulnerable and helpless in adoration . . ." *Womb and bowels, womb and bowels –'* said Mr Griffith-Jones. 'Is that good writing? Or is it ludicrous?'

'Not to me.'

'We have two parts of her anatomy coupled together twice in three lines. Is that *expert* and *artistic* writing?'

'He is describing a woman in a highly emotional condition.'

The Judge joined in: 'Is it a piece of good English?'

Mr Hough: 'In context it is.'

Mr G.-J.: 'And in the last line of that page there is the phrase "bowels and womb" again. Is that writing of high *literary* merit?' And the prosecution pressed on, with hard persistence, pressed on and the scene took much longer, more beyond endurance than one could make it last with words on paper. It was a scene of wilful bullying, and like such scenes it was embarrassing to watch.

'I am asking you whether a work of high literary merit has that kind of repetition?'

Mr Hough: 'Knowing Lawrence, yes. It was his method. He was trying to describe –'

'Never mind what he was trying to describe. Is it good writing to repeat again and again "womb and bowels"?'

'Yes. It was his method.'

'It may well be his method. But has this kind of repetition any literary merit?'

'I would say so.'

Mr Griffith-Jones now read aloud another passage (page 204 of the Penguin edition). 'We have had two four-letter words appear repeatedly in twelve lines – is that a realistic conversation between a gamekeeper and a baronet's wife?'

'I don't think so,' said Mr Hough. 'I think as a passage this is a failure.'

Mr G.-J. (heavily): 'You grant me this much? In this book which is of such merit there is at least one passage which is a failure?'

'There are several,' said Mr Hough.

Mr G.-J. (reading a paragraph, p. 232): 'As a *literary critic* and an *expert*, do you regard this as good writing to repeat that offensive word three times?'

'I think in this case it is.'

Mr Griffith-Jones read the letter which is the finale of the novel. He read the passage of it that begins, 'So I love chastity now . . .' He read it very badly, not on purpose, but like a man who reads a foreign language, a man who cannot see. The effect was unexpected. The power and beauty of Lawrence's writing carried. Up in the gallery, on the court benches, in the jury box, people were sitting absolutely quiet, listening, their hands still, listening deeply moved.

Unaware, isolated, prosecuting counsel read on. He read the after-dinner conversation at Wragby. 'Does that conversation present an accurate picture of the way gentlemen of that class talk together on that kind of occasion with their hostess present?'

Mr Hough: 'I think it is quite convincing.'

Mr G.-J.: 'And the entire rest of the book, let's face it, is about sex? Even the old nurse – Mrs Bolton – is dragged in without any point at all so that Sir Clifford may feel her breasts?'

'There is very much point. This is most relevant . . . The decay of Clifford. Clifford is shown to have become like an unpleasant child.'

Mr G.-J.: 'Is there any particular literary or sociological advantage in having this described?'

'Yes, I think there is. These are representations of false and wrong sexual attitudes, and this is an important part of the book.'

'Where do the good attitudes come in?'

'Well, in the relationship between Connie and Mellors, who really loved one another.'

The judge raised an eyebrow. Mr Hough repeated his answer.

Mr G.-J.: 'Are you an expert on good sexual relationships?'

Mr Hough (calmly): 'I do not share the sexual ethics of D.H.L., I was never a disciple of his doctrine, but I think it is important and should be clearly stated.'

'Listen to this,' said Mr Griffith-Jones, ' "Lift up your heads O ye gates, that the King of glory may come in." We have looked up the correct quotation which is, 'Lift up your heads O ye gates; and be ye lift up, ye ever-lasting doors; and the King of glory *shall* come in.' Do you not think that if – in a book of literary merit – he is quoting from the Twenty-Fourth Psalm, he might look it up?'

Mr Hough: 'Oh, no. Writers often misquote. And in this case it is the gamekeeper who is speaking –'

'Do you think that the inclusion of the words from the Scriptures adds literary merit to the book?'

Here Mr Hough allowed himself once more to be flippant. 'I think it is the only sentence of this passage that *has* any literary merit.'

The second witness called turned out to be one of the most effective and impressive witnesses of the whole case. One saw climbing onto the witness stand a woman of homely appearance with a pleasant, open face, the kind of person one is apt to think jury members would welcome as a forthright and respected aunt; and indeed some of them were lifting trusting faces at her entrance. She was Helen Gardner.

'And are you,' said Mr Gardiner QC, 'the Reader in Renaissance English Literature at Oxford University? The author of books on T.S. Eliot, John Donne, and the Metaphysical Poets? A member of the Radio Critics' Panel?'

Miss Gardner said she was all these things.

'It has been said,' Mr Gardiner asked her, 'that the four-letter words form the whole subject matter of the prosecution, and that one word occurred thirty times?'

Miss Gardner stood up there unruffled. It is not at all easy to come out well in that witness-box. It is very hard to lie successfully about a point of fact; it is impossible to get away with an opinion not sincerely held. You stand up there, very much exposed, all the eyes are on you; the jury, the bench, the two counsel are ready to pounce, to twist, to fling your words back at you. And at the end it all depends not on what you know and the ability to express it, not on courage and unflappability – though they all count – but on *what you are*. It shows. And that was why in this case nearly all those witnesses scored so heavily. They had come (at their own expense and risk) because they felt it their duty to do so; they were people of patent honesty and honour, people of splendid goodwill . . . and, of course, considerable abilities.

So Miss Gardner stood there and shone with goodness and integrity. She captured the hearts of the public gallery (many hardened murder-trial queuers among them), she may have captured the jury . . . 'I do not think words are brutal or disgusting in themselves,' she said; 'they are brutal if used in such a sense or context. The very fact that this word is used so frequently in this book means that with every use the original shock is diminished. By the time one has read the last page one feels that Lawrence has gone far to redeem this word.'

Mr Gardiner: 'What do you gather was Lawrence's original intention?'

'To make us feel that the sexual act is not shameful and the word used in its original sense is not shameful either,' she said with complete simplicity. 'Those passages succeed in doing something extraordinarily difficult, and very few writers have attempted with such courage and vision to put into verbal media experiences that are difficult to verbalize.'

'Do you feel any embarrassment in discussing this book in a mixed class?'

'Good gracious no,' said Miss Gardner.

'What, in your view, is the theme?'

'I think Lawrence felt very deeply the degrading conditions in which many people lived without beauty or joy and in slavery to what he calls, from William James, the Bitch Goddess Success, and he thought the most fundamental wrong was in the relationship between men and women – in sex; he thought through a better relationship there the whole of society might be revivified. Padding? *Oh, no!* It is a remarkable though not wholly successful novel, and though it doesn't rank with the greatest of Lawrence's work, I think certain passages are amongst his greatest. The ride through Derbyshire – the narra-tive of Mrs Bolton – Oh, Mrs Bolton – a character worthy of Dickens.'

Mr Griffith-Jones had no questions. The prosecution did not choose to cross-examine.

The next witness was Joan Bennett, the Cambridge don and critic (*George Eliot, The Victorian Novel*, etc.). She looked like a distinguished intellectual, in fact rather like Janet Flanner. She had a tendency to answer quickly, and then to qualify. Mr Griffith-Jones kept his eye on her.

Lawrence's view, she said, was that the physical life was of great importance; many people lived poor emasculated lives, they only lived with one half of themselves; Lawrence dealt with sex seriously, very seriously . . . Promiscuous intercourse was shown as unsatisfactory, giving no fulfilment or joy, as being rather disgusting . . . He thought that marriage was a complete relationship, marriage, not quite in the legal sense, but a union between two people for a lifetime was of the highest importance, of almost sacred importance –

'What did you say?' said the Judge. '*Of almost sacred impor-tance.*' He wrote it down.

Mr Gardiner: 'And have you got one son, three daughters and eight grandchildren?'

'I have,' said Mrs Bennett.

Mr Griffith-Jones was ready for her. 'Does not this book show a picture of a woman who has sexual relationships with people who are not her husband?'

'Yes.'

'Does this adulterous intercourse show a regard for marriage as it is generally understood by the average reader?'

'What average reader?' asked Mrs Bennett, faithful to precision. 'If you mean an intelligent child –'

Mr G.-J.: 'If you *can* come down to our humbler level from your academic heights will you answer my question – does this book show regard for marriage?'

'In what sense do you mean marriage?'

The Judge leaned toward her: 'Lawful wedlock, madam!'

Mrs Bennett said bravely, though in not too sure a voice, 'Lawrence believed it can be – as I think the law allows – broken in certain conditions.'

Down swooped Mr Griffith-Jones: 'Is not that precisely what Lawrence himself did? He ran off with somebody else's wife, did he not? Did he not?'

MR GARDINER'S re-examination consisted of one question.

'Did D.H. Lawrence's one and only marriage last his lifetime?'

'It did,' said Mrs Bennett.

'I call,' said Mr Gardiner, 'Dame Rebecca West.'

Dame Rebecca went into that box and said her say. There was no prodding *her* into the question-and-answer shafts. She made the points she found necessary to make, she made them in her own way and she made them well, and that was that.

The story of Lady Chatterley, she said, was designed as an allegory; the baronet and his impotence were a symbol of the impotent culture of our time which had become sterile and unhelpful to man's deepest needs, and the love affair with the gamekeeper was a return of the soul to a more intense life. Lawrence was not a fanciful writer; he knew he was writing about something *quite real* – he saw that in every country in the world there were populations who had lost touch with life and who could be exploited. All the time he was governed by this fear that something was going to happen – fascism, nazism – something that did happen in the shape of the war . . .

Of course one could find individual passages which appeared to have no literary merit. By this time Dame Rebecca was addressing the court and jury as she might some fairly alert committee. 'But the same is true of Shakespeare and Wordsworth, they all have some terrible lines. *Lady Chatterley* is full of sentences any child could make a fool of. You see, Lawrence was a man without a background of formal education and he also had one great defect which impairs this book, he had absolutely no sense of humour. And a lot of the scenes are, I think, ludicrous. But in spite of the ugly things, the ugly words, it is still a good book.'

Witnesses of sufficient eminence, or who have shown a deal of character, were not likely to be cross-examined. They might boomerang. Dame Rebecca was not questioned; the prosecution left well enough alone.

MR GARDINER said, 'I am calling the Bishop of Woolwich!'

This was the moment of thrill for the regular crime reporters, who now made a dash for their telephones. The Bishop looked delightful, like a well-groomed and angelic poet, and he wore his pectoral cross and violet silk cloth with a romantic air. He admitted to being Dr John Arthur Thomas Robinson, the father of four children, the author of several works on the New Testament, and to having long experience in teaching and ministering to university students. He had read *Lady Chatterley's Lover* in the summer.

He was cut short by Mr Griffith-Jones: 'I submit that the Bishop cannot be heard – his qualifications do not entitle him to give evidence about the book's literary merit.'

Mr Gardiner said the Bishop had come to give evidence on its ethical merits.

Mr G.-J.: 'Ethical merits are not mentioned in the Obscene Publications Act.'

Mr Gardiner: 'My Lord, the Act mentions art or learning or other objects of general concern.'

The Judge: 'I agree with you, ethics must be considered an object of general concern.'

So the Bishop was allowed to proceed.

'Clearly,' he said, 'Lawrence did not have a Christian valuation of sex, and the kind of relationships depicted in the book are not necessarily of the kind I should regard as ideal. But what Lawrence is trying to do, I think, is to portray the sex relationship as something sacred . . . I might quote Archbishop Temple: "Christians do not make jokes about sex for the same reason they do not make jokes about Holy Communion, not because it is sordid but because it is sacred." I think Lawrence tried to portray this relation in the real sense as an act of holy communion, in a lower case. For him flesh was sacramental . . .'

The Judge took it down ostentatiously.

'Lawrence's descriptions of sexual relationships cannot be taken out of the context of his whole quite astonishing sensitivity to the beauty and value of all organic relationships. Some of the descriptions of nature in the books seem to me extraordinarily beautiful, and to portray an attitude to the whole organic world in which he saw sex as the culmination.'

Mr Gardiner: 'Can you make a distinction between the book as it is, and as it would be with the sexual passages left out?'

The Bishop: 'I think the effect of that would be to suggest that what Lawrence was doing was something sordid and could be put before the public only if the passages about sex were eliminated. I think that is a false view. I think neither in intention nor in effect is this book depraving.'

'It has been said that it puts promiscuous and adulterous intercourse on a pedestal.'

'That seems a distorted view. In the last pages there is a tremendous and most moving advocacy of chastity: "How can men want wearisomely to philander?'' '

The Bishop's cross-examination took place after the luncheon adjournment. By that time on that day one of the unusual features of this trial had become more distinct, and that was the invasion of the professional sanctity of the court by the outer world. The Old Bailey is very much a place of its own, a highly specialized place where (apart from the occasional sensational trial) humdrum, brutal, shabby crime is dealt with day after day in a steady, drab, conscientious grind. The prisoner sits in the dock, the contests are fought between teams of professionals and their attendants. Of course, there are other people in court, but they don't count. They are there because they must: if the accused has partisans they are helpless people, frightened, involved; his wretched wife perhaps in a back row, a humbled father; or they are there out of some unengaged curiosity, or to do a job, law pupils, the regular crime reporters, a pack of Pavlov dogs sitting in their pew waiting for their cues of sex and violence. This, then, was one of the rare occasions when the court was packed with outside people of conscience, heart and mind, people who were passionately concerned about the outcome, and who were not wholly – at least outside the actual court – mute and powerless: writers, poets, educators, Lawrence enthusiasts, literary journalists, English, American, Canadian . . . The French, or members of other Latin nations, did not participate.

Mr Griffith-Jones started with this question to the Bishop:

'Do you tell us that this book is a valuable work on ethics?'

The Bishop answered that it had positive value from an ethical point of view.

'It is not a treatise on marriage, but Lawrence made it clear that he was not against marriage relationships –'

Mr G.-J.: 'I don't want to be offensive to you, but you are not here to make speeches. Just answer my questions. Are you asking the jury to accept this book as a valuable work on ethics?'

'I would not say it had an *instructional* value –'

'Is it a book Christians ought to read?'

The Judge: 'Does it portray the love of an immoral woman?'

The Bishop: 'It portrays the love of a woman in an immoral relationship, so far as adultery is an immoral relationship.'

By now Bench and prosecution were seen to have spun themselves into the old fallacy: a book dealing with immorality is an immoral book. It is neither law nor logic, but it is an easy web for juries to get lost in, and the Churchman at any rate was being shown as having tied himself into apparent knots.

'*Is* this a book Christians ought to read?' asked Mr Griffith-Jones.

'Yes, I think it is. And because –' But the Bishop was not allowed to explain; the prosecution stopped him in his tracks. And by evening the headlines proclaimed: Bishop's Defence of Lady C – Book All Christians Ought To Read.

'SIR WILLIAM EMRYS WILLIAMS!' A director of Penguin Books, Secretary-General of the Arts Council, knighted in 1955.

'Will you explain why you printed 200,000 copies of this book?'

'That is nothing out of the ordinary. An average first printing of a Penguin would be 40,000 to 50,000 copies, but for some books we print as many as 250,000.'

'Why did you not think of putting in rows of asterisks?'

Sir William: 'That would make it a dirty book.'

'What about dashes for the four-letter words?'

'That would make for unwholesomeness.'

'Do you think you could have sold a large number of copies of an *expurgated* edition?'

'Quite the same number.' (There is in fact such an expurgated edition published in Britain, and it sold nearly a quarter million copies in nine months last year.)

'PROFESSOR VIVIAN DE SOLA PINTO!' Professor of English at Nottingham University; perhaps one of the greatest D.H. Lawrence authorities living today.

Mr Griffith-Jones (cross-examining): 'Professor, just let me make sure what your ideas of beauty are?' He reads.

Professor Pinto: 'An able piece of realism.'

Mr Griffith-Jones (furiously): 'Cunt! Cunt! Cunt! Cunt! Fuck! Fuck! Fuck! Fuck!'

'The Reverend A.S. Hopkinson!' Vicar of St Catherine Cree, London; General Director of Industrial Christian Fellowship; Anglican Adviser to Associated Television.

'. . . A study in compassion . . . A book of moral purpose.' ('A book of?' said the Judge.) '. . . All comes from God, thus sex comes from God; it is utterly wrong to link sex with sin. The words? The words are about activities that are an essential part of human life; it would be a mistake to replace them with blanks . . . Yes, I would like my children to read it, I should like them to discuss it with me and their mother.'

The Judge asked: 'You have no objection to your children reading this book?'

'Only one of them has, to my knowledge,' said the clergyman, 'and he found it rather dull.'

Mr Griffith-Jones: 'As a minister of the Church, you would have the highest opinion of the marriage vows?'

'Yes.'

'Would you not agree that this was a book about a man and a woman who have little regard for the marriage vow at all?'

'No.'

Mr G.-J.: 'I am sure you do not hold the view that we can throw our marriage bond overboard?'

'No, I do not.'

'That is what this woman is doing! That is what this whole book is about – she throws her marriage bond overboard in order to get sexual satisfaction. That is what this book teaches.'

'With respect, I should say that the marriage goes wrong, and afterwards she takes the wrong course.'

Mr G.-J.: 'None of you experts in this case is able to say Yes or No to any question! Listen to this, ''Lift up your heads O ye gates . . .'' ' He read the whole Psalm passage again. 'Is that shocking? Blasphemous?'

'That was not the author's intention.'

'We are not concerned with the author's intention. Answer my question, will you? Were you shocked to find a Psalm in such a passage?'

'I did not recognize the Psalm.'

'MR ST JOHN-STEVAS!' M.A. Oxford and Cambridge; Ph.D. Columbia; LL.D. Yale; Academic Lawyer and Qualified Barrister; author of *Obscenity and the Law*; legal adviser to the Committee which sponsored the Obscene Publications Bill; a Roman Catholic; student of Moral Theology; and still a very young man.

He said he would put Lawrence among the great literary moralists of our literature.

'Lawrence was essentially concerned to purge, cleanse, reform. I have been horrified by the representation of him in some newspapers, in papers which I think he wouldn't have deigned to read!

'I have had the misfortune to have to read through a vast number of books of a pornographic and obscene nature, and I find it difficult to make comparisons with *Lady Chatterley*, so great is the gulf between them.'

Mr Hutchinson asked him if he found the book consistent with the tenets of his own faith.

Mr St John-Stevas said: Quite consistent. Of course Lawrence was neither a Christian nor a Catholic, but one could say he was a writer essentially in the Catholic tradition. 'I mean by that the tradition that the sex instinct is good in itself, is implanted in man by God, is one of his greatest gifts. This tradition was opposed by the movement which started at the Reformation and has grown in Protestant minds that sex is something "which is wrong", which is essentially evil.'

'I call the Headmaster of Alleyns!' D.S.O.; former Military Governor of Berlin (not cross-examined).

'I call the Master of the Temple!' Canon of Lincoln Cathedral (not cross-examined).

'Mr Roy Jenkins, M.P.!' (Not cross-examined.)

All that day, and the next day, and the next, that procession of defence witnesses went on, professors, editors, schoolmasters, critics, poets, clergymen of the Church of England, psychologists. . . .

THERE CAME to many of us a most moving moment, when counsel called:

'Edward Morgan Forster!' And in came Mr E.M. Forster – alone – he had been sitting waiting on a bench in the hall the best part of the morning, waiting to be called. Now here he was, in a mackintosh, old only in years, looking very firm and calm.

The greatest living writer perhaps in the English language had come into this court, and of course there was no sign of recognition; that is not within the rules or spirit of the place. But Mr Jeremy Hutchinson, very likely seized by a desire to do something, chose the one gesture of favour or respect that can be made in a courtroom – he asked the judge if Mr E.M. Forster might be given a chair. His Lordship said: Certainly. But Mr Forster said, no, no, he didn't want one, he didn't want a chair. Then he spoke.

'I knew Lawrence quite well. In nineteen hundred and fifteen . . .' And there came a sense of the past, and the years.

How would he place him in English literature, asked Mr Hutchinson.

'I would place him enormously high. The greatest imaginative writer of his generation . . . He is part of the great puritan stream of writers, Bunyan, Blake . . . Though that may seem a bit paradoxical at first sight. A preacher . . .'

But Mr Forster's passage was all too brief. Mr Griffith-Jones said he had no question, and Mr Forster was gone.

'I CALL SIR STANLEY UNWIN!'

'Miss C.V. Wedgwood!'

'Mr Walter Allen!' Novelist and literary critic.

'In your professional capacity, how many novels do you read a year?'

'Up to two hundred.'

'How would you describe *Lady Chatterley's Lover*?'

Walter Allen: 'A tract and the work of a genius.'

'Miss Sarah Beryl Jones!' Classics Mistress and Senior Librarian at Keighley Grammar School. A little grey-haired woman, who speaks her own form of oath.

The Judge: 'What did you say?'

Miss Jones (bright and fussy): 'The whole truth as far as I am able to speak it.' She is made to eat those words.

Mr Gardiner: 'Do girls grow up earlier now than they used to?'

Miss Jones: 'In my experience, yes.'

'Is there a good deal of literature available to them on sexual matters?'

'There are technical works, and there are what you might call dirty books.'

'How far do girls understand the four-letter words?'

Miss Jones: 'I have inquired of a number of girls – after they left school – and most of them have been acquainted with them since the age of ten.'

'Has *Lady Chatterley's Lover* any educational value?'

'Considerable value, if taken at the right age, which is normally after seventeen, because it deals honestly and openly with problems of sex which are very real to the girls themselves. Girls are very good at knowing what is good for them. Girls read what they want to read and they don't read what they don't want to read.'

'Miss Ann Scott-James!' A most smartly dressed young woman.

Mr Griffith-Jones rises at once to object.

'I understand you are the editor of a Ladies' Page?'

Miss Scott-James: 'Not a Ladies' Page. It hasn't been called that since 1912. A Woman's Page.'

'Do you claim any particular qualification to be a literary expert?'

'Of a popular kind. And I was a classical scholar at Oxford.' She adds disarmingly, 'It's not a negligible qualification.'

Mr G.-J.: 'Does that make you a literary expert?'

'I was brought up in a very literary family. My father –' But Miss Scott-James is whisked out of the box.

'Mr Stephen Potter!'

'When I read the book again, I was surprised by its power! . . . And the words only shock the eye, and that soon goes because they do not shock the brain. I think what D.H.L. was trying to do was something very difficult and courageous, he was trying to take these words out of the context of the lavatory wall.'

'Dr Clifford James Hemming!' Writer, lecturer, educational psychologist.

'Young people,' he said, 'reading *Lady Chatterley* might find themselves for the first time confronted with a concept of sex which includes compassion and tenderness.

'Young people nowadays are subject to constant insinuation of shallow and corrupting values . . . Books and papers tell the young girl that if she has the right proportions, wears the right clothes, uses the right cosmetics, she will become irresistible to men, and that this is the supreme achievement of women, to become irresistible to men. And as far as the men are concerned, it is suggested that to have a pretty woman in your arms is the supreme thrill of life, and to seduce a woman is manful in yourself and something to envy in others. The contents of *Lady Chatterley* are an antidote. They show all that makes sex human . . .'

Mr Gardiner: 'Are the detailed descriptions justified? Are they of any sociological value?'

'Oh, yes,' said Dr Hemming. 'It is now recognized that for young people to grow up and marry with brutish and ashamed attitudes is most harmful. The rejection of our bodies can lead to mental ill health. This book would act as a positive antidote to those promiscuous and dehumanizing influences.'

There was no doubt that the prosecution and the Bench were flabbergasted to be hearing what they heard. The views of apparently respectable professional men and women . . . Chaos, it must have seemed to Mr Justice Byrne, had come again.

Mr Griffith-Jones, in cross-examination, asked, not unexpectedly: 'Let us see what amounts to an antidote.' And he began his now-familiar tone-deaf reading. 'Is *that* an antidote to promiscuous sex among young people?'

Dr Hemming: 'Yes.'

'That was a description of what was happening just before the act of intercourse?'

'Yes.'

'That was promiscuous intercourse by Lady Chatterley?'

Dr Hemming: 'Yes, but it is quite different from the street-corner promiscuity which is one of our problems today.'

Mr G.-J.: 'I was not limiting my meaning to street corners. Is there anything to suggest that *she* wouldn't have gone on and on, from man to man, until she found someone who satisfied her?'

Dr Hemming: 'That is a conjectural question. I do not believe she would have led that kind of life.'

As one can see, Constance Chatterley had ceased to be a character of fiction. To the defence she was poor Connie; to the other side, Lady Chatterley, a traitor to her class, a shocking example, and the guilty party to a divorce action of the most undesirable nature.

Mr G.-J.: 'Here we have another one of the bouts. Listen.' (He reads.) 'Does that strengthen the antidote much, does it?'

Dr Hemming: 'I don't see why not.'

' "As he found her", what do you think these words mean?'

'Getting into closer intimacy.'

Mr G.-J.: 'What do you mean?'

'What Lawrence means.'

'What do *you* mean by that?'

'A continuation of the physical act of love.'

Mr G.-J.: 'What do you mean by that? I shall go on asking you until you tell us in plain good English words what you think that means!'

Dr Hemming: 'He was caressing her.'

'Where?'

'It doesn't say.'

'Where do you think?'

No answer.

'Where?'

And so it went on.

Sometime later, a witness, an Oxford don, read D.H.L.'s own comment. ' "It's the one thing they won't let you be, straight and open in your sex. You can be as dirty as you like. In fact, the more dirt you do on sex the better they like it. But if you believe in your own sex and won't have it done dirt to, they down you. It's the one insane taboo left – sex as a natural and vital thing." '

TO UNDERSTAND the conduct of the prosecution case, it may perhaps be well to bear several rather contradictory things in mind. One: prosecuting counsel acts as an advocate; it is his job to present one side, and to present it strongly, to the best of his abilities. This, however, is somewhat weakened by the concurrent principle by which the prosecution is held to present all the facts fairly and not to press for a conviction *per se*; and so it can be said that counsel's job is not to press a case beyond its merits.

Two: a criminal trial is the trial of an issue of fact; was this act committed, and was it committed in such and such a way, yes or no? Did this man stab his wife, did that man steal a load of cheeses? It is not a matter of opinion, it is a matter of facts – the knife, the prints, the eyewitness, the alibi. And this is where the prosecution here, and the whole legal machinery, ran into trouble. They were dealing with something pressed into a Procrustean framework devised for something else; they were dealing with what was in reality an issue of judgment or opinion by a procedure created for the pinning down of fact.

Obscenity, unlike murder and theft, is not self-evident fact; it involves, in (US) Judge Bryan's words, 'questions of constitutional judgment of the most sensitive and delicate kind'; it involves definitions, definitions depending on – relative and changeable – community standards, on private feelings, on opinions. And below the standards, the feelings and opinions, lie the powers of what are perhaps our deepest and most irrational taboos. In regard to sex, and even more so in regard to certain words, England is still Disraeli's Two Nations, and the thought barrier between them is complete.

And so, three: in a true issue of fact, counsel's feelings or opinions are of no account and must never be expressed. In this case counsel did express feelings and opinions. For one thing, because he could hardly help doing so in the context. But they also were, and this was crystal clear to everyone present, his own feelings and opinions, and he believed in them to the exclusion of anybody else's. He, like the witnesses, was the man he was, and that comprised, evidently, that he had never in his life been conditioned to regard with respect any modern classic in the realm of purely imaginative writing. Confronted with a very difficult one, he displayed his natural reactions.

And it must be for something of all these three considerations that the cross-examinations were so indignant, so ineffective and so very much beside the point.

'The Dean of the Faculty of Arts at Liverpool University!'

'The Editor of the *Manchester Guardian*!'

'The Provost of King's!'

'Sir Allen Lane!' Founder of Penguin Books.

'Mr C. Day Lewis!'

'The Former Precentor of Birmingham Cathedral!' and Director of Religious Education.

'. . . By reading it, young people will be helped to grow up as mature and responsible people . . .'

The prosecution made a point of cross-examining nearly all the clergy. Their position was most vulnerable. (In fact, the Bishop of Woolwich was rebuked by the Archbishop of Canterbury after the trial.)

Mr Griffith-Jones: 'Is there anything to suggest that marriage is sacred and inviolable?'

'It is a novel.'

Mr Griffith-Jones repeats the question.

'I think it is taken for granted.'

'Let us see. Mellors, the gamekeeper, did not regard marriage as sacred and inviolable?'

'He was very much attracted by Lady Chatterley.'

'Of course he was. Everybody who commits adultery is very much attracted by the man or woman with whom he does it. Just answer my question please.'

The Judge: 'Does the book really deal with anything other than adultery?'

'Mr John Connell!' the writer and critic.

'I disagree utterly and totally about all those suggestions about indulgence and promiscuity and padding. The book is concerned with two intertwined themes in human life and English society – sex and class. And it deals with a tragic situation.'

Mr Hutchinson: 'What about an expurgated edition?'

Mr Connell: 'I was unfortunate enough to be sent one for review the other day. I found it: a) trivial, b) furtive, c) obscene.'

A reader, having reached this stage, may well feel that the portents now were for acquittal. All those witnesses, the sheer weight of numbers must have left their mark. Had they? We were far from certain. The lawyers and defendants were only faintly hopeful. A hung jury, perhaps. The American journalists present looked at us with pity. The more enlightened court decision of their country had not been allowed to be heard in evidence.

'Do you know,' Mr Gardiner had asked, 'of any civilized country where this book cannot be bought except in Lawrence's own Commonwealth?' Mr Griffith-Jones had objected, 'What happens in other countries is not relevant,' he said. Mr Gardiner put forward that it would be evidence of literary value. 'I'm against that,' had said Mr Justice Byrne.

The regular reporters told one with satisfied cynicism, 'They won't get away with it – no British jury will swallow those words.' So one went on staring at this British jury. Most of them looked like pleasant people. The women seemed at their ease. There were two of them besides the twelfth juror; one very pretty young woman with a gentle face – ought one to pin hopes on her? – and one middle-aged, more of the housewife type. The second day she had appeared without a hat. A favourable sign? One man often dozed. Another looked worried. Another sullen. The foreman, the twelfth juror and one or two of the men laughed and talked as they walked through the vestibule, a most unprecedented thing.

IF THE CASE had any turning point at all, it must have been the exchange with the most quietly and fervently assured (as well as one of the most brilliantly intelligent) of the witnesses, Richard Hoggart, on Day Three. Mr Hoggart, Senior Lecturer in English at Leicester University, is a young man from the Midlands, dark and short, born, like Lawrence himself, into the coal-mining working class. He started his education at an elementary school.

He had called *Lady Chatterley* a highly virtuous, if not a puritanical book, and Mr Hutchinson had invited him to enlarge on that.

'I was thinking of the whole movement of the book, of Lawrence's enormous insistence on arriving at relationships of integrity. I was struck on re-reading it to realize how much of it is contemporary; it tells us a great deal about our society at a level which we do not usually probe, and with an insight which we do not usually attain . . . It makes you consider your relationship to society, it teaches you to question your place and your being . . .'

Mr Hutchinson: 'It has been suggested that the only variations in the sexual descriptions lay in where they took place.'

'A gross misreading,' said Mr Hoggart firmly. 'I don't mean highbrow reading. I mean an honest reading.'

Mr Hutchinson asked him about repetition of words.

'Indeed, yes. It's one of Lawrence's characteristics, and one he uses to great effect. He hammered home and almost recreated words. Shakespeare repeated ''nothing'' five times in one passage.'

Mr Hutchinson asked if the four-letter words were genuine and necessary.

No one who saw him on that morning will ever forget Richard Hoggart, how he stood up there talking in his serious, clear-minded, communicating way. And now he uttered the words we had so far only heard from the lips of the prosecution.

'They are totally characteristic of many people,' he said, 'and I would like to say not only working-class people, because that would be wrong. They are used very freely indeed, far more freely than many of us know. Fifty yards from this court this morning, I heard a man say that word three times as I passed him, one, two, three, I heard him. He must have been very angry.

'These are common words; if you work on a building site, as I have done, you will hear them frequently. But the man I heard this morning and the men on the building site use this word as a word of contempt, and one of the most horrifying things to Lawrence was that the word used for sex has become a term of violent abuse, and has totally lost its meaning. He wanted to re-establish the proper meaning of it.

'When I first read it, the first effect was one of some shock, obviously because it is not used in polite literature. But as one read, one found the word losing that shock. We have no word in English which is not either an abstraction or has become an evasive euphemism for this act; we are constantly running away from it or dissolving into dots. I realized that it is we who are wrong. Lawrence was wanting to show what one does in the most simple, neutral way . . . Just like that, with no snigger or dirt. That is what one does.'

Mr Griffith-Jones rose to cross-examine. And he under-estimated Mr Hoggart's effectiveness, virtue and strength; the passage that followed was the prosecution's biggest moral defeat in the case.

Mr Griffith-Jones: 'You described this as a puritanical book. Is that your genuine and considered view?'

'Yes.'

Mr G.-J. (with gentlemanly superiority): 'I think I must

have lived my life under a misapprehension of the word "puritanical". Will you help me?'

Mr Hoggart (earnest and friendly): 'Yes, I will. Many people do live their lives under a misapprehension of the meaning of puritanical. In Britain, and for a long time, the word has pretended to mean somebody who is against anything which is pleasurable, particularly sex, but the proper meaning of it to an historian is somebody who belongs to the tradition of British puritanism, and the main weight of that is an intense sense of reponsibility for one's conscience. In that sense the book is puritanical.'

Mr Griffith-Jones said: 'I am obliged to you for the lecture.' (He reads a sexual passage.) 'Is that puritanical?'

Mr Hoggart: 'Yes. Heavy with conscience.'

'I am not asking you if it is heavy with conscience. I am asking you if it is puritanical.'

'Yes. It is one of the side issues of puritanism.'

Mr G.-J. (reading a passage from the Michaelis episode): 'Puritanical?'

'Yes – puritanical, poignant, tender, moving, and about two people who have no proper relationship.'

Mr G.-J.: 'I should have thought that could be answered without a lecture. This is the Old Bailey, and not [with thin distaste] *Leicester* University.'

A further passage.

Mr G.-J.: 'That is about all there is to keep those two con- nected? It was done purely for the satisfaction of her sexual lust, wasn't it?'

Mr Hoggart: 'No, it was done because she is lonely and lost, and she feels through the sexual act she may feel less lonely and lost.'

Mr Justice Byrne: 'It is just an immoral relationship between a man and a woman?'

Mr Hoggart: 'Yes.' (Suddenly, eagerly.) 'In Milton, in *Paradise Lost*, there is a great passage in which Adam and Eve come together in this way . . . Highly sensual . . .'

Mr Griffith-Jones then read that extraordinary page about

the source of life. Again he read as though it were some foreign text; again the court sat rapt. ' "The weight of a man's balls" – puritanical?'

'Yes, it is puritanical in its reverence.'

'Reverence for what?' screamed Mr Griffith-Jones. '*The balls?*'

'Indeed, yes,' said Mr Hoggart gently.

AT THE END of Day Four, Mr Gardiner said that, although they still had thirty-six witnesses in reserve, of 'the same sort of character and standing', the defence would call only one more. The prosecution now had the right to call witnesses in rebuttal, but Mr Griffith-Jones said he did not propose to call any evidence. And so the case had reached the stage of the final speeches. The speech for the defence and the speech for the prosecution were two speeches made from two different levels, addressed to two kinds of people. Only one question remained: Which kind was the jury?

Mr Gardiner rose to speak the next morning. His manner was quiet though firm, and he anticipated a good many prosecution points.

'It might be suggested,' he told the jury, 'that you should ignore the evidence given by the witnesses on the ground that it was given by professors of literature, by people who are living rarefied lives and are not really in touch with ordinary people. And indeed, no higher class of experts could have been called on any similar occasion.' Now the most important single fact here was that Parliament had expressly provided that evidence may be called both by the defence and by the prosecution; yet when the prosecution's turn came to call evidence, they called none at all. 'Not one single witness has been found to say anything against Lawrence or this book; we have only got to go by what Mr Griffith-Jones said himself when opening the case.

'. . . Hardly any question has been put to witnesses [by the prosecution] about the book as a whole. The technique has been that used before the new Act: to read out a particular passage and to say, is that moral?

'. . . This is a book about human beings, about real people, and I protest at the statements that have been made about the characters, about Constance, as though she were a sort of nymphomaniac. When it is said that this is just a book about adultery, one wonders how there can be things which people cannot see? I suppose somewhere there may be a mind which would describe *Antony and Cleopatra* as a play about adultery, the story of a sex-starved Roman soldier copulating with an Egyptian queen.

'As a book published at 3/6, *Lady Chatterley* will be available to the general public and it may well be said that everyone will rush to buy it. This is always the effect of a wrong prosecution.

'Witnesses have been asked if it was a book they would like their wife or servant to read. This may have been consciously or unconsciously an echo of the Bench of years ago: "It would never do to let the members of the working class read this." I don't want to upset the prosecution by suggesting there are a certain number of people who do not have servants. This whole attitude is one Penguin Books was formed to fight against. It is the attitude that it is all right to publish a special edition at five or ten guineas, but quite wrong to let people who are less well-off read what those other people read. Is not everyone, whether their income is ten pounds or twenty pounds a week, equally interested in the society in which we live? In the problems of our relationships, including sexual relationships?

'. . . It would be very easy to say to you for counsel for the prosecution, "You and I are ordinary chaps, don't you bother about those experts – they don't really know what goes on in the world at all." Lawrence, members of the jury, was a man of the people. There are students of literature in all walks of life . . . If it is right that the book should be read, it should be available to the man working in a factory as it is to the teacher working in a school.

'. . . In England we have before banned books by Hardy, G.B. Shaw, Ibsen, Wilde, Joyce, and even Epstein's statues.

But is Lawrence to be always confined to dirty bookshops? This would be the greatest irony in literary history.

'. . . A book is not obscene merely because part of its subject matter is a relationship between people who are not married, or who are married to someone else. If that were so, ninety percent of English literature is obscene.

'. . . Can it be seriously suggested that anyone's character will be changed by reading words that they already know?

'I submit that the defence has shown on balance of probabilities that it is for the public good that this book should be generally available . . . If this is not a book to which the Section of the new Act applies, then it is difficult to conceive of any book by such an author to which it can apply.

'We are a country known throughout the world for our literature and our democratic institutions. It is strange indeed that this is the only country where this Englishman's work cannot be read. Lawrence lived and died suffering from the public opinion, caused by the banning of this book, that he had written a piece of pure pornography. For the first time this case has enabled the book to be dragged out into the light of day. The slur was never justified. All the time the book was a passionate and sincere work of a moralist who believed he had a message for us in the society in which we live. Whether we agree with what he had in view or not, is it not time we rescued Lawrence's name from the quite unjust reputation and allowed our people – his people – to judge for themselves? I leave Lawrence's reputation and the reputation of Penguin Books with confidence in your hands.'

Mr Griffith-Jones' speech followed.

'This is a case of immense importance, and its effects will go far beyond the actual question which the jury has to decide.

'. . . It has been emphasized that you have heard no witnesses called by the prosecution. It may sound a good point to reiterate again and again, but it is an empty point, and not the kind of argument on which you are to decide the case. The law restricts me to calling evidence only as to the literary, artistic and other merits of the book. As to the merit of the book as literature, I have from the first conceded that Lawrence was a great writer. These are matters upon which the prosecution never sought to argue, and upon which it would have been wholly irrelevant and redundant for me to call evidence. On whether the book is of educational or sociological merit, I am happy to leave that aspect to the book itself. I cannot believe that you, or any other jury, would wish evidence to be called simply to hear these words: This book is not a great educational document, nor is it of great sociological value.

'Members of the jury, there are standards, are there not? There must be standards which we are to maintain, standards, of morality, language and conduct, which are essential to the well-being of our society. They must be instilled in all of us, and at the earliest possible age, standards of respect for the conventions, for the kind of conduct society approves, for other people's feelings, and there must be instilled in all of us standards of restraint.

'You have only to read your papers and see day by day the results of unbridled sex . . . It is all for lack of standards, lack of restraint, lack of mental and moral discipline . . .

'. . . It is true, as Mr Gardiner has anticipated, that I would urge upon you that you alone will have to decide, and not the various witnesses whose views you have heard. You will not be brow-beaten by these witnesses, you will judge the case as ordinary men and women, with your feet firmly planted on the ground. Were the views you have heard from those most eminent and academic ladies and gentlemen really of so much value as the views which *you* – without perhaps the eminence and the academic learning – possess yourselves? I do not question the integrity and sincerity of those witnesses, but suggest that they all have got a bee in their bonnet about this book . . .

'When one sees some of them launching themselves at the first opportunity, at the first question, into a sermon or a lecture – according to their vocation – one cannot help feeling that, sincerely and honestly as they feel, they feel in such a way that common sense perhaps has gone by the board.

'One witness said that sex was treated "on a holy basis".

Can that be a realistic view? Is that a way a boy leaving school would read it? The Bishop of Woolwich went one better and called it something as sacred as an Act of Holy Communion. Do you think that is the way girls working in a factory will read the book in their luncheon break? Or does it put the Lord Bishop wholly out of touch with the large percentage of the people who will buy this book at 3/6?

'A book of moral purpose, the Reverend Hopkinson has said. *What* moral purpose do *you* read into the book?

'I suggest that Miss [*sic*] Rebecca West is capable of reading what she said into the book, but is that typical of the effect that book will have on the average reader? Are they going to see an allegory in it? Is the baronet and his impotence going to be read by them as as symbol? One wonders whether one is talking in the same language . . .

'Members of the jury, is there any moral teaching in the book at all? How can there be when right until the end, when they decide to get their respective divorces, not a single word is spoken between them during their thirteen bouts, other than sex? All they have done before they decide to run away with each other is to copulate thirteen times . . .

'It has been suggested that the shock of using the foul words wore off as one got used to it. Is that not a terrible thing if we forget the shock of using this language?'

And here Mr Griffith-Jones took up the book once more. Once more he read. He read the Psalm passage again. 'Do you know *who* the King of glory is? Do you?' He read another. 'Here we come to a little striptease . . .' He read again the last letter; he read, for the first time, two pages of Connie's last night with Mellors before she leaves for Venice.

He shut the book. 'You will have to go some way in the Charing Cross Road, in the back streets of Paris, or even Port Saïd, to find a description that is as lurid as that one.

'It is for the jury to decide this case, and not for the so-called experts. This book has to be read not as bishops and lecturers read it, but as ordinary men and women read it, people without any literary or academic qualifications. Do you think, as I submit, that its effect on the average person must be to deprave, to lead them into false conceptions, to lower their general standard of thought, conduct and decency, and must be the opposite of encouraging that restraint in sexual matters which is so all-important in present times? This is what you must ask yourselves. And if you decide that it has a tendency to deprave, then you have to ask yourselves what public good is being done by this book to outweigh the harm. Is there such a public need in the interest of public good for the publication of this document?

'There can be but one answer.'

There was still the Judge. Juries are apt to look up to the Judge, and to look at him to clarify their minds. Mr Justice Byrne began his summing-up on the afternoon of Day Five and continued on Day Six. He began:

'In these days the world seems to be full of experts. There is no subject you can think of where there is not to be found an expert who will be able to deal, or says he will be able to deal, with the situation. But the criminal law is based on a view that a jury is responsible for the facts and not the experts.'

The Judge's voice was discreet in tone, polite and quietly persuasive. He spoke for two and a half hours all in all, and here are some extracts from what he said.

'There is no intent to deprave necessary to be proved in order that this offence should be committed. The intention is quite irrelevant.

'. . . This book is to be put upon the market at 3/6 a copy, which is by no means an excessive price in these days when there are not only high wages, but high pocket money . . . Once a book gets into circulation, it does not spend its time in the rarefied atmosphere of some academic institution; it finds its way into the bookshops and onto the bookstalls and into the public libraries where it is available to all and sundry to read.

'. . . The book has been said to be a moral tract, a virtuous and puritanical production, and a book that Christians ought to read. What do *you* think about that?

'Is it right to say that the story is one of a woman who first of all before she was married had sexual intercourse, and then after marriage when her husband had met with disaster in the war, and became confined to a wheelchair, she was living with her husband in this dreary place, Wragby, and committed adultery on two occasions with somebody called Michaelis, while her husband was downstairs in the same house. After that she proceeded to have adulterous intercourse with her husband's gamekeeper. And that is described, you may think – is it or is it not? – in the most lurid way, and the whole sensuality and passion of the various occasions is fully and completely described.

'. . . You will have to consider the tendency that this book will have on the moral outlook of people who buy it, people possibly without any knowledge of Lawrence, or of literature, and people perhaps quite young, the youth of the country.

'. . . If you are satisfied that the book is obscene, you must go on to the further question: are the merits of the book as a novel *so high* that they outbalance the obscenity so its publication is *for the public good*? . . . I would repeat the observation made by Mr Griffith-Jones who said, "Keep your feet on the ground." In other words, do not allow yourselves to get lost in the higher realms of literature, education, sociology and ethics.

'One witness, Mrs Bennett, said, "A reader who is capable of understanding Lawrence could get much of what his view is." Who, members of the jury, are the people capable of understanding Lawrence? You have to think of people with no literary background, with little or no learning . . .

'It has been said that the book does not deal simply and solely with sexual relationships, but that it deals with other matters, such as the industrial state of the country and the hard lives people are living. Whether you find there is very much in the book about that or not is for you to say . . . You may ask yourselves whether, unless a person is an authority on literature, he would be able to read into the book the many different things the many witnesses said he intended to be in the book . . .

'Mrs Bennett said that Lawrence believed that marriage, not in the legal sense, but the union of two people for a lifetime was of the highest importance. Members of the jury, what is marriage if it is not in the legal sense? What are they talking about? This is a Christian country, and right through Christianity there has been lawful marriage, even if it is only before a registrar.

'The Bishop of Woolwich said Lawrence was trying to portray the sex relationship as something sacramental.' The Judge looked up, '*Where are we getting?* Do *you* find that the author was trying to portray sex as something sacramental? Then we had the Master of the Temple, and he was full of praise for the book. Then we had Professor Pinto who said that in some measure it was a moral tract – does *that* coincide with *your* view? Do you find that the relationship between Lady Chatterley and the gamekeeper was really moral? Did you find one spark of affection between these two? Or were they merely having sexual intercourse and enjoying it?

'You heard one witness say that it is possible to feel "reverence for a man's balls"; what do you make of that? Does it coincide with your view of the matter? Well, members of the jury, there it is, there it is . . . You must ask yourselves whether as you *read* the book, you find you can agree with all the things the witnesses said Lawrence was trying to say . . . You are not bound by the evidence – you have to make up your own minds.'

Well, and so they did.

The world now knows that verdict, but for us, who waited on that day, it was a long three hours before we heard – still incredulous in relief – those words: Not Guilty. A ripple of applause broke out, stentoriously suppressed; there was no other comment. It is customary for the Judge to express thanks to the jury; Mr Justice Byrne did not do so, and the words were spoken by the Clerk.

SELECTING THE JURY FOR THE TRIAL OF JACK RUBY
For The Murder Of
Lee Harvey Oswald

Dallas, Texas, U.S.A.
February–March 1964

WHATEVER THE outcome, the trial will go down in history. In years to come, they will have the court records, the books (rather too many of them), the admirable photographs of the present scene and the present cast – the city, the courtroom, the participants whom circumstances, or their own wills, propelled to decide this issue. In years to come, they will look at these, scan the faces, and speculate – just as we, here and now, the spectators-in-the-flesh of the yet unresolved events, scan the live faces and try to guess. Will he have a fair trial? Did he have a fair trial? The best trial he could get?

For that is all that is left, all we can hope to have now: a manifestly fair trial. The notion is not the monopoly of Mr Melvin Belli. We – that is, the American people (or a large part of them) and the world (or a large part of it) – are obsessed by the desire – creditable, civilized, pathetic (because what we can get will be confused and little and too late) – to see justice done on behalf of the remaining, wretched piece of humanity. The desire is the life ring thrown into the sea – the sop to tragedy, to our bid for order, truth, relief.

A good trial does not take place at will or in a void. It is the product of a community, its customs, its habits of thought and feeling, and of men – ultimately, a handful of men: the prosecuting attorneys and defence attorneys, their hand-picked juries, and the judge. Men – within limits – can rise to great occasions. So, there is still cause for hope, though the first stages have not been propitious.

There has been that surely fantastic indulgence in publicity and publicity-seeking. Both sides have talked too much, both sides have tried to condition the public mind. There has been vacillation, indiscretion and the lamentable publication of Jack Ruby's first-person story. The change-of-venue issue – a perfectly legitimate one in itself – was allowed to degenerate into an unseemly squabble.

The actual opening day of the trial was – to put it mildly – ragged. Perhaps inevitably so; it is physically impossible to cope with the contemporary broadcasting media and the press in courthouses designed for another age. And so the corridors were choked with cameramen and apparatus, and the moving of the prospective jurors in and out of the courtroom was slowed down.

Ruby himself was hustled in and past throngs of unsearched men and women, a replica – or nearly so – of the situation of Nov. 24.* Everybody is thoroughly frisked on his way into the courtroom, but there is no control whatsoever over persons entering the courthouse and the corridors. And in fact, as we know, at least one other crackpot with a mission and a gun has already been discovered next door.

There were delays and hanging about, press conferences by the attorneys, and an early adjournment. And thus the sense of inevitability, the sense of the terrible, smooth swiftness of justice that marks the opening of a trial in London, for instance, was lost.

Judge Joe B. Brown bumbles about the scene, flings a word to Belli's colleague Joe Tonahill, calls for water, swallows a pill or stands still to be photographed, or does his go-out-and-get-a-

---

*When Oswald himself was hustled in past an unsearched crowd and was thus shot by Ruby.

cup-of-coffee stuff. At one point he appears in the pressroom, pipe in mouth, his robe on a coat hanger in his hand: 'How're you doing, boys?'

This is the homespun touch – and there is nothing wrong with it, if it is genuine, and it is genuine here. Judge Brown runs, as he loves to say, an informal court – justice without the trappings, justice with a minimum of props, with simplicity, warmth, human ease, accessibility. These are, perhaps, or could be, the hallmarks of the most perfect form of judicial administration. But they also make the greatest demands on the man himself, on his strength, his courage, his independence, on his ultimate ability to make himself inaccessible when the need has come.

ON THE SECOND DAY, when the actual jury selection gets under way, things begin to jell. If there is no speed, there is at least coherence. Judge Brown's opening words are, 'Be seated and *no smoking.*'

The first potential juror called is a man, now all but sunk back into oblivion. After a few exchanges, it becomes evident that he longs to be picked for this jury. His name is Hilliard M. Stone, his age 35, his answers careful and articulate. District Attorney Henry Wade, calm, seated in his leather swivel chair, leads the man competently through routine information:

'You have been called as a prospective juror in the case against Ruby. What business are you in? Where do you live? Married? Children? Which church preference? Ever been on a jury?'

Then Wade comes quickly to the point. In Texas law the jury does not merely determine guilt or innocence; it must also assess punishment. This is by no means universal in the U.S.:

'The sentence for murder with malice can be anything from two years' imprisonment to the death penalty. Have you any religious or conscientious scruples against death in the electric chair for one convicted of murder?'

This is a crucial question. Any juror who declares himself opposed to capital punishment in all circumstances can be disqualified by challenge for cause, and Wade has declared that the prosecution will do so throughout this case.

Mr Stone gives some thought-out answers that pay tribute to what he calls 'a pretty big question', but the long and short of it is that he is not opposed to capital punishment. He mentions society and the value of amputating gangrened limbs.

Then Wade explains, as he will to every jury candidate, the law as to insanity. The law presumes, he says, every person to be sane. Jack Ruby has the presumption that he is sane as he sits there now:

'Burden is on the defendant or his attorneys to establish his insanity by preponderance of evidence. Burden is on us [the prosecution] to establish his guilt beyond reasonable doubt. Will you follow that law?'

The prospect says, 'Yes, sir.'

Now the prosecution rests. The candidate is handed over to Mr Belli's questioning. We have now reached the clash of wills. The defence professes to be convinced that no fair jury can be found in Dallas, and Belli not long ago said that he was ready to wager his life that he would get his change of venue.

Indeed, in the elevator back in the large hotel two gentlemen – rosy with morning, replete with breakfast, unlit cigars in mouth – had drawled to one another. 'Why try the fellow? *I* seen him.' And when a reporter chipped in that precisely what the nationwide audience of the live television transmission did *not* see was the identity of the killer, the same man snapped back, 'Well, police *did*,' and stepped off with a wave of dismissal and disgust: 'Aw, the law's an ass.'

But is he, and his likes and his *point*, peculiar to the city of Dallas, to Texas, to the country as a whole? It happened to have happened in Dallas; it *could* have happened elsewhere.

At any rate, 'We all seen it.' It is the extreme, the logical payoff of the mass media – or, rather, of the licence that we have given them to invade our public life. We shall either have to curb these media or stretch the laws to accommodate them.

Meanwhile, we have to pay the price. If, by a fair trial for Ruby, we mean a trial without preknowledge anywhere, we are being ostriches or indulging in legal fiction.

However, preknowledge – in a less succinct form – is an ingredient of every contemporary trial of major interest, and it has been found that preknowledge, though it probably cannot be erased from the subconscious mind, does not *necessarily* lead to bias and unfairness. The minds of jurors, once inside a court and exposed to other influences and an often quite different presentation of the evidence, have been found to change. Much depends on the atmosphere of the court itself, and here dignity and an aura of patient impartiality are of the essence.

BELLI, IN his well-groomed, gay clothes, but looking tired, rises. His task is formidable. Later, the burden of proof – that Jack Ruby shot and killed Lee Harvey Oswald with malice aforethought – will rest with the prosecution. But now Belli must carry the burden; he must force the prospective juror to disqualify himself.

By and large there are two things he will try first, to get rid of this or any other prospective juror: make each one admit that he has formed an opinion about Ruby's guilt (and Stone has already said that he has not) or get the court to accept the argument that every one of those who actually saw the killing of Oswald on the television screen must, in fact, have a fixed notion of that guilt.

If Belli can do this, the juror will be excused for cause – and both the defence and the prosecution, subject to the judge's ruling in each case, can challenge for cause an unlimited number of times. Failing, Belli must use up one of his precious 15 peremptory challenges, which he can use at his whim to dismiss a prospective juror.

Belli's wings appear clipped from the start. We have expected fireworks; we get sober if repetitious probing, blocked by a barrage of objections from the D.A.'s table.

Mr Stone, asked about his newspaper reading, looks down his nose; he doesn't keep up with that sort of thing: 'I usually pay no attention to these kind of cases in the newspaper.' He admits to having seen one rerun of the television scene. He says, sensibly and truthfully, 'I saw a man in a hat move forward and a lot of confusion.' Only later, in the morning paper, did he see the large picture which actually showed and named Ruby in the act.

'You *had* already seen that man shoot Mr Oswald on TV, hadn't you?'

Stone: 'So they said. As far as I know, there was a shooting.'

All this time, Ruby sits, small and still, a little behind the big Belli's chair. He appears nervous but does not move much. From time to time he licks his lips. His skin is pallid, moist, almost transparent. There is something ineffective about the man – damp, soft. The pointed nose is spinsterish. The small, round, nut-brown eyes are either fixed or swivelling. His expression is furtive and unhappy.

Henry Wade, burly, robust, sits relaxed but very much all there, occasionally buttressing an objection by Jim Bowie, his assistant. Time passes – an hour, another hour. Wade, despite the court's opening instruction, has begun to smoke. The cigarettes look tiny in his fist. The judge sustains every objection by the prosecution. Belli gets nowhere. Presently we come to the point where the judge makes his crucial ruling:

Belli: 'The defence wants this witness excused on the basis that he was witness to the event.'

Judge Brown: 'That depends on his attitude – what he can put out of his mind.'

Belli: 'I respectfully submit that seeing the TV rerun is just the same as being there.'

Judge Brown turns to the juror: 'If I ask you – considering everything you have seen, read, heard about the case – can you put that out of your mind and enter the box with a free and open mind?'

'Yes.'

Judge Brown: 'I would call him qualified, Mr Belli.'

Henry Wade rises and agrees that to have been a witness to the event is not by itself a disqualification.

Belli persists.

Judge Brown mops his brow copiously, then puts his specs in his mouth – a great breath – wipes them with a baby-blue tissue. The dais is a kind of half-enclosure, a little like an open confessional stall in a church. The judge lowers his chair sideways and reclines. The outside world can still see his face – it is a fine, round, humorous face, with a look of a handsome owl. He is waiting.

The jury candidate, a little rattled, is also waiting, prevented as he is from answering three-quarters of the questions.

Belli: 'Have you any feeling on the subject of insanity?'

'None.'

'Have you any experience with the subject of epilepsy?'

Objection.

Sustained.

Belli: 'Opinion about blackouts?'

Objection.

Sustained.

Belli: 'Do you know the jailhouse scientists?'

Objection.

Judge Brown: 'Sustained. Get down to the credibility of the witness.'

Belli: 'Did you follow the political careers of anyone in the D.A.'s office?'

Objection.

Belli: 'Do you feel that, if there were a change of venue, it would be a reflection on Dallas?'

Objection.

Sustained.

Bell: 'Do you feel there is a Dallas image?'

Objection.

Sustained; from his lazy position, the judge is quick on the trigger.

Belli: 'Have you read anything about the oligarchy in Dallas?'

Objection.

Judge Brown: 'Just qualify the juror.'

Belli: 'Do you feel that Mr Ruby can get a fair trial?'

Objection.

Belli now is casting about: 'Do you have any Jewish friends?'

Stone: 'I suppose so.'

Belli: 'Do you have any prejudice about Ruby belonging to a minority race?'

'No, sir.'

Belli: 'Do you have a great respect for Mr Stanley Marcus?'

'I don't know him.'

Judge Brown: 'Mr Belli, you must qualify or disqualify!'

Belli: 'Did you see the swastika signs on Jewish stores at the time of the President's visit to Dallas?'

'I was unaware of them.'

Belli: 'Did you discuss the case with anyone?'

'Not since yesterday.'

Belli: 'Do you think that Mr Oswald would have given us any information had he not been shot?'

Objection.

Belli: 'Certainly we should ask this question. We are being precluded . . .'

Judge Brown: 'You may have your exception.'

Belli: 'Did you discuss whether Oswald would have given us any further information?'

'Yes.'

Belli: 'What side of the question did you take?'

Objection.

Sustained.

Judge Brown: 'Do you want to challenge the juror?'

Belli: 'I don't want to challenge.'

Judge Brown (grimly jovial): 'You are going to have to.'

Belli: 'Your Honour says that this juror is qualified. I disagree. This man is witness to the event and has discussed all the phases of the lawsuit. I don't think it is enough to ask this man if he has any prejudice or nonprejudice . . . Your Honour is precluding us from getting a fair jury.'

Judge Brown: 'I think I am going to be the guide set up by the laws of Texas and I don't think you are.'

Belli: 'Your opinion of Jack Ruby is what?'

Objection.

Sustained.

Belli: 'You have never at any time felt that Dallas was on trial because of the assassination of the President?'

Stone: 'I am sure public opinion comes and goes. I have not felt Dallas was on trial.'

Belli: 'Did you feel that Dallas being on trial had its character impugned again with the shooting of Oswald?'

Objection.

Sustained.

The court is about to rise now for the luncheon recess. Belli still hangs on. But one knows that his round is lost.

THE VERY process of jury selection – that marathon, that contest within a contest at the threshold of American cases – is now unique to the United States. Continental European countries do not handpick their juries and in Britain the selective process, though still on the books, has become obsolete. Parties can still challenge for cause in England; each side may still exercise a small number of peremptory challenges, but in practice they are hardly ever used.

In England even a jury for a murder case is usually constituted in something under five minutes, the time it takes for the clerk to read out the names and for the jurymen to cross the floor. They are picked at random. The English have come to believe in the efficacy of absolute anonymity (neither addresses nor occupations of jurors are ever disclosed). The expectation is that the 12 presumably divergent attitudes will fuse somehow into the representative voice of the community. It is a kind of mystique; the only rational thing about it is that it saves public exposure, time and money. The jury is regarded as a Delphic oracle from which the veil may not be lifted – a species of sacred animal, dumb until the brief and final word, and indeed for ever after. Nobody may interview the members.

Of course it might, and occasionally does, happen that a juror will be found to have been deaf or ignorant of the English language or to have been the judge's mother. On the whole, though, strangely enough it works.

The American principle of selection looks to be the more enlightened one, though in practice there turns out to be something redundant, if not self-defeating, in the bipartisan playing and withholding of the trumps and counter cards – the two kinds of challenge. Perhaps the solution might lie in a middle course – for the American juries to be scrutinized a little less and the English ones a little more.

WHEN THE Ruby case resumes at 1:45 p.m., there are a few more abortive questions. Then Henry Wade accepts the juror for the prosecution. Belli once more moves for him to be disqualified for cause. The judge overrules the motion. Belli uses his peremptory challenge. The juror is excused. The next prospect moves in.

THE PATTERN, more briefly, will repeat itself. Again and again and again. Judge Brown has ruled, in effect, that a juror cannot be disqualified simply because he was a witness to the act on the TV screen. A decisive point has been reached.

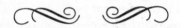

THE TRIAL OF JACK RUBY
For The Murder Of
Lee Harvey Oswald

Dallas, Texas, U.S.A.

❧ AFTER THREE and a half months of universal speculation and half-knowledge, after four weeks of trial at the county court at Dallas, after two hours and 19 minutes of jury deliberation, we have seen Jack Ruby tried and sentenced. What are we left with – has the trial answered or attempted to answer any questions? Was the prosecution case of murder with malice a just one? Was Ruby as wisely defended as he might have been? Did he have a fair trial? Was justice done? Did justice appear to be done? Was justice seen to be done?

ON MARCH 4, on the 15th working day in the court in Dallas, Ruby was at last arraigned. District Attorney Henry Wade, grizzled, broad-backed, charged with energy, planted himself in front of Ruby and intoned the indictment in the sing-song voice reserved for that form of words.

'How do you plead, Jack Ruby?'

Ruby, with Defense Attorney Melvin Belli hovering by his side, spoke a colourless 'Not guilty'. Mr Belli, anxious impresario, made an effort to inflate the plea: 'We plead not guilty by reason of insanity.'

'Very well,' said Judge Joe Brown.

'I want him to repeat it, too,' said Mr Belli.

'He's said it,' snapped the judge. 'That's enough, get on.'

And get on they did. The prosecution did not make an opening speech. Wade, instead of telling the jury what he would do, went ahead and did it.

I. PROSECUTION

THE PROSECUTION'S task was a single and straightforward one. The murder, in the extraordinary circumstances of this case, was common knowledge. The facts, the shooting of Oswald by Ruby, were not in dispute, so what remained to be proved beyond a reasonable doubt was 'malice'. In other words, did Ruby kill Lee Harvey Oswald after cool reflection? That was going to be the focal point of the state's case. Malice, under Texas law, can be formed in one second, in a 'twinkling of an eye'. A longer span of time, though mattering not a scrap in law, would obviously be more convincing to a jury.

The district attorneys presented their evidence in coherent form – chronologically (as far as possible), as a story. They succeeded in doing so with order and dispatch. Their case took three days.

On Day One the first three witnesses, two men and a girl, members of the advertising staff of the Dallas *Morning News*, began with the beginning, the morning of Friday, Nov. 22. We heard of Ruby sitting in the newspaper office, with its view of the Texas School Book Depository, fussing over the weekend advertisements for his nightclubs. The presidential visit getting on its way below, the first news of the assassination seeping in, the rush to a TV set, Ruby's emotion – not much noted in the general surge.

Mr Belli asked, 'Did he have a fixed stare . . . ?'

The witness, a pretty girl, hesitated, cast a glance at Jack Ruby and said, 'About the same as here.'

The next seven witnesses were newsmen and police officers and a car-park man who had encountered Ruby at various points and times between the Friday afternoon and Saturday night when he was following the press – 'making like a reporter', as he had described himself to one of them.

A radio man told how Ruby had turned up that first night bringing a big paper bag of sandwiches and various soda pops for the comfort of the press. 'He [Ruby] seemed pleased in the sense of being in on something.'

Note that the prosecution did not have to prove that Ruby is sane. In law he is assumed sane until and unless proved otherwise by the defence. In practice, nevertheless, it could not come amiss to build up for the jury a Ruby sane, calm and collected. The defence, of course, was out to build up the opposite.

Mr Wes Wise of TV station KRLD said that Ruby was in tears when they were talking about the two western saddles that were to have been given by the city as a present to the Kennedy children.

Assistant District Attorney William Alexander: 'Was he excited?'

Wise: 'Touched.'

Mr Joe Tonahill for the defence (trying to sew it up): 'He broke down and cried?'

Wise: 'I would not describe it as breaking down and crying – I'd say there were tears in his eyes.'

A reporter on the *News* described how Ruby got into police headquarters on the Friday night. He got into the elevator wedged between newsmen, concealing his lack of a press badge by bending over a reporter's notebook and pretending to be scribbling. Later a policeman called out, 'Hey, Jack, what are *you* doing here? . . . He said he was helping, and he *was* help-ing . . . He seemed to enjoy being in the midst of excitement.'

Belli: 'He was buzzing round?'

'Not buzzing. Standing still.'

With the eleventh witness the case reached the events of Sunday morning, Nov. 24, and established one cast-iron fact of time. Mr Doyle Lane, Western Union supervisor, gave the following testimony: He was on duty when Ruby came in to send a $25 money order to one of his stripper girls in Fort Worth (Little Lynn, the girl who had telephoned Ruby long-distance an hour earlier that morning and asked him to send some money at once as she had to pay her rent). The Western Union man knew Ruby as a customer. The defendant appeared cool and calm. The money order (produced in court) was stamped for time by a clocking device at 11:17 a.m. Nov. 24. It takes about three minutes to walk from the Western Union office to the city hall. Oswald was shot there at 11:21.

Belli: 'Did Ruby seem at all in a hurry to leave?'

Witness: 'No.'

In the afternoon on Day One, after identification of the gun, a .38 sold to Ruby over the counter on Jan. 19, 1960, we heard the first of the six crucial prosecution witnesses, the six police officers who were present in the basement at city hall and who saw, handled or heard Ruby during and after the act.

The first on the stand was Detective J.R. Leavelle, the man in the light tan suit and the Texas hat we saw on the television screen walking on the right of Oswald, his left wrist handcuffed to Oswald's right. Officer L.C. Graves was on Oswald's left, Captain Will Fritz walked on before. They came out, '. . . the floodlights directly shining on us . . . a glare . . . a great number of people in the basement'. Leavelle saw Ruby out of the corner of his eye: 'I recognized him as someone I knew but could not recall his name.' He saw a hand with a gun: 'I could not tell whether it came from his pocket.' After the shot, Leavelle tried to protect his prisoner, 'kind of swung him around'.

'And then?'

'Oswald grunted and hollered and sank to the floor.' Leavelle, still tied to him, was pulled down – then loosened the handcuff, straightened up. Oswald never spoke again.

Ruby, meanwhile, had been disarmed by other police officers, seized, pounced upon, flung down. Leavelle heard him say . . .

Here came a forceful interruption by the defence. It was

argued that anything said by Ruby after that point was inadmissible as testimony. The law lays down that what a man says before he is warned that he is under arrest – and Ruby pinned down to the floor by policemen certainly was under arrest – cannot be used in evidence against him; that is, it cannot be repeated in front of a jury at his trial. However, the law also lays down that what a man says *immediately* following an act – still in the heat, as it were, of that act – is *res gestae*, part of the total of the act and thus admissible. Much depends on the interpretation of 'immediately'.

Judge Brown ruled that Ruby's utterances were admissible, and so we heard what Leavelle said he heard: 'I hope the son of a bitch dies.'

On that Leavelle was cross-examined by Mr Belli: 'You say you heard this three or four minutes, or how long after the shooting?'

Leavelle: '. . . Approximately one minute. I do not know the exact time.'

Belli: 'He never at any time said, when he was on the deck or on the ground there, "I shot him," did he?'

Leavelle: 'I didn't hear him say it.'

Belli: 'And there were other people who said, prior to your hearing Jack Ruby say "I hope the S.O.B. dies," there were other people that said, "Oswald is shot, Oswald is shot," right? At least we heard it over the radio.'

Leavelle: 'That's what I understand, yes.'

Belli: 'And that was before Jack said, "I hope the son of a bitch dies"?'

Leavelle: 'I would assume so, sir.'

Belli: 'He could have been saying that in response to a lot of people saying, "Oswald is shot, Oswald is shot," as far as you know?'

Leavelle: 'That's possible, yes.'

Subsequently Mr Belli established some material points. Ruby, at the shooting, was carrying $2,015.33 rolled up in his pockets (a reason suggested for carrying the gun). The time of the shooting was 11:20–11:21. It did take some three minutes to walk over from the Western Union office to city hall.

Mr Belli likes to do his questioning standing or pacing between defence table, witness stand and jury box. It is a habit frowned upon in Texas courts. The San Franciscan's agile prowling visibly irritated District Attorney Wade.

Wade: 'Judge, I think he can ask questions sitting at the table over here.'

Judge Brown: 'I think so, too.'

Belli (from his chair): 'Did you feel that Jack was kind of peculiar in the past?'

Leavelle: 'No, sir. I do not think so.'

Presently Leavelle stepped down. A doctor testified to Oswald's cause of death, and the court adjourned.

DAY TWO was occupied entirely with the examination of Detectives Graves, D.R. Archer and Thomas McMillon. Graves was on the stand for barely one hour. It was he who had grabbed the gun, held tight the cylinder – so that Ruby, whose finger was still on the trigger, was unable to get off a second shot – and wrenched the gun out of Ruby's hand.

Detective Graves heard no words said. Not even the ringing ripple, 'Oswald's been shot! . . .'

During cross-examination, Mr Belli did a bit of gun-play. He demonstrated the rather awkward grip – index finger laid along the barrel, middle finger on the trigger – with which Ruby is supposed to have held and pulled the gun: 'Most unusual handling of a revolver [the inference being that Ruby was in some sort of a convulsion]?'

Graves (unyielding): 'It would be for *me*.'

Graves repeated that he had heard nothing said. Mr Tonahill broke in to ask if he had heard Leavelle say to Oswald, 'I hope someone shoots *you*, you son of a bitch.'

'I did not hear this.'

Mr Belli ended by asking, on his feet, 'Now, to sew this up so that we can throw it in the trash basket – there was no connection between Ruby and the Dallas police force?'

Graves: 'That I don't know.'

Mr Belli insisted.

Graves: 'Not as far as I am concerned.'

Once more Mr Belli repeated the question.

Graves: 'I still don't know, Mr Belli.'

The next witness called was Detective Archer, who had been on duty in the basement. *He* had heard a good deal. He saw the shooting and, about 12 seconds later, he heard Ruby say, 'I hope I killed the son of a bitch.' Archer also heard cries of 'Who is he? Who is he?' and Ruby calling out as he was lying on the floor, 'I'm Jack Ruby. I'm Jack Ruby – all you guys know me.'

And now came the first entirely fresh piece of evidence. Detective Archer told that, as Ruby was being led from an elevator into the jail office on the fifth floor, he said to him, 'Jack, I think you killed him.' To which Ruby replied, 'I intended to shoot him three times.'

The ensuing cross-examination was conducted in a tough tone. Belli wanted to know if Archer had gone over his testimony with the D.A. Archer admitted that he had. How often? Three times. Belli wanted to know whether Archer had included the bit about 'I intended to shoot him three times' in the report he had made to his superiors at the time. Archer thought he had not. Belli demanded to see the report. He was told by the D.A.s and the judge that he could not. (There is, in fact, a Dallas city ordinance which forbids defence attorneys to subpoena police officers' reports.) Mr Belli insisted.

Judge Brown: 'Court has made up its mind.'

Mr Belli invoked the Constitution, the Bill of Rights, the Supreme Court . . .

Judge Brown: 'Ah don't want to hear anything more about it.'

THERE WAS worse to come. Almost immediately Detective McMillon took the stand. He said that he heard Ruby shout to

Oswald as he lunged at him: 'You rat son of a bitch, you shot the President.' McMillon entered the scuffle on top of Ruby, handcuffed him and helped to take him to the jail upstairs. On his way through the seething basement, Ruby kept crying, 'I hope I killed the S.O.B.' And in the jail office, McMillon overheard Archer's 'Jack, I think you killed him.' Ruby's answer had been . . .

The defence cut in. New objection against disclosing the defendant's words after arrest. The judge ruled them admissible. Defence objected again. The judge overruled. The defence entered an exception (a formal protest, put on record, necessary for an eventual appeal). When the tumult died down, McMillon was able to corroborate Archer's earlier evidence. In fact, he improved upon it. According to him, Ruby's reply was, 'I meant to get off three shots, but you-all moved in on me so fast I couldn't get the other two away.'

McMillon continued. A Captain King had stepped up and said, 'Of all the low-life scum things, this takes the cake – why did you do it?' Ruby answered, 'Someone had to do it, someone had to do it, and you guys couldn't do it.'

What a defence can do after a damaging piece of evidence has come to light is to try to shake the witness. Yet a cross-examination is a perilous thing; you can never tell which answer will get out of line.

Belli: 'Did you call him "Jack"?'

McMillon: 'Yes, I did . . . He had some dealings with the police before – he got arrested.'

The three defence counsels leaped to their feet. Mr Belli exploded:

'You arrested him? For arson? For larceny? For child kidnapping? For robbery? For moral turpitude?'

Detective McMillon sat stubborn and shrugged. *He* didn't know.

Mr Belli finally made him admit that it might well have been something to do with an expired beer licence. 'Your Honour, I insist the jury must disregard this.'

Judge Brown: 'All right, the jury will disregard it.' He

neither looked at nor addressed the jury on this point.

Mr Belli: 'You cannot unring a bell, can you?'

The Judge: 'All right, get on with it.'

The jury, the eight men and the four women, sat with unmoved faces.

After the luncheon recess on Day Two, Mr Belli plunged at once into the continued cross-examination of Detective McMillon.

Belli: 'Who did you talk to during the recess?'

McMillon: 'Mr Wade – Mr Alexander – Mr [Jim] Bowie.'

Belli: 'Where?'

McMillon: 'In Mr Wade's office.'

Belli: 'What were your instructions?'

McMillon: 'They instructed me to tell the truth.'

Then let's have it, Mr Belli said, and in sequence. He tried out when and where exactly the 'of all the low-life scum things' dialogue between Captain King and Ruby was supposed to have taken place. McMillon could not remember.

In the elevator? On the fifth floor? In the jailer's office? McMillon refused to be pinned down.

Belli: 'But Ruby *was* arrested? Did you discuss that with the D.A.?'

McMillon: 'We discussed that point some.'

Thereupon Mr Belli once more demanded to see those police officers' reports. He looked at the judge and began to shout about the appeals court and motions of mistrial. The reports were handed over from the D.A.s' table. (Why? Mr Alexander was overheard explaining to a reporter, 'Because the goddam liberal Supreme Court makes them available to the defence.') Mr Belli was not satisfied. They were photostats. Where were the originals?

Judge Brown: 'You can't have them.'

Belli quoted the rule that entitled a party to 'the best evidence available'.

Judge Brown: 'The state has proffered these – you take 'em for what they are, Mr Belli.'

Belli (impassioned): 'Are we back in the Middle Ages, so that we cannot see original documents?'

Judge Brown (cheerfully): 'Yeah.'

Mr Belli made the best of what he got. McMillon, we now learned, had made two reports. The first was in his own writing and dated Nov. 24. The second was a transcript of an oral report made on Nov. 30. The first did not contain those extremely damaging words attributed to Ruby. The second one did.

There were other words in those reports. They had so far not entered McMillon's testimony. Mr Belli got them in. Ruby, the jury learned, was heard to say after the shooting, 'You-all won't believe this, but I couldn't have planned this thing. I couldn't have timed it so perfect.'

On the morning of Day Three the film strips of the shooting were shown in court, projected first in normal, then in slow motion, then in stills. Ruby watched avidly. It must have been – did he realize it? – one of the strangest experiences a man ever had.

Afterward they called Captain Glen D. King. The captain, in uniform, made a good impression as a witness, careful and straightforward. He had not observed the shooting. He saw 'a lot of movement, heard a lot of noise . . .' Later on he talked to Ruby upstairs in the jail office. The crux of his testimony was that Ruby said to him, 'You didn't think I was letting him get by with it?' Captain King was quite positive he heard this.

For the rest, the captain corrected the line attributed to him by McMillon. 'I did not say, ''Of all the low-life scum things,'' I said, ''You dirty scum,'' or ''You filthy scum, you are the scum of the earth.'' ' And he did not ask Ruby, 'Why did you do it?' And consequently did not hear Ruby's alleged, 'Someone had to do it and you guys couldn't.' Nor did he hear, 'I hope the S.O.B. dies,' nor 'I meant to shoot him three times . . .'

The last state witness called was Police Sergeant Patrick Dean and he gave what was probably the most damning prosecution evidence, a straight indication of intent. The sergeant was on duty in the basement – heard the shot – saw the commotion – ran to join the scuffle, and *some 10 minutes later*, so he said, was sent to take a Secret Service man, Forrest Sorrels, up to the fifth floor. They found Ruby in the jail office, stripped to his shorts. The Secret Service man questioned Ruby.

Sergeant Dean: 'Ruby said something to the effect that he thought about the killing two nights prior when he saw Oswald on the show-up stand [during the press conference at police headquarters].'

Ruby was asked, 'Jack, why did you do it?' Sergeant Dean reproduced Ruby's alleged answer not in the pat, word-perfect quote so favoured by police witnesses, but obliquely, in a rambling sentence.

Dean: 'Ruby said he believed in due process of law, but he was torn up by the events and could see no sense in a long and lengthy trial and he knew the outcome would be inevitable – would be the death penalty [for Oswald], and he was shaken and emotional and despondent since the assassination, and this man not only shot the President but Officer Tippit, and his [Ruby's] sister was just out of the hospital and was nervous and very emotional, and they were both torn up, and he wanted to spare Mrs Kennedy having to come back to Dallas for the trial . . .'

Mr Belli burst in with a motion for mistrial: '. . . This man's constitutional rights have been violated.'

Motion denied.

Wade: 'Coming back to Friday, Nov. 22. Tell us what Ruby said.'

Dean: 'He said when he first noticed the sarcastic sneer on Oswald's face, that was when he first thought he'd kill him if he got the chance.'

Wade: 'And then?'

Dean: 'He said he wanted the world to know Jews do have guts.'

Wade: 'What was the word?'

Belli (beside himself, on his feet, at the top of his lungs): 'JEWS – *J-E-W-S*! I want that word to ring out, Your Honour.'

Tonahill (also on his feet): 'We want it on the record that his testimony is highly prejudicial from a racial standpoint.'

ON THAT afternoon, Mr Belli had a last go at Sergeant Dean. Belli was unable to shake the sergeant on the premeditation testimony.

Mr Belli also demanded to see this man's original police report. As it happened, the report – two reports – were in the sergeant's pocket. He surrendered them.

Belli: 'It is *written* here that you took the Secret Service man upstairs to Ruby at approximately noon?' (That would make the time – between the criminal act and Ruby's incriminating words – 40 minutes and not the 10 minutes Dean had told about.)

Dean said the written report was wrong.

Belli: 'Would you call 11:30 a.m. "approximately noon"?'

After some hedging, Dean admitted that he would not. He launched himself into an explanation as to the mistake. He had miscalculated the length of a television interview he had given immediately after the shooting. Only later, on a rerun, had he realized that the interview was a matter of short minutes. He had lost track of time.

This may well be true. If it is not, a higher court may have to decide whether a conversation held 40 minutes after the act can be considered part of the original act.

At the last, Mr Belli wanted to settle if Ruby had been questioned about the possible connection with Oswald. Sergeant Dean was positive: 'Ruby confirmed there was no previous communication with Oswald whatsoever.'

And at 2:55 p.m. on March 6, the state rested.

Twenty-five minutes later, on the same afternoon, the defence opened. Mr Belli demurely stepped before the jury box and made a brief opening statement. The gist of it was an appeal to enlightenment and reason, and it was frequently interrupted by one or more of the district attorneys.

II. DEFENCE

THE FIRST witness was a girl who had worked at Ruby's club, and for the last few days she had been expecting hourly to have a baby. While she was waiting in the packed, sweltering corridor to give her evidence, the Dallas prison escape got underway. Two bolting prisoners charged into the corridor, one brandishing a homemade (soap, boot-black, syrup) pistol. Little Lynn (the witness' professional name) dodged for cover – 'Pregnant Strip-Teaser Scared by Jail-Break,' as the headlines, accurately, had it the next day. A few minutes later Mr Belli was able to conduct the witness to the stand.

Considering everything, Little Lynn – 19 years old, helmet mop of hair, dark glasses, baby-doll mouth and chin – showed remarkable composure. It was she who telephoned Ruby that morning, Nov. 24, long-distance from Fort Worth, asking him to send the $25 money order. It was because of that telephone call, the defence contended, that money order, that Ruby drove to the Western Union office near the city hall and that everything did happen: '. . . He sounded as if he was crying, had been crying, or was about to cry. I said, "Jack, Jack?" He didn't seem to hear me . . .'

She had also talked to him Saturday night: 'He was far away. I told him I had come to work and found he had closed the club. He got very mad at me. "Don't you care about the President?" he yelled.'

'Sounding abnormal?'

'He didn't sound like Jack. Not like his voice. He had a laughing voice – there was laughter in it – he kep' up everybody's spirits when we were upset.' (How many sides, one thought, are there to a man?)

WHAT THE defence was trying to do was quite clear to all. Their case, revealed many weeks ago with calculated candour, was temporary insanity. Now, under Texas law, which abides like England's with the M'Naghten Rule, a man is held to be insane if at the time he did not know the nature or quality of his act; or if he did know, he did not understand that it was wrong. (Many think this is an antiquated, clumsy, almost childish test, and altogether out of line with such knowledge of the human mind as we now possess. But the fact remains that, for the present, neither Texas nor England has chosen to replace M'Naghten with the Durham Rule, established by a U.S. Court of Appeals, which states that a defendant is not guilty by reason of insanity if 'his unlawful act was the product of mental disease or mental defect'.)

Consequently, having chosen to plead temporary insanity, the defence had to prove that Jack Ruby, at the time he shot Oswald, was either out of his mind to the point of not knowing right from wrong or did not know the nature of his act. And to get to this point at all, his attorneys had to prove (Step 1) that Ruby suffered from a defect or disease, (Step 2) that this defect or disease was capable of producing mental blackouts, fits, or spells of temporary insanity, (Step 3) that such a fit or spell occurred precisely at the time of the shooting of Oswald.

Before calling the actual medical evidence, Messrs Belli and Tonahill did some groundwork by calling lay witnesses to conjure up an impression of Ruby as an offbeat, unstable, possibly psychotic personality.

On Monday, Day Four of the trial, their first witness of weight was Barney Ross, world welterweight champion in the 1930s. He first knew Ruby in Chicago when they were boys together: 'We were in a group that ran around together on the West Side.'

Belli: 'Was it a tough neighbourhood?'

Ross: 'Not the easiest [neighbourhood] – but nice enough. There were about 10 or 12 of us – I knew him from when I was 15 to 33 . . . Jack got into screaming fits. He used to turn almost purple and walk away from us.'

Ruby, leaning forward with his fixed look, his mouth slightly open, drank this in.

Ross: 'If you criticized a deal he liked, he'd holler and scream and run away – get his steam up – give us a mean look and walk away for two or three days. And we'd miss him. And after he'd get so gentle he wouldn't step on a fly or caterpillar. We called him Sparky, because he was a hustler, even when he was a teenager he kept his eyes open for ways of making money . . .'

Belli: 'Did he ever get into any trouble with the police?'

Ross: 'I don't think so.'

The next witness was a man who had stayed at Ruby's apartment in November, George Senator – a man about 50, a defenceless witness, truthful, mild, not very quick.

Tonahill: 'Tell us what happened after the assassination?'

Senator: 'Ruby woke me up at 3 a.m. [dawn of Nov. 23].'

Tonahill: 'What did he say?'

Senator: 'He said he didn't see why it had to happen to a nice family like that.'

Tonahill: 'How did he look? Just tell the jury how he looked.'

Senator: 'He had a look I had never seen before. He was deeply upset. He kept saying, ''What will happen to the wife and children?'' '

Mr Senator then told a tale about a strange dawn peregrination, when Ruby insisted that they both get up and out, then and there, take the car out, drive downtown, pick up a boy with camera and flash bulb, and photograph the 'Impeach Earl Warren' sign on the North Central Expressway: 'He was very disturbed about that sign.' They photographed it. It was still dark. They milled around and had breakfast at an all-night place. Senator went back to bed and, later on, about his business. He was with Ruby again the next morning, Sunday, in the hour or two before the murder: 'His condition was changed. He was more solemn and grievous [*sic*].' They shaved, dressed, had coffee, looked at the papers, saw a bit of TV. Little Lynn telephoned from Fort Worth. Ruby got ready to go downtown.

Tonahill: 'Any reference, innuendo to Oswald?'

Senator: 'Never mentioned his name to me.'

Next came a very pretty dancer, Penny Dollar, who used to work at Ruby's club. She told how she once saw Ruby kick a taxi driver down the stairs, then bang the man's head on the sidewalk. Ruby suddenly stopped, looked dazed and cried, 'Did I do this? Did I do this?'

Penny Dollar: 'It just stuck in my mind that he could do this and not realize what he had done. I'm not a doctor, but in my opinion he is mentally sick.'

Then Mr Ike Pappas, reporter for WNEW, New York, played the sound tape he had recorded at the time of the shooting. 'Oswald is shot! Oswald is shot!' can be heard, but not Ruby's alleged 'You son of a bitch.' Mr Pappas himself, who at the time stood only six feet away from Oswald, testified, 'I did not hear Ruby say anything.'

And at 3:40 p.m. the defence called the first of their expert witnesses, a clinical psychologist, Dr Roy Schafer, Ph.D., Yale University.

Dr Schafer had spent some hundred hours giving Ruby a series of standard psychological tests (which served to form part of the basis of other doctors' findings). He attempted to explain the nature, scope and purpose of these tests. The prosecution chafed and Judge Brown got restive: 'Get down to the meat of this thing.'

Mr Belli implored that it would be impossible to ask the ultimate question – to ask at this point whether Ruby was legally sane – without having laid the foundations on which such an answer could be based: 'Deny us this testimony and your Honour will deny us all modern scientific testimony in the world. If you shut up this great Yale psychologist, we might as well shut our briefcases.'

'I will exclude this testimony,' said Judge Brown.

Mr Belli (passionately): 'Is your Honour trying to tell a jury in Dallas in 1964 not to hear the testimony of this great man?'

All the district attorneys leaped up and wild tri-cornered wrangling ensued. The jury was sent out, and the argument went on until D.A. Wade sprawled back in his chair and said, 'Aw, we'd have been finished by now. Let's let him testify.'

So, the judge overruled himself, the jury came back and Dr Schafer was allowed to give his evidence, which, sustained with great detail, was in effect this: that Ruby, by the tests, showed a physical brain damage, probably due to a long-forgotten head injury; and that it was the type of brain damage which, under certain emotional or mechanical stimulation, might cause a person to go into a temporary 'fugue state'.

Wade: 'Would a person be capable of completing any purposeful act in such a [pretending to stumble on the outlandish word] f-f-fugue state?'

Dr Schafer: 'They would.'

Wade: 'If they carried out a purposeful act, would they know what they were doing?'

Dr Schafer: 'It depends on what you mean by purposeful.'

Wade: 'Let's get right down to killing. Isn't that a purposeful act? Would he remember what he did afterwards?'

Dr Schafer: 'He might not.'

Wade: 'You mean that if a man picked out a person from a mass of 200 people, killed and remembered every bit of it, you'd turn him loose on society again?'

Dr Schafer (with composure): 'I don't believe I said anything like that.'

Wade: 'With all these ink blots and pictures, did you make out if Ruby knew right from wrong when he shot Lee Harvey Oswald?'

Dr Schafer said he had no way of knowing that, one way or the other. The court adjourned.

The whole of Day Five was taken up with the testimony of two expert medical witnesses for the defence: Dr Martin Towler, psychiatrist and neurologist of the University of Texas, Galveston, and Dr Manfred Guttmacher, psychiatrist attached to the Baltimore courts.

Dr Towler was one of the three doctors who in January did an electro-encephalogram (EEG) on Ruby ordered by the court. (The three were Dr Robert Stubblefield, nominated by the court; Dr John T. Holbrook, by the prosecution; and Dr Towler, by the defence.) The kernel of Dr Towler's evidence, which lasted several hours, was that Ruby's EEG showed that Ruby had a 'seizure disorder which probably is a psychomotor epilepsy variant [PMV]'.

Dr Towler spread the EEG, the recorded impulses of Ruby's brain, out on the ledge of the jury box and for about an hour explained the tracings to counsel and the jurors.

Ruby craned his neck and seemed fascinated at first, but as it went on, out of his earshot, he appeared to become listless again, or bored. Judge Brown thumbed through a magazine, and neither showed interest nor asked a question.

By then the judge's non-participation had become a frustrating element. The presence of a presiding mind, the sense that a man of principle, integrity and some intellectual grasp is at the helm, is a *sine qua non* of any healthy trial.

Dr Towler, sandy-haired, stocky, appeared a serious, careful witness.

Belli: 'You used the words "seizure disorder" to describe Ruby's condition. Can you tell me some of the symptoms?'

Dr Towler: 'Patients may feel an overwhelming sense of despondency or despair.'

Belli: 'Can you tell us what they do in these spells? Can they carry on normal activities?'

Dr Towler: 'They may perform their usual day-to-day tasks . . .'

Belli: 'Does a man know what he was doing in these spells?'

Dr Towler: 'He may remember nothing, or may recall bits of what took place . . .'

Belli: 'Did you receive any fee?'

Dr Towler: 'None whatever.'

Wade: 'What is your diagnosis?'

Dr Towler: 'Seizure disorder.'

Then Mr Wade asked the essential question: 'Was Ruby in a seizure state when he shot Oswald?'

Dr Towler: 'I have no opinion. I have no way of knowing that.'

During one of the short recesses on that day, there took place the following incident. Oswald's mother, who had been barred from entering the courtroom, was sitting in the corridor outside, gibbering to herself. Judge Brown sat himself down next to her, and for a full five minutes there they were, posing, smiling and looking into each other's faces while a score of cameramen took their photographs.

WITH DR GUTTMACHER the defence reached the apex of their medical case. Dr Guttmacher had used the groundwork – the psychological tests and the EEG – and had himself minutely examined Ruby in the jail. Now came the full synthesis.

Belli at once went to the heart of the matter: 'Do you have an opinion as to whether Ruby realized the nature and consequences of his act, or knew the difference between right and wrong?'

Dr Guttmacher answered flatly: 'I do not think he was capable of distinguishing between right and wrong, or knew the nature and quality of his act at the time of the homicide.'

Dr Guttmacher never budged from that opinion. He remained certain that Ruby was neither morally nor legally responsible during the shooting. He was, however, less certain as to what had caused that temporary state. He said he could not be sure that it had been in fact a psychomotor epilepsy seizure, but called it 'a disruption of the ego, an episodic discontrol . . . a state of diminished consciousness. All his defences crumbled. The hostile, aggressive part of his makeup, which is very strong, became focused on this individual, Oswald.'

Dr Guttmacher then proceeded to give a compressed case history. He talked of Ruby's quite appalling family background and heredity, the father 'a drunken immigrant tyrant; the mother, ineffectual, a certified paranoiac'. So, at the age of 7 or 8 until 15, Ruby had to be farmed out to various foster parents and grew up in a half-dozen different homes. One brother had to be treated in an institution for acute depression, and a sister for involutional melancholia.

'I think we are dealing here with a very abnormal individual – a vulnerable individual – psychotic, violent.'

Ruby was watching Dr Guttmacher with a kind of dead-chicken stare. He looked more and more diminished as the days went by, more and more like a wretched, scraggly, half-plucked broiler, blinking or staring under a strong hypnotic light.

'His swaggering and boastfulness were only a façade –'

'A what?' asked District Attorney Alexander.

'A mask,' Dr Guttmacher said politely. 'The assassination

of President Kennedy imposed a tremendous emotional impact on him. He was struggling to keep his sanity during this period. He felt an unusual degree of involvement in the tragedy.'

Belli: 'What did he tell you about President Kennedy?'

Dr Guttmacher: 'He told me, "I fell for that man." He admired the President as the head of a model family. And as a Jew, as a member of a minority group, he had an intense feeling for Presidents Roosevelt and Kennedy because of their stands over civil rights . . . So, after the assassination he didn't want to go on living any more: "I feel like a nothing person." He wanted to leave Dallas . . .'

Mr Wade, lying back in his chair, chomping on his unlit cigar, drawled. 'Your Honour, this is all rambling . . .'

Belli (bouncing up, clear and loud): 'I resent this cornball talk of rambling. It is insulting to this learned gentleman – and it is unworthy of a sophisticated city like Dallas.'

Wade (lazily): 'I still think he's rambling.'

Belli (blazing): 'That's because you don't understand it.'

Wade (crying to the judge): 'Are you going to let that lawyer refer to us as ignorant, as ignoramuses?'

After this, it really got out of hand. Belli, pointing at District Attorney Alexander, shrieked, 'This man called the people of Dallas peasants!'

Tonahill (booming): 'And *he* took the Lord's name in vain.'

The judge: 'Everybody sit down.'

During a calm period, Belli asked if Ruby had any guilt feeling about having killed a human being.

Dr Guttmacher: 'He has an intellectual realization of the wrongness of his act, but there really isn't any guilt feeling. I think he feels, at a deeper level, that he is an exterminator. When I asked about Oswald's wife and children, Ruby said, "You have no right to ask me that question. You have no right to ask me that." He denies the humanity of this individual [Oswald].'

Yet Ruby also told the doctor, 'If only I had been kept longer at the Western Union office, if only I had been married, it would not have happened.'

Belli had been positive, in conference with the press, that he would call Ruby to testify. His next question indicated that he was having second thoughts: 'Could Jack take the witness stand this week?'

Dr Guttmacher: 'I wouldn't want to predict his reaction. He might either crack up on the witness stand or present a more normal aspect than I would expect. I think this man could become flagrantly psychotic.'

Belli's clinching question was:

'When this seizure state grips you, can you do anything about it at all?'

Dr Guttmacher: 'It is a pathological mood state, beyond control.'

As we know, Ruby was not called.

The cross-examination of Dr Guttmacher was conducted by D.A. Alexander. He addressed his questions to the witness in a half-incredulous, half-contemptuous tone: 'When did that "fugue state" begin?'

Dr Guttmacher: 'In my opinion, when he walked down the ramp there and saw all the people, the bright lights.'

Alexander: 'Did he know what he was doing?'

Dr Guttmacher: 'He was very much like a sleepwalker.'

Alexander: 'Picking one man among 200 in a fugue state? Saying, "You rat S.O.B., you killed the President"? . . . Shooting him dead? . . . Saying, "I hope the son of a bitch dies"? Saying, "I meant to shoot him three times"? When did he come out of this fugue state?'

Dr Guttmacher: 'It could be a matter of less than a minute.'

Alexander: 'As little as two seconds?'

Dr Guttmacher: 'As little as 10 seconds.'

Alexander: 'Your diagnosis?'

Dr Guttmacher: 'I think he has psychomotor epilepsy [PME]. There is no doubt about that. We have no data to tell whether at that moment it was a spasm of PME or whether it was episodic discontrol.'

Alexander: 'Your diagnosis?'

Dr Guttmacher: 'A mental cripple, carrying an unbearable load, who cracked.'

Alexander: 'A *bad* personality?'

Dr Guttmacher: 'A *sick* personality.'

Dr Guttmacher's testimony was the high-water mark of the defence case. The jury, who had listened to Dr Schafer with huffy neutrality and followed Dr Towler's EEGs with open boredom, had looked interested and alive. So when, on the next morning, Day Six, Mr Belli announced first thing, 'The defence rests,' it was not wholly a surprise. As Belli stood up to rest his case, the judge leaned forward, smiled, shook his head as if in disbelief, and for a moment stopped chewing his tobacco.

III. REBUTTALS

THE STATE lost no time in calling rebuttal witnesses. Ira Walker, a TV technician, said that he was sitting in his sound truck outside city hall at about 10:30 a.m. on that Sunday morning. Ruby came up to him and asked, 'Have they brought him down yet?' He meant Oswald, of course. A little time later, Ruby appeared again and asked the same question.

Next, newsman Frank Johnston, of U.P.I., said he was standing in the basement to the right of Police Officer Leavelle when Oswald was brought in. He heard Ruby yell, 'You rat son of a bitch,' then the gun went off. The defence asked Johnston if those words could have been uttered by someone else. Mr Johnston said, 'Yes.'

Next, Dr Sheff Olinger, neurologist, first medical expert witness for the state, a young man, self-assured. Mr Alexander asked him: 'Does Ruby's electro-encephalogram show organic brain damage?'

Dr Olinger: 'Not in my opinion.'

Alexander: 'Does the EEG indicate PME?'

Dr Olinger: 'The findings would be consistent with PME. However, they are not by themselves sufficient to establish it.'

Alexander: 'Do you agree with Dr Towler's finding?'

Dr Olinger: 'I disagree.'

Alexander: 'All told, you would not diagnose PME or psycho-motor variant in Jack Ruby?'

Dr Olinger: 'I would not.'

Mr Belli treated the witness to a terse little classic in cross-examination: 'Is there any abnormality in Ruby's EEG?'

Dr Olinger: 'A change – a deviation – not strictly normal – not abnormal.'

Belli: 'Your are *not* a specialist in EEG? Nor in neurology?'

Dr Olinger: 'I am in practice in neurology since 1959.'

Belli: 'You are *not* on any of the national boards? You have *not* taken any of the specialists' certificates?'

Dr Olinger: 'That's essentially it.'

Belli: 'You are *not* specialized in any medical field? You *are* licensed to practice?'

During a recess, Mr Belli was assaulted with questions. Why was Ruby not put on the stand? He warded them off with, 'He weeps copiously. We would have had that Niagara of tears, but the jury would not have appreciated it.'

Next, the second medical expert for the state, Dr Robert Stubblefield, psychiatrist. *He* has an impressive string of qualifications: Professor and Chairman of the Department of Psychiatry, Southwestern Medical School at Dallas; Chief of Service of Psychiatry, Parkland Memorial Hospital, Dallas; St Louis City Hospital, diplomate of this, consultant to that. He is not, however, an expert in the field of EEG. Dr Stubblefield, it will be recalled, was one of the three doctors who examined Ruby in January by order of the court.

Alexander: 'Doctor, you are not employed by the prosecution?'

Dr Stubblefield: 'No.'

Alexander: 'You are receiving no financial remuneration from the prosecution?'

Dr Stubblefield: 'No.'

Judge Brown: 'Nor from the court, for that matter.'

Alexander: 'Were you able to form an opinion as to whether the defendant was sane at the time of the shooting?'

Dr Stubblefield: 'I have no opinion about that.'

Alexander: 'Jack Ruby was at the Western Union office, calm, deliberate and normal. He proceeded from there at a normal pace to the city hall. He made his way into the basement, took out a gun and shot Lee Harvey Oswald. He was grappled to the ground and thereafter stated, ''I'm Jack Ruby – you guys know me –'' '

Defence objection.

Tonahill to the judge: 'I didn't hear you sustain that objection.'

Judge Brown: 'I don't have a chance – you all talk so loud.'

Objection overruled.

Mr Alexander, continuing: 'He further stated, ''I hope the S.O.B. dies . . .'' '

Objection overruled.

Alexander: '. . . further stated, ''I meant to get off three shots –'' ' Objection. Overruled. 'Further, ''Somebody had to – you guys couldn't –'' '

And so on, through every one of Ruby's alleged sayings.

Alexander: 'I ask if you, as an expert in psychiatry, can form an opinion whether Ruby was of sound mind on Nov. 24, knowing the difference between right and wrong and the nature and consequences of his deed?'

Dr Stubblefield: 'If I assume the facts as you state them, I would have the opinion that he did know.'

Mr Tonahill, in his carrying voice: 'Trouble is, all those facts aren't so.'

After three more medical experts, an expert of another kind. Alfred Breneger, a retired army colonel and pistol-shooting instructor, a cheery-looking character who spoke with some gusto of his own shooting career. He was called to refute the defence suggestion that Ruby's unusual handling of the gun, 'middle finger on the trigger', might be due to a convulsion.

The colonel said that using the middle finger was a common practice 'when you are in a hurry, when you have no time to use the sight. We call it instinct shooting.'

The state rested its rebuttal. Mr Wade was heard to make this aside: 'We've got some other doctors, but we want to get this thing over.'

ALTHOUGH IT WAS already half past five p.m., the court went into this new phase at once.

Mrs Eleanor Pitts, Ruby's Negro cleaning woman, testified that she always telephoned Ruby before she came because 'I was scared of Sheba, the dog'. Ruby rang her up on Sunday morning, Nov. 24 – sounding strange, she said – and made an appointment for her to come to clean the apartment that very afternoon. She was to telephone him before coming in, as she always did. Thus, the defence implied, there was no pre-meditation.

On the morning of Day Seven, the defence produced a counter-doctor, whose testimony occupied half of a weary morning. Dr Walter Bromberg, psychiatrist, Clinical Director of Pinewood Psychiatric Hospital, Westchester County, N.Y., certified by the requisite boards. He saw Ruby for a total of 18 hours in December and mid-January.

Dr Bromberg: 'I feel he was mentally ill and did *not* know the nature of his act. I feel he was in a state of suspended mental consciousness due to complicated mental illness . . .'

Belli: 'Suicidal tendencies?'

Dr Bromberg: 'Here we have a man with a low self-esteem – the feeling that he was a nothing person. When you find this type, you find suicidal tendencies.'

The cross-examination, even by the standards of that court, was tough.

Wade: 'You've testified a number of times for Mr Belli and his associates, haven't you?'

Dr Bromberg: 'On two or three cases, I would say.'

Wade: 'And they are paying you $350 a day?'

Dr Bromberg: 'That depends on the hours I spend.'

Wade (gruff sneer): 'That's your fee, isn't it – $350 a day.'

Dr Bromberg: 'Yes, sir.'

Wade: 'And they pay travel and expenses?'

Dr Bromberg: 'That's right.'

Wade: 'When you were psychiatrist at the Mendocino State Hospital in California, you recommended that sex criminals should be released to run around in the community?'

Dr Bromberg: 'I said that they should be given some freedom on the hospital grounds as part of their treatment.'

Wade: 'Did Ruby have that there psychomotor epilepsy?'

Dr Bromberg: 'He had that condition.'

Wade (shouting): 'He wanted to be a hero, didn't he?'

Dr Bromberg: 'A martyr, rather. He shows a messianic trend. It is very common in epileptics. He wanted to rescue the Jewish people from the charge they didn't have guts.'

Wade: 'Don't you think shooting a man on television in grandiose circumstances would give a man a feeling of being a hero?'

Next, Rabbi Hillel Silverman, of Dallas Congregation Shearith Israel, youngish man, clean-shaven. He had known Ruby for about 10 years and had been worrying about him: 'Let me give you an instance. During Rosh Hashana, Ruby telephoned me after a service, crying and screaming remorse that he and his sister had had an argument and not been able to sit together during the high holiday services. He talked to me for 45 minutes, begging me to patch up the quarrel so that he could sit with her the next morning. So, I called up the sister and she told me that Ruby had shoved and pushed and actually struck her. Now, Jack had no memory of that when I called him back.'

The rabbi spoke simply and with conviction. He was also convincing. A good man, if ever there was one, and on the witness stand these things show: 'One afternoon he came out to the house and brought his dogs. We were standing on the front lawn talking, the dogs were running around. Jack suddenly stopped what he was saying, waved to the dogs and started to sob: "I'm not married. I have no children. This is my wife," he pointed to one of the dogs, "and these are my children. This is the only real family I have." He moaned and cried, and in a few minutes he had recovered and talked about something else.'

Tonahill: 'Did you see him after the assassination?'

Rabbi Silverman: 'He came to the service at the temple the night the President was killed. He seemed to be in a sort of trance.'

Tonahill: 'Do you think he knew right from wrong?'

Rabbi Silverman: 'It is my opinion that he did not know right from wrong then. It is also my opinion that he does not know right from wrong at this moment.'

The defence would have been well advised to rest their rebuttal here. Instead, they dragged on, calling 11 more minor witnesses, none of them leaving any particular impression or scoring any important point.

IV. SURREBUTTALS

SURREBUTTAL BEGAN AT the tag-end of this same afternoon. There was a drained feeling about the trial then. The state produced three more doctors: Dr Robert Schwab, neurologist, graduate of Harvard College and Cambridge University, Harvard Medical School, author of a hundred articles on EEG, Director of EEG at the Massachusetts General Hospital. He said, 'I would not say that Ruby's brain waves are unusual. They do not represent convulsions or seizures. They could be found in a person who has a history of brain damage, but they could also be found in those who have not.'

Belli: 'Do they suggest any abnormality?'

Dr Schwab: 'They suggest a non-specific, mild abnormality.'

And that, under lengthy cross-examination, remained that.

Next, Dr Francis Forster, Professor of Neurology, Dean of the University of Wisconsin School of Medicine, and one of the doctors called in by President Eisenhower at the time of his stroke.

Professor Forster was definite that the EEG did not support a diagnosis of PME. He, moreover, ridiculed the possibility of Ruby's acting in a blackout during the shooting: 'A person in a

PME seizure could never have done the things which witnesses say Ruby did.'

Dr Roland Mackay, neurologist, from Illinois, the last of the state's medical men, also said that the EEGs did not indicate epilepsy or PME. Mr Belli shook him so far as to add, 'They do not exclude it.'

Mr Belli asked Dr Mackay about PME variant, as if it were a well-accepted medical term.

Dr Mackay: 'As far as I know, Dr Gibbs is the author of the only paper on that subject.'

Belli: 'Just as Pasteur was the author of the only work on anthrax?'

Dr Mackay: 'Dr Gibbs is an eminent man and I agree with him on almost anything else. I think he is in error on this particular point.'

A rumble of objections because Dr Gibbs had not been here to testify. (Dr Gibbs had so far refused to appear for the defence. He said he would come only if asked to by the court.) Mr Tonahill said promptly, 'He *will* be here.' Mr Belli wheeled around: 'Did you get him, Joe?'

Tonahill: 'He'll be here from Chicago on the midnight plane.'

It was after 6 p.m. District Attorney Wade announced the closing of the state's surrebuttal. This was their end; after that third chance, no further testimony would be called.

THE TRIAL THEN entered into a hectic phase in which chaotic waiting alternated with endurance tests. Judge Brown had declared that he would wind up the rest of the testimony straightaway, if it took all night. But the defence surrebuttal witness, Dr Gibbs, was manifestly not on hand.

'All right,' Mr Belli said to the newsmen, 'Brother Tonahill will give you an example of a real southern filibuster – we are going to talk till morning.' After some confusion, the judge changed his mind. The court decided to adjourn.

Dr Gibbs made it on Day Eight. Dr Frederic Gibbs, authority on brain-wave tests.

Belli: 'Did you find from the EEG tracings what Jack Ruby is suffering from?'

Dr Gibbs: 'I have determined that Jack Ruby has a rare form of epilepsy. Not the form with seizures, but the type that afflicts one half of one per cent of all epileptics, and it has a very distinctive epileptoid pattern.'

Belli: 'Was your finding clear or borderline?'

Dr Gibbs: 'It was clear.'

Belli: 'Does this type of disease appear rarely in the tracings?'

Dr Gibbs: 'It is rare. Like leprosy – it is rare, but when you've got it, you know you have it.'

Belli: 'You have examined 50,000 separate EEGs, have you not?'

Dr Gibbs: 'I have.'

Belli: 'And in 253 cases, PME was unmistakable?'

Dr Gibbs: 'Yes.'

Belli: 'And this one, Jack Ruby's, is unmistakable?'

Dr Gibbs: 'It is.'

Mr Alexander (in cross-examination): 'Do I understand that PME variant is a disease?'

Dr Gibbs: 'It is a form of the disease of epilepsy.'

Alexander: 'It is not in the American nomenclature of diseases?'

Dr Gibbs: 'There is a great deal of lag in medical nomenclature. It will be.'

Alexander: 'Do you have an opinion as to whether Ruby knew right from wrong and the nature and consequences of his act on Nov. 24?'

Dr Gibbs: 'I have no opinion.'

And there we were again, 13 medical experts later, where we had started at the beginning.

As Dr Gibbs was about to leave the stand, Mr Belli said: 'One minute. The judge may have a question, or the jury . . .'

Judge Brown: 'I have none. And I'm sure the jury has none. And if they had any, I wouldn't let them ask them.'

The defence surrebuttal rested by 10:30 a.m. Those among the reporters present who were accustomed to the well-regulated presentation of a case settled on their benches ready to listen to the final arguments. They were mistaken. The judge retired with the state and defence attorneys to discuss his charge while the trial remained recessed. (In Texas the charge is a brief written document containing the judge's instructions or directives to the jury as to law. It does not sum up or survey the testimony. It is also in keeping with Texas law that the charge is drafted by the prosecution, and then presented to the defence for proposed recommendations.)

Presently Melvin Belli and Joe Tonahill, howling protest, popped out from the judge's quarters trailed by newsmen. The charge as written by Wade, Mr Tonahill asserted, called for a directed verdict of guilty of cold-blooded murder. Mr Wade told another news-gang that his assistants had prepared a charge, but that the judge was not going to use it. 'We don't care what's in the charge,' Wade said, 'as long as there's room at the bottom for the jury to write a verdict of guilty.'

Then it seeped out that the defence had found some 40 objections to make in the first four pages of the charge alone. Among other things, the charge failed to state clearly that the burden of proof of guilt fell upon the prosecution. The judge told Mr Phil Burleson of the defence to present the objections in writing. Four secretaries were sought and hired.

The day wore on. The judge gave his permission for the final courtroom speeches to be broadcast, and the radio stations were holding off and rearranging programmes and installing apparatus in the courtroom. Later on he changed his mind. Meanwhile, he wandered about the massed reporters, the swelling crowds, snapping, 'We'll get this thing to the jury today. We'll get it there tonight if it takes till 4 a.m.'

V. NIGHT SESSION

AT 8 P.M. that Friday, March 13, with the courthouse overflowing with humanity and litter, with counsel, staff and newsmen in an indescribable state of grubbiness, nervous exhaustion, fatigue, the court resumed its session.

The judge took 17 minutes reading through his charge, taking drinks of water in between. The contents were confined to legal directives. They were addressed to the jury, but the judge read as if he were addressing no human being on this earth, and as if what he was reading were a catalogue.

'If you find the defendant guilty of murder with malice, the penalty under this verdict can be death in the electric chair or a term in the penitentiary ranging from two years to life.

'If you find the defendant guilty of murder without malice, the penalty under this verdict can be a term in the penitentiary from two to five years.

'If you find the defendant not guilty through insanity, which is the verdict you would return if you are convinced that he cannot distinguish right from wrong, you must rule on his mental condition now. If you rule him insane then and now, he must go to a mental hospital. If you rule him sane now although insane then, he would go free.

'You will not consider the failure of the defendant to testify in his own defence, nor will you consider any experience or knowledge you may have, nor any fact or matter not in evidence in this case.'

Then the judge spoke to Mr Wade: 'How long d'you want?'

'Two hours,' Wade said lightly.

Judge Brown: 'Two hours, Mr Belli?'

Belli: 'We should like at least three, your Honour.'

Judge Brown (amiably): 'Two and a half?'

Belli: 'All right.'

Each side now had two and a half hours to speak in, dividing it among themselves as they pleased. (The prosecution has both the first and the last word.)

Judge Brown: 'Who's first?'

Mr Wade pointed at Alexander.

'Next?'

Belli said: 'Burleson.'

'Next?'

Wade said, 'Frank Watts.' The order was finally fixed as Alexander for the state answered by Burleson for the defence answered by Watts for the state answered by Tonahill for the defence answered by Jim Bowie for the state answered by Belli for the defence answered by Wade for the state.

D.A. Alexander, tall, gaunt, tense, with his long dangling arms, equine head and uncertain smile, strode toward the jury box. 'May it please the court, ladies and gentlemen of the jury . . .

'Malice . . . malice can be formed in the twinkling of an eye [snapping his fingers]. This man who loved [drooling out the word] President Kennedy so much and Jacqueline Kennedy and the children [takes two steps forward], he wouldn't stir himself enough to walk five blocks to see the parade. The defence claims that he suffers from some weird psychomotor variant they seem to have developed for this man.'

A small table had been placed below the jury box holding a few poor objects – the exhibits. The money order, some photographs, the gun. Alexander picked up the gun and hammed the shooting.

(Breathlessly) 'Did you realize how fast it happened until you saw those movies? It was 12 seconds from the time it starts until they are in the jail office. [Relaxing] Now that's fast – fast, folks. Oswald sank down, gutshot and dying, while handcuffed to an officer. And *he* was still trying to get off a shot [lips drawn back over teeth, snapping the gun]. Those boys were fortunate. Graves was a lucky man! Leavelle was a lucky man!'

Alexander flailed his arms, contorted his face and limbs. It was lurid and coarse, and hideously fascinating.

'Jack Ruby knew right from wrong [*fortissimo vibrato*] when he fired at Oswald with malice, cursing as he did it and repeating the curse over and over again after Oswald fell.

'I am not going to defend Oswald to you – it is American

justice that is on trial – but Oswald was entitled to the protection of the law – just as *you* [swinging round and pointing], Jack Ruby, are demanding for yourself. Lee Harvey Oswald was a living breathing American citizen. [Softly] Lee Harvey Oswald loved life, just like you, the jury, love life, and he had the right to draw every breath that God and Dallas County would allow him, but his lips are sealed. [Screaming] He is dead! He is silent! Taking secrets to his grave!'

Belli leaped to his feet. 'Just a moment, just a moment – there can be no question of secrets on the part of Oswald. The FBI has stated . . .'

Judge Brown (placidly): 'Jury'll disregard it.'

'Jack Ruby said, "To hell with justice." He went to kill for fame and money, and I tell you that he mistook the public temper of the time. He has mocked American justice while the spotlight of the world was on us.'

Then it was young Burleson's turn, and he had his moments: 'The only malice in this case comes from the blistering lips of some police officers – this happened in their own back yard, and was a breach of their own security . . . What prompted Jack Ruby's act was seeing the sneering, smirking Communist killer of the President of the United States.'

Frank Watts for the prosecution: 'He charged down the ramp at city hall like the Germans around the Maginot Line.' And: 'The blood is still red on the hands of Jack Ruby.'

Ruby sat with his arms folded. His eyes did not flicker.

THEN JOE TONAHILL in all his bulk, standing close against the jury box, began gently and in a hushed voice: 'Many times during this trial when my nature – our natures – responded to assaults, we have done things in a louder voice than it is necessary to hear us . . . It was because I was shocked at the deliberate attempt to distort facts.

'Ladies and gentlemen, when you took your oath each and every one of you shook hands with the Lord . . . [Swelling] I'd never thought I'd live to hear a jury told that Oswald, too, loved life. [Changing tone to spitting contempt] They would have you take Lee Harvey Oswald by the hand and walk with him.'

Wade [rumbling from his chair]: 'We didn't say anything about taking him by the hand and walkin' with him.'

'They lost their great opportunity, and now they are so wrought up they have to get someone to substitute for Oswald – they would have you send a sick man, suffering from psycho-motor epilepsy, to a penal institution to satisfy their political ambitions . . . their frustrations . . . [Gentle again, but manly] Jack Ruby, this G.I. – Jack is a good man, a patriotic man, the best he could be. He's a sick man – goes to the rabbi saying, "Nobody loves me," calling dogs "my wife and my children," throwing people down the stairs, howling in depression . . . You heard the experts' testimony of his brain damage and psycho-motor epilepsy . . . [Very softly] Ladies and gentlemen, write a verdict the world will praise you for . . .'

As it grew late, the scene took on a hallucinatory quality – the harsh lights, the packed room, the pressing crowds outside, the unceasing shower of words hammering upon consciousnesses tired beyond sleep.

Tonahill – there was a sense that he would never stop – was now flaying the prosecution: 'They've got to stand or fall on McMillon's testimony and [all stops out] McMillon L-I-E-D. He *lied* in his teeth because he didn't hear what he swore on that witness stand that he heard. His is the perjury Mr Wade must digest! I am not embarrassed by these people – I am ASHAMED of them. The uncouth, ungentlemanly, un-Texan conduct of the district attorney . . .'

And suddenly one knew what it was, the extraordinary unreality of these speeches: this was the long-discarded forensic art of the Victorians, the courtroom style of blood and thunder and tears. We were in another century. Dickens would have been at home here. With the invective, the froth, the violence, the sob stuff, the hysteria. Here, in that electronics-conscious backwater, there was re-enacted what Dickens saw and heard, enjoyed, exposed.

'A good government doesn't take the life of a man with a weak mind. But Jack Ruby's scalp added to Henry Wade's belt will mean something to him, I guess. And Bill Alexander . . . Bill Alexander would like to travel. He'd like to see the rolling hills of Texas, see the bluebonnets and the dogwood, and the pine woods on his way to Huntsville to watch the execution. He'd go – he'd LOVE to go. Can't you see the pleasure in his eyes, his great tarantula-like eyes, if you gave him the death sentence?'

Joe Tonahill stood still. He leaned over the jury rail. 'I just want to look at you for a minute.' He did. In silence. Then he whispered, 'I see great courage . . . great faith . . . what you do here will be long remembered.'

Then Jim Bowie did a turn for the prosecution. It was a more muscular version of Alexander's performance. Where Alexander had writhed with histrionic hate, Bowie shook his fists, squared his shoulders, flexed his knees. He did everything but push-ups on the floor.

By the time Belli came on, we were mentally deaf. The jury looked glazed; one of the women was succumbing to sleep.

'Let us see now, in the early hours of the morning, when great discoveries have been made in garrets and basements, let us try to rediscover a justice that has never really been lost in your great city . . .'

On the whole, Mr Belli was out of style, and his speech was closer in manner and content to our time. Yet there was the defeating knowledge that nothing he might say would matter very much now. Everything had got out of hand. We were too numb to think or feel. Sheer physical weariness had taken over. Yet Belli spoke – had to speak, he could not have stayed silent – for an hour.

The burden was that Jack Ruby is a sick, sick man, and that 'Who, in November, in this troubled city, was not a candidate for what Jack Ruby did?' He ended: 'Look at this verdict from the vantage point of 40 or 80 years – they may laugh at us then for what we tried to do now with our poor tools.'

As Belli went back to the defence table, Tonahill was crying.

D.A. Wade, assesssing the court's mood, cut short his own time. He was compact and pugnacious and every sentence came from the top of his lungs: 'Jack Ruby is a glory seeker who wanted the limelight, who wanted to go down in history. You can bet your last dollar that if this man is set free the Communists will be darned happy. They believe in executing them on the spot. They don't believe a man is innocent until proved guilty . . .

'Turn this man loose and you'll turn civilization back a century, back to lynch law. What will you want the history books to say about you? You want them to say that we slapped this man's wrists and gave him a little penitentiary sentence?

'Now Jack Ruby and his defence ask mercy and sympathy – I ask you to show him the same sympathy as he showed Lee Harvey Oswald in your Dallas police department. You want the world and Communism to know that we believe in a world of law.'

Upon these words, at 1:05 a.m., the case was sent to the jury. The jurors decided not to begin deliberations then, but to go to bed, and start a few hours later.

VI. LAST MORNING

THE JURY met at 9:15 a.m. At 11:34 a.m. they sent word that they had found a verdict. The court reassembled. The judge had arranged for a live television camera to record this session. 'This is for posterity,' he explained. The camera was in place. The jury filed in. Twelve men and women who had made up their minds and hearts in two hours and 19 minutes. They did not look at the defendant.

In Texas, the jury foreman does not have to speak the verdict. It is written by him into the judge's charge in the appropriate space. The charge was handed up to the dais. Judge Brown moistened his thumb, in a gesture we knew well, and flicked the pages. Then, in gabbling monotone, he read, 'We, the jury, find the defendant guilty of murder with malice as charged in the indictment and assess his punishment as death.'

There was a fraction of silence. Stunned silence. Then Belli broke into his strangled cry, 'I want to thank the jury . . .'

Ruby, to whom all eyes had travelled, was unchanged. The guards seized him and he was bundled out. Voices rose, cameramen poured in, leaping on tables, taking chairs and ledges by assault. The circus went ragging. But it was over.

As I made my way out with an uncontrolled face, I brushed against the judge. He stopped. 'Take it easy,' he said. Behind me, Henry Wade and his minions were tramping down the stairs. Below, the broadcasting units stood in wait. As I reached the street, I heard an aide break urgently into the cry of our age: 'Microphone! Microphone!'

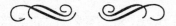

THE WORST THAT EVER HAPPENED

THE TRIAL OF TWENTY-TWO FORMER STAFF OF AUSCHWITZ CONCENTRATION CAMP

Frankfurt, West Germany

ON DECEMBER 20, 1963, there opened in the high court in Frankfurt, West Germany, the trial of 22 former members of the staff of the concentration camp Auschwitz. The name on the record was *The Trial of Mulka & Others;* in history it will go down as the Auschwitz trial. It was the first large-scale case of its kind tried by Germans, before a German judge and jury; the charges were murder and collective murder.

There was snow on that first winter morning, and it was still dark outside. One did not know who was walking beside one in the street. A temporary court had been rigged in the town hall – the regular courtrooms were not large enough to hold the press – a tribune, benches and, for the accused, four rows of wooden school desks. Each desk bore a white cardboard square with a number: 1 to 22.

On an easel stood a board with a large plan, something between a map and an architectural print, which was to become grimly familiar to us throughout the months: it was the ground plan of 8,000 acres in southern Poland, KZ Auschwitz (Main Camp) and KZ Auschwitz II (Extermination Camp Birkenau). Nobody knows exactly how many people were killed at

Auschwitz between 1940 and 1945. The estimates were between two million and four million dead.

By 8 a.m. the accused men began to file in. There is an intense desire to look at their faces; to see, to know, to find perhaps a key to deeds that most of us on this earth have heard about and are haunted by or try to belittle or forget or choose not to believe. A few of the men here look inscrutably ordinary; the faces of the rest are dreadful – pinched, closed, hard; carved by cruelty, brutality, vacuity.

Meanwhile the floor has filled with waves of lawyers in black robes; they are defence counsel, 18 of them, middle-aged men, for the most part, with reputations of considerable experience. One of them – a tall, theatrical figure – is Dr Hans Laternser, who defended members of the Wehrmacht High Command at Nuremberg. Facing this massed defence corps, the forces of the prosecution, seated on a raised platform of their own, look frail and few. Four blond young men.

We rise and the judges walk in, followed by the jury, and take their places together on the tribune. Three judges and six jurors, three of them women, and at this stage they are still unknown quantities. The presiding judge, Hans Hofmeyer, swiftly opens with a brief ritual, and (after half a dozen defence lawyers have jumped up with motions on points of form) the first phase of the trial is under way. This – according to German criminal procedure – is the judge's examination of the accused.

A microphone and a single chair have been set out below the tribune.

Accused No. 1, Robert Mulka, former *SS-Obersturmführer* and Camp Adjutant, takes the floor. He is a silver-haired man of 68, dressed in pinstripe trousers and black coat, and he looks like a not undistinguished clergyman in mild distress.

'Please, sit down,' says the judge.

Mulka is led through his life history, which, like all of their histories, is bound to that of our times. Born in Hamburg. Commercial training. Volunteered in First World War. 2nd Lieutenant. 1919: joined a Baltic formation 'to fight Bolshevism'. 1920: employed in an agency. Same year: sentenced to 8 months in prison for embezzlement. (Here he showed some agitation and protested his honour as a German officer.) Dismissed from the Army Reserve. 1931: founded his own import-export business. World War II: volunteered for the Waffen-SS. Sent to Auschwitz from early 1942 to March, 1943. Adjutant to Camp Commandant Rudolf Höss from May, 1942. 1945–48: interned by the British. Subsequently sentenced to 1½-year prison term for 'knowledge of events at Auschwitz'. Sentence quashed on appeal. Resumed his business career.

Mulka is married, has two children. He was arrested, on the present charges, in 1960, and is now at liberty on bail of 50,000 marks (£3,600).

The charge is complicity in mass murder. It is alleged that in his capacity as adjutant he was instrumental in carrying out the Nazi extermination programme: he was responsible for the construction of gas chambers, supply of poison gas, organization of transport.

He now denies that his functions at Auschwitz had been anything of the kind. He just sat in his office and did his paperwork. 'It may sound unbelievable,' he says, 'but I never set foot inside the actual camp.' (Mulka's fellow accused put on cynical grins.)

The Judge: Did you ever make any attempts to find out about the sixty thousand human beings locked up in there? Did they have shelter? Did they have food? Was there a water supply?
Mulka [Compressing his lips spinsterishly]: I never heard of any complaints.
Judge [Suddenly stern]: Who was *able* to complain? *Whom* could they complain to?
Mulka [Remaining stubborn and cool]: No one was allowed inside. It was punished by death.
Judge: Did it never dawn on you that there was something very, very wrong at Auschwitz?
Mulka: I asked no questions. I was careful.
Judge: What did you do when people were beaten to death?
Mulka: It did not come to my knowledge . . .

Judge: But *you* were supposed to be the right ear of the commandant?

Mulka: I did not enjoy the commandant's confidence.

Judge: Then why were you assigned as his adjutant?

Mulka: I have no answer to that.

Judge: How did your men live?

Mulka: Like all soldiers. Off duty they sang and played cards. We had a band. A magnificent band. [Recruited, it appears, from prisoners who had been in the Warsaw Philharmonic.] It played outside Villa Höss on Sunday mornings. And we had entertainments, a play or some sort of a show at least once every other week.

Judge: Herr Mulka, what did you think these camps were for?

Mulka: Protective camps. Where enemies of the Reich were being re-educated.

Judge: Did you see the lists with arriving prisoners' names? Did you know that some names had a black cross put against them?

Mulka: I seem to recall that.

Judge: Did you know what the black cross meant?

Mulka: No.

Judge: It meant Return Undesirable [*Rückkehr Unerwünscht*]. Did you know about the Black Wall? About the standing cells? The Gravel Pit? Block Eleven? Did you know that the rations were calculated to keep a man alive for a maximum of three months?

Mulka: No. No. No.

Judge: When you were working in Supply, did you ever request delivery of Jewish Resettlement Material, the code name for Zyklon-B gas?

Mulka: I, personally, never arranged for Resettlement Material.

Judge: Did you know there were gas chambers?

Mulka [Long silence]: Yes. But I had no occasion to speak about them.

Judge: Never to your commandant?

Mulka: Commandant Höss was a strange, unapproachable

man. I avoided asking him questions.

Judge: Did you know that there was a standing rule that all children under sixteen were to be gassed with their mothers?

Mulka: I never saw any children.

Judge: And what did *you* think of the arrival of those thousands of people at the camp?

Mulka [Weakly, an old man not sure of his ground]: One wanted to liberate the Reich from the Jews.

Next came Karl Höcker, No. 2, who was Adjutant from May, 1944, until January, 1945. (Age 52. Elementary education. Unemployed 1930–32. Assistant cashier. Joined General-SS in 1933; Waffen-SS in 1939. Sent to a chain of concentration camps: Neuengamme, Majdanek, Auschwitz. Interned by British. Sentenced to 9 months by a German court in 1953. Obtained post as chief cashier; dismissed June, 1963. Currently living on unemployment relief. Married, two children.) The charge is complicity in mass murder. Höcker, too, is out on bail. He looks neither good nor bad, bright nor stupid, maintains he gave no orders, saw nothing, knew nothing. The judge asked him whether one of his duties had been the keeping of a secret diary.

Höcker: On principle, all decisions over the life and death of a prisoner came from the Führer, and all orders for executions or punishment were secret. I never read them. I merely entered their completion into the secret diary.

Judge: Did you ever have doubts as to the legality of such orders?

Höcker: Whatever came from the Reich Security Office was a lawful order.

Judge: Did you know that no one is obliged to obey a criminal order?

Höcker: I didn't study law.

He had no idea, Höcker presently tells the judge, that women and children had been killed 'on purpose'.

Judge: Then why did you think they were sent to Auschwitz?

Höcker: Well, we thought they were a public danger.

Judge: You believed that innocent children were killed in order to protect the public?

Höcker: Well, they were Jews.

The 22 defendants were not the men who created and ruled Auschwitz. Hitler and Himmler committed suicide at the end of the war, and Commandant Höss was hanged by the Poles in 1947. Richard Baer, the last commandant of Auschwitz, was finally found and arrested in December, 1960, but he died of heart disease while in custody, before this trial began. Of at least 6,000 men who worked at Auschwitz, many of whom have never been identified, there were only these 22 defendants. They fell roughly into two categories: the middlemen of death, the officers and administrators and doctors, who did their jobs by delegation, from behind their desks, keeping up an appearance of detachment; and the troopers, the ruffians, who did the dirty work with their own hands and did more of it than they were asked, and liked it. The most feared names were Boger, Hofmann, Kaduk, Baretzki, Klehr. And here is Wilhelm Boger, the No. 3 man, the SS investigator who invented the Boger Swing, a kind of trapeze that held the victim upside down while he was beaten, which, Boger boasted, kept the escape rate down (a model of the unspeakable thing is exhibited in court). He now refuses to speak himself. 'My decision is unshakable,' he declares self-importantly. His lawyers concur, 'We have weighed the pros and cons most carefully.'

NOW ANOTHER one stumps up to the tribune, clicks his heels, draws himself to attention, then grasps the microphone and begins to bellow, 'I was sentenced to death by the Soviets! Proceedings against me here are illegal –'

Judge Hofmeyer – who is beginning to reveal himself as a man of patience and authority – cuts quietly into the shouting.

'We know about that, Herr Kaduk, and shall deal with it in due course. Meanwhile we want to learn something about yourself.'

The defendant's hysteria is punctured; he admits to being born in Silesia, primary education, 57 years old, butcher, fireman and male nurse by occupation. Volunteered for the SS in 1940? 'Yessir!' 'What were your reasons?' 'Not political . . . politics don't interest me . . . the chess club . . . all the comrades were in the SS.' He was put through a special *Unterführer* course, promoted and sent to Auschwitz. 'Just like that?' asks the judge. 'Had you applied?'

Kaduk says, 'An order is an order, isn't it?' (The prosecution later produced evidence showing that assignment to concentration camps was highly selective.)

'And what were your functions there as block guard?'

Kaduk barks, 'Quiet, order, cleanliness.'

The charges against this man, Oswald Kaduk, are frightful. He is accused of trampling a young boy to death because he overslept; he is accused of throttling two elderly prisoners one night, when he was half drunk, by laying a walking stick across their throats and standing on the stick. Once the rope broke during an execution, and Kaduk was seen to flog the condemned man first, then hang him up again. Once more we have to ask, what does such a creature look like? Is there a special mark? Yes; up to a point. The face is sly, brutish, shut. But there are limits to what flesh and bone are able to convey.

Now Kaduk holds forth. '*I* had a breakdown. [A laugh] Why? If *you* had seen such things – I never drank as much in my whole life as I did at Auschwitz.' It must not be thought that because the accused is not silenced that the bench is not in control. German legal procedure allows an accused man to have his own say in his own words; he is, in fact, allowed a good deal of rope.

'Why did the Russians sentence you to death in 1947?'

Kaduk [contemptuously]: 'This Auschwitz business. Former prisoners denounced me. [The sentence was commuted to 25 years' hard labour. Kaduk served 9 years in East Germany, then was released. Now he is off again] . . . The *inhuman* treatment . . . comrades died like flies . . . and now *we* are being reproached! I should have stayed in the East. They warned me. They'll persecute you in the West, they said to me. I chose the West – and bitterly regret it. I never dreamed of such injustice!'

When he is asked about the crimes he is accused of, Kaduk, like Boger before him, stands on his legal right not to give evidence.

Franz Hofmann, a stoker, talks a good deal. A brother had been in the SS, so there was a spare uniform hanging in the closet. 'I didn't have any expenses, see? I was unemployed.' Hofmann was sent to Dachau in 1933, and, regularly and rapidly promoted, served in concentration camps for 12 years. 'Let me tell you something, when my wife and children joined me at Auschwitz, I applied for domestic help and got permission to employ a prisoner. We had the girl to live with us. We gave her clothes [impressive pause]. She was fed [another pause]. Why, we treated her like a real, like a free, human being.'

This Hofmann – 57 years old – is already serving a life sentence for murder. Two murders, we learn, committed at Dachau. He is round-headed, double-chinned, stout and nervous. He looks like a low brute, a common thug, less crafty than Kaduk, and very stupid.

'The gas chambers were terrible, of course,' he says easily. 'But those who weren't gassed had a real chance to survive.'

ONE BY ONE, day after day, through those winter months, these nightmarish figures took the floor. Each one was asked if he would like a chair; all were given the *Herr* before their name; all were treated with detached politeness. Some killed by injecting disinfectant into human hearts, others by making people stand in freezing water, others operated the poison gas. Some used pistols or clubs or an empty bottle or their boots. Some are truculent or surly, some show themselves cooperative and brisk. Many are given to bureaucratically precise details about dates and figures. All are evasive as to their own part. Not one – so far – has shown a sense of proportion; there has been no sign of understanding or repentance, no spark of pity.

Yet it is through these men that the immeasurable suffering that was Auschwitz is taking on ever clearer and more unbearable shape. Through Stefan Baretzki, No. 11, we get the sense of hunger. We knew about the impossibly low calories: now this uncouth little German-Romanian with the rodent's face makes it real. Summer or winter, rain or snow, the prisoners stood for roll call in the yard at dawn; if the count didn't come out right they might have to stand for two hours, three hours, more; then they were marched to work. Marched for miles, on feet wrapped in rags, or bare feet in wooden clogs, to work a 12-hour day in stone quarry or gravel pit. For breakfast they had been given a mugful of brownish ersatz coffee. Bread? 'No bread . . . never bread in the morning . . . nothing solid . . . not during the day . . . bread was at night . . . after they got back [after another march, another roll call] . . . soup and bread . . . margarine sometimes.' For the rest of the 24 hours: nothing.

Through another accused, Bruno Schlage – once warder in Block 11, now a janitor in civil life – we get confirmation of that fiendish invention, the standing cells. These cells were shaped like an upright coffin and so narrow that a man could just stand in them. There was no window and no door. Only a hole near the bottom through which the prisoner had to crawl in on all fours.

Judge: People did die there of exhaustion?
Schlage: Not that I know of. Well, maybe somebody fainted now and then . . .

Schlage is an old man with a game leg. His face is wooden. One of the prosecutors asked him, 'Did it ever occur to you to make a prisoner's life a little easier for him?'

'No. I thought that someone might tell on me.'

Through Dr Franz Lucas, Defendant No. 14, we learn of still other things. Dr Lucas, a gynaecologist who joined the SS in

1937, is a heavy, middle-aged man, gray suit, gray hair, who moves slowly and speaks in a low, unhappy voice. He is the first of the defendants who does not speak the language of the oppressor. Sent to Auschwitz in 1943, 'I was entirely unprepared . . . I remember the ghastly sight of the first prisoners . . . The overcrowding, the sanitary conditions were bestial. Everyone was seriously undernourished. There were people who suffered from a frightful disease called noma which only attacks patients whose resistance has sunk to the lowest point. This disease eats a hole into the cheeks so that one can see the teeth. I have never encountered it in civilian life.

'In the evening I was invited to drink a glass of schnapps with my colleagues. I was asked if I had any idea of what was going on at Auschwitz. Had I already heard of gas chambers? After I had been enlightened, I told them that as a physician it was my duty to preserve life, not to take it. I wrote to my superior officer; he answered that orders were orders, and besides, we were in the fifth year of war.' Lucas then went to seek advice from the Bishop of Osnabrück, who happened to have been a schoolmate of his father's. 'The bishop told me that an amoral order should not be obeyed, but that resistance should not go so far as to endanger one's own life.'

Dr Lucas is accused of complicity in collective murder by having carried out selections on the ramp, where arriving prisoners were divided into two groups – those who would work and those who would die. He denies the charge. He always avoided, he claims, going on duty when the transports came. 'I faked stomach trouble, colics, that kind of thing.' He was transferred to another camp and in 1945 was threatened by a German court-martial; with the help of a Norwegian, a former prisoner, he managed to escape and remain in hiding until the end of the war.

Another defendant who stands out from the pattern is Emil Bednarek, who was not a member of the Nazi élite but a prisoner himself. A Pole, by birth if not by language, he was arrested by the Gestapo on suspicion of belonging to the Polish resistance movement. The camp authorities made a practice of using prisoners of suitable mentality to act as their assistants; these were made block prefects, *capos*, and enjoyed considerable privileges – more food, no health-breaking work, power. *Capos* survived. They were usually recruited from professional criminals rather than from political prisoners. Bednarek, however, became a *capo*, and even by camp standards an exceptional one. He clubbed his wards to death, the charge sheet says, and made elderly, exhausted people do exercises until they collapsed and died. 'Ridiculous,' is his answer. 'All lies.'

Klehr – Josef Klehr, age 59, carpenter and male nurse – was head of the Gas Commando and a member of the SS Sanitary Corps.

Judge: What do you have to say to the charge that you pushed living people into an open fire? [Corpses, during one period, were burned in pits.]
Klehr: Untrue.
Judge: There will be witnesses who will testify that you did.

The judge speaks of two women, mother and daughter; one of them had been selected for the gas chamber, and they clung to each other, not wanting to be separated. Klehr was seen to make an end of it by coming up from behind and knocking both women into the fire pit. He denies this. He does admit that he administered a number of phenol (carbolic acid) injections 'by order'.

The prosecution exhibits a photocopy of a written demand for five kilograms (11 pounds) of *Phenolum purum*, *pro injectione*, signed by Klehr. A member of the court remarks that a prescription for phenol for injection must be pharmaceutically unique. The judge calculates: 5 kilograms = 5,000 cubic centimetres = enough to stop the lives of 1,000 human beings.

Klehr's victims were hospital patients. During an epidemic or when the beds were getting full, there would be a selection. The doctors walked through the wards, and on their way out they simply left the registration cards of the superfluous on a table. Their names would be copied on a list and sent to the Political

Division to be OK'd. In due course the list would be returned, accompanied by the completed individual death certificates. The cause of death entered on these certificates was changed every eight days. One week pneumonia; heart failure the next. All were signed by an M.D. Afterward the victims would be delivered up to the male nurses.

Klehr used to do his work in a room marked DOCTOR'S OFFICE. He sported a white coat he had had especially made.

The sick people were led in, arms tied behind their backs, chests bare, and put upon a chair.

> *Judge*: Was anything said?
> *Herbert Scherpe* [another accused nurse]: No. I think they knew nothing – they were so very weak. I don't mean that they couldn't have got well.
> *Judge*: You mean if they had been given something to eat?
> *Scherpe*: Yes. Children were told they were going to be vaccinated.

Klehr, or others, shot the phenol into the heart. Death was usually instantaneous. The bodies slumped on the floor, were dragged out on the double by a detail of prisoners. The job was called *Leichenschleifen*, body-hauling, and it carried extra rations.

The death register of the hospital of Auschwitz I is still extant. The number of dead entered between the summers of 1942 and 1944, the period when the accused men Josef Klehr, Herbert Scherpe and Emil Hantl were block *Führers*, is 130,000.

'Well,' says Klehr, 'they were hardly people anymore, they were half dead already, walking skeletons.'

THAT FIRST phase, the examination of the accused, lasted over two months. We all knew from the outset that it would be a very long trial, and a slow-moving one. There was the sheer number of defendants and their counsel; there were the hundreds of witnesses expected, the overwhelming mass of oral and documentary evidence to be presented, and the formidable task of sifting and coordinating it. There were also the pinpricks of the multiple technical points – much leaned upon by the defence – which had to be dealt with at every session. To all this had to be added the extreme thoroughness of the court and the choking mass of paperwork involved. It was decided early that hearings would be held only three days a week (anything more would have been unendurable), and the trial was expected to take six months, or even eight. No one dreamed then that it would go on for nearly two years.

Everything in legal omniscience was done to avoid having to begin all over again because of a mistrial. There were appointed two spare judges and five spare jurors – understudies, as it were. They had no function other than to be mutely present throughout the whole proceedings; thus if anything should happen to a judge or juror, a spare would be legally qualified to take over.

Of the three acting judges, two speak little. Judges in Germany are civil servants and quasi-anonymous. Not much is known about them, and the press does not insist. The presiding judge, *Landgerichtsdirektor*, now *Senatspräsident*, Dr Hofmeyer, is a man in his 50s, lightly built, with a pleasant round face and a quiet pleasant voice and provincial accent. He tries, as judges will, to keep the temperature down. Though patient and courteous, it would seem unwise to underrate his toughness; and he has a gift of being able to convey a freezing degree of moral condemnation.

Occasionally the bench appears swamped by the untiring interruptions by the defence. Dr Laternser, the Nuremberg veteran who comports himself more like an opera tenor than an advocate, simply will not sit down when told to do so. The remedy is often a brief suspension of the hearing.

The prosecuting attorneys – *Oberstaatsanwalt* Dr Hans Grossmann, *Staatsanwälte* Vogel, Wiese and Kügler – may not be as smooth or experienced as some older hands; what is impressive is the strength of their conviction: they do not seem to stand here as functionaries dealing with a job but as men driven by a mission, the exposure of a German past by a new Germany.

The jury, as ever, remains the unknown quantity. All we know is that none of the six was in the Nazi Party; the rules allow screening to that point.

German criminal procedure is markedly different from British and American procedure. Their *Schwurgericht* is a hybrid form of jury trial; the judges and the jury do not merely sit together, they deliberate and decide together, and they decide on sentence as well as guilt. The verdict is arrived at by majority; a simple majority is enough for an acquittal, while a two-thirds majority is necessary for a conviction.

The accused in this system – the inquisitorial system prevalent in most of continental Europe – is not a party to his trial but an object of investigation. He is examined at every stage, and the fount of all examinations is the judge, who does not act here, as in our adversary system, as the arbiter between prosecution and defence, but is himself the probe exposing the evidence on both sides. The accused may refuse to answer all questions, or certain questions. He is not, and cannot be, put under oath, and he has the right to defend himself by telling lies. His previous convictions, or clean slate, are disclosed to the court from the start.

The stages of a trial are the examination of the accused by the presiding judge, followed by supplementary questions by the junior judges, the jury, the prosecution and defence; the examination of witnesses and documents; the closing speeches of the prosecution and defence; verdict and sentence. A trial ends with the judge's delivering a – usually written – post-verdict summing-up of the facts and considerations which led to the decision. The death penalty was abolished in West Germany in 1949. Consequently the maximum sentence that could be given to any of the defendants here is life imprisonment.

But then what was at stake in Frankfurt was not the fate of these 22 accused men. They had to be judged because it would have been indecent to condone and forget offences such as theirs. What was at stake in Frankfurt was the establishment of truth: a unique opportunity of testing what many Germans, and non-Germans, still like to evade, in the hardest, straightest arena of all, an open court of law. A German court, it must be repeated, not at Jerusalem, not at Nuremberg under an alien code, but under the German criminal code as established nearly a century ago.

But why – as was asked then and is still asked – why did the trial come so late, 20 years and more after the events? Though the reasons for this are complex, the answer is simple: it was technically not possible before. Given the dislocation and confusion of German civil life after the defeat, it needed time to find the will and organize the means. West Germany is a federation administered by the *Länder*, the individual states, which delays the prosecution of a diffuse and complex case. Many potential witnesses were dead; hard evidence was dispersed; incriminating documents, if not destroyed, were in the East Zone or in American, Russian or Polish archives.

Then in March, 1958, one Adolf Rögner wrote to the Public Prosecutor of Stuttgart that he knew the whereabouts of a 'human monster named Wilhelm Boger'. Two months later Hermann Langbein, a survivor of Auschwitz and Secretary of the International Auschwitz Committee in Vienna, was able to furnish evidence against Boger and produce 11 witnesses. In October, Boger was arrested. The wheels began to turn. By the end of the year the new Central Office for Research into National Socialist Crimes of Violence had opened at Ludwigsburg. At the same time a Frankfurt journalist found a bundle of half-charred documents in the apartment of a former Auschwitz prisoner who had kept them as a souvenir. The journalist handed the documents over to Dr Fritz Bauer, attorney general of the state of Hesse. Prosecutions can be pursued with greater or lesser zeal. In some German offices Nazi crimes have been investigated with energy, in others with reluctance. Dr Bauer became the moving spirit behind the Auschwitz investigation. He believed that it was necessary to present the facts to Germany and the world in the clearest and the most dramatic way. Dr Bauer is an anti-Nazi veteran – resistance movement, concentration camp, exile – a kindly, brilliant, excitable man, shining with a sort of nonconformist goodness ('I couldn't hurt a fly; could *you*?') who wore himself out over the case. He spoke of the prosecuting attorneys as 'my boys'.

In 1959 Ludwigsburg was able to supply the names of Franz Hofmann, Hans Stark, Pery Broad, Viktor Capesius and Klaus Dylewski. In April, Kaduk was found living under his own name in West Berlin. Eventually some 1,300 witnesses were questioned, many of them living outside Germany, and a huge file was collected. The Supreme Court in Karlsruhe ruled on the problem of venue. In 1963, after five years of preliminary investigation, the trial was able to open in Frankfurt, the capital of Hesse.

ON FEBRUARY 24, 1964, the first live witness was heard: a small, thin man in his 60s, a G.P. from Vienna, deported to Auschwitz as a Jew. His name is Dr Otto Wolken, and his voice is calm.

'May I begin with two or three remarks? I have come without any feelings of hatred or revenge. I had the good fortune to survive; twenty years have passed. Yet we must not forget that the murder machine could never have run if there had not been thousands of individuals willing to serve it.'

He describes the daily condition. Twelve hundred men crammed into a windowless stable built to hold 500: 'They lay literally packed like sardines inside a can.' The plague of fleas, 'billions of fleas. At Auschwitz II it was rats, they were large bold animals, they gnawed not only at the dead but at the bodies of the sick and dying.' He speaks of the lines for the stinking latrines; he speaks of hunger. 'If a few drops of soup slopped over on the ground, people would fling themselves on it in a heap, trying to spoon it out of the mud into their mouths.' He speaks of his own arrival. After he had been made to undress and give up his belongings (nothing ever remained, not a comb, a scrap of photograph), he was taken to a washroom already full of naked people. There they stood, they waited and they stood, hoping that a bit of food might be brought to them. None came. They were able to lick a little water from the taps. After dark, still without clothing, they were shooed outdoors. It was a cool spring night with a light drizzle. 'We stood and waited the whole night.' In the morning the SS came, and they were shaved and were tattooed with a number.

There was separation ever after between men and wives, parents and children. They did not see one another again; they did not know who was dead, who still alive. Only gipsies were kept together in a so-called family camp.

Doctor Wolken says that he must speak of some things. One morning he saw a group of naked women being beaten onto trucks. 'We were standing at roll call before our barracks. The women cried out to us, the men, to help them. We only stood and trembled.' The trucks moved off to the crematorium; a last car was marked with a red cross. 'That was the car that carried the Zyklon B.'

The children. Child detachments were routed up at 6 a.m. and made to stack potatoes until 6 p.m. 'The children were so stone-tired that they fell into their bunks; they couldn't even eat.' Children who caught scarlet fever were taken into the gas. Doctor Wolken asked one small boy, ' ''Aren't you afraid?''

'He said to me, ''No, I'm not afraid, it's all so terrible here, it can only be better up there.'' '

It was at this moment that one of the women jurors began to cry.

The next witness was Frau Ella Lingens, M.D. and LL.D. Not Jewish. Sent to Auschwitz in 1943 for having helped a Jewish family to escape. She was put to work in the hospital block. 'It was only if you got some special job that you had a chance to survive. Calories were 700 to 800 maximum a day. No ordinary prisoner could hope to live longer on that than four months.' In her case she was given the saving job because an SS doctor found out that she had been to his old university. 'He felt sentimental. There isn't an SS man who cannot claim that he saved at least one life. There were few sadists. Only five to ten percent were instinctive criminals in the clinical sense. The rest were normal people who perfectly well knew good from evil. They knew what they were doing.

'During the terrible winter of 1943–44, 20,000 out of 30,000 women died. They weren't gassed, they just died. Sickness, lack of food . . . I saw diseases one normally only learns about, like pemphigus, an extremely rare disease that attacks the skin and kills in a few days. The common camp diseases were spotted fever, typhus, typhoid and T.B. We'd have 500 women or more in a ward with about 180 beds.' There were no medical supplies. 'We couldn't even wash them. All suffered abominably from lice.' When there was no more room, there would be a selection. 'I saw the blankets torn off sick, naked women with the words. ''*You* won't need that anymore.'' I saw corpses stacked in the yard three feet high the length of the hospital block.'

There was one exception – one island of peace, Dr Lingens called it. It was because of one man, an SS officer called Flacke. He was good to the prisoners, his block was clean, there was even food. 'We never knew how he did it. The women called him Daddy. I don't know what became of him. I spoke to him one day. I said, ''You know, there's no sense for us in going on, there's no hope, when the end of the war comes we shall all be killed. They cannot afford to let any witnesses survive.'' And Flacke answered me. ''I hope that there will be enough of us to prevent it.'' '

The judge said, 'Do you mean to say that everybody at Auschwitz was able to decide for himself whether to be good or bad?'

'Exactly.'

Next came a former SS officer, a camp physician, Dr Wilhelm Münch (tried and acquitted after the war by a Polish court). He tells of his effective refusal to serve in gassings and selections. 'A human reaction was possible only during the very first hours. A man who had been at Auschwitz for any time was unable to react normally. He became an accomplice, he was trapped.'

How was it possible? Those SS men were brought up in the

climate created by the Nazis. Himmler said in a speech to the SS
in 1943:

> . . . How the Russians are doing, how the Czechs are doing, is not
> of the slightest concern to me . . . Whether foreign populations live
> prosperously or die from hunger interests me only insofar as we
> might need them as slaves for our own civilization; in any other
> respect it doesn't interest me at all. Whether ten thousand Russian
> females drop with exhaustion digging an anti-tank trench for us,
> interests me only insofar as the trench gets finished for Germany
> . . . We Germans, who are the only people in the world with a
> decent attitude to animals, will also have a decent attitude to those
> human animals, but to care about their welfare would be a crime
> against our own blood . . .

Herr Hermann Langbein of the International Auschwitz
Committee speaks of his work in the registration office. 'At
Dachau, too, I had to keep the death lists. There, it was a bad
day when we had to book ten deaths; at Auschwitz we did shift
work, day and night, on seven typewriters.'

There was also a secret monthly report (to which Herr
Langbein had access through his job) which gave candid figures
about 'Special Treatment Actions'. He was able to note the
contradictory directives coming from Himmler's SS Headquarters at Oranienburg, which were reflected by the divided
policies in the camp itself: Commandant Höss aimed at the
liquidation of the greatest possible numbers, while SS
Untersturmführer Grabner, the head of the Political Division,
wanted to lower the death rate in order to get more work out of
the prisoners.

'Life counted for nothing. To have killed a man in the evening
was hardly worth mentioning next day. The personal power of
an SS man was enormous. There were many who were neither
fanatical nationalists nor anti-Semites – there was one officer
who had the most beautiful manners with the prisoners, and
men like [the accused] Dr [Willi] Schatz or Dr [Willi] Frank
never did harm to individuals. Yet in that atmosphere no one
had scruples about sending people into the gas.'

Soon there is corroboration. Frau Maryla Rosenthal (deported five days before her wedding day with her non-Jewish fiancé and her mother – both died at Auschwitz) worked as interpreter in Boger's department. He treated her decently, she says, and gave her his own food. He rescued her when a woman *capo* had got her sentenced to a punishment squad, and certain death, for careless dusting. Boger used to say to men sent to him for interrogation, 'I have a talking machine here that will make you speak.' He took them to another room. She could hear the frightful screams. 'After several hours the victims were carried out on a stretcher. I could not recognize them.' When Frau Rosenthal cried, Boger told her, 'Here, you've got to cut out all personal feelings.'

Two times we heard a witness who survived Boger's machine. They were among the very worst moments of the trial. When one witness, a man in his 50s, saw the model of the Swing in court he cried. His crime had been to allow a Polish prisoner to say a word to his mother across a fence. The witness described how Boger tortured him until he was unconscious. Three times he was revived by buckets of cold water. Afterward he was put for several days into a standing cell. In the cell next to his, another man, Heinz Rothmann, had been left to die of hunger.

The judge recalled a warder of those cells, the accused Schlage. 'Were you under orders not to feed the prisoner?'

Schlage shows himself as impervious as before. 'Food issues had nothing to do with me.'

The judge: 'There are things one cannot get over. Those gruesome installations in which men slowly died. At the end their bodies had to be literally scraped out through the hole near the floor.'

Schlage admits that this had been so. But none of his business.

The second survivor, a Polish architect, had been tried for treason by a German court and acquitted. The SS arrested him on release. Interrogations by Boger. Six weeks – *six weeks* – in a standing cell with his hands tied behind his back. Food every third day only. Other men, whom he names, were given no food or water whatsoever.

Men were put into these cells because they had attempted to escape, were suspected of plotting to escape, refused to betray. One man was there because he had picked some apples off a tree.

'No door ever opened. One might shout, scream, curse. One might call Hitler names. *No one ever came.* Starvation is no easy death. Hunger stops on the fifth day. On the seventh day thirst begins. The men screamed for mercy, licked the walls, drank their own urine. After the thirteenth day they could no longer speak. One could still hear their groans. On the fifteenth day they died.'

In court, Boger sat silent through this evidence. At times one thought one saw a thin smile flicker across his face.

AT THAT time, seven of the accused were still free on bail. When the trial opened, their number had been 13; since then Mulka, Schlage and others had been arrested in open court as the evidence against them became grave. The seven men still free – among them Adjutant Höcker, Dr Lucas and the two dentists, Drs Schatz and Frank – were legally entitled to their liberty. In German law a man on trial – even for murder – is not kept in custody unless or until the case against him is very strong and there is reasonable suspicion that he may choose to escape. The meticulous justice of the Frankfurt court was perhaps in itself a tiny triumph over that vast injustice of the past.

The rest of us, the press, the public and – far worse – the witnesses, have to rub shoulders with men on bail, in elevators, or in the cloakroom, or lining up for a beer. They stamp about with their heads held high. Their photographs and crimes had been splashed over many a front page, yet they were not protected by police when they entered or left court or went to eat and drink in public places. The men of Auschwitz were not protected because they did not need to be protected. The spectators, the public, never threatened them.

Yet the public was there, watching. The German press and

radio provided admirable coverage of the trial. The serious papers, notably the *Frankfurter Allgemeine Zeitung*, which published the work of Bernd Naumann, carried columns of first-rate reporting and perceptive comment after every court day through the whole of the trial.

The public gallery in the court was filled chiefly by the very young, boys and girls with a teacher, students on their own. They were learning at first-hand what they had never before had much opportunity to learn. Outside the courtroom many Germans were concerned about the trial and spoke of it with distaste, hostility. 'Why rake it up again – what good can it do? Those men were not the only ones – anyway, it's too late.' There is a desire nowadays among people who were grown-up during the Third Reich, even, surprisingly, among those who hated it and took risks to defy its worst commands, to be done with it all and not think of it again for the rest of their lives. The young, who were born after the events, are more disturbed and curious and shocked. They want to know what happened, and how, and why, and they hold their elders to account for what the elders want to forget. I heard a son attack: 'Mother, how could you let it happen?' and her answer, 'You don't know, you can't *know*, what it was like – we were all afraid.'

As the first winter turned into spring and that spring into early summer and still no end in sight, the court had to move out of the town hall, where its presence was causing inconvenience to the normal business of city administration. The new quarters, chosen once more for size, were a festival hall near the outskirts of town. So now the court sat in what was a casually converted cinema theatre on a second floor above a restaurant. The judges and jurors occupied a platform at the end where the screen would have been, the prosecution was placed at right angles on a slightly lower platform: there were benches set out for the accused and their lawyers and their guards, while the public sat in the back rows. The vast balcony was reserved for press and for TV cameramen.

On June 7, the prosecution introduced a curiously direct piece of evidence, the Broad Report. It was written shortly after

the war by one of the accused himself, Pery Broad, and handed
to the British. The report, about 10,000 words long, was now
read to the court. Here are some extracts.

Concentration camp Auschwitz was situated near the (Polish)
town of the same name on marshland between the river Weichsel
and its tributary the Sola. It was founded in 1940 . . . At first it only
consisted of what was called the Main Camp. Its heavily guarded
entrance lay on the road connecting Auschwitz town with the village
of Raisko. From the road one could see the luxurious villa of the
commandant. One could not look into the camp, which was surrounded by a high concrete wall and a chain of watchtowers. Inside,
there were twenty-eight blocks of two storeys each housing the
prisoners, the hospital, the administrative offices and the kitchen.
The camp was protected by two tall, electrically charged, barbed-
wire fences which were lit up at night by a chain of strong lamps.
The towers were fitted with searchlights. Inside the first wire fence
there was a strip of gravel 10 feet wide, the so-called neutral zone.
Whoever stepped into this zone was shot on sight. In this Main
Camp 20,000 to 25,000 men and women were imprisoned.

Three miles farther on lay the notorious Camp II, Birkenau, built
up in 1941–42. It later held 50,000 to 60,000 men and 30,000
women. If one took the train at night from Bielitz to Auschwitz one
could see the endless string of glaring lights along the fence of
Birkenau.

Conditions there were even more unbearable than at Auschwitz
I. With every step one took, one's foot sank into tough mud. There
was hardly any water. The prisoners were kept in primitive stone
buildings, the walls of which were still damp, and in horse barracks
without windows. They slept on wooden bunks three tiers high, six
men to a bunk. Most bunks even lacked straw. The two daily roll
calls meant standing in wet, cold and mud for hours. If it rained
during the day, the prisoners had to lie on their bunks in their wet
clothes. No wonder that hundreds died each day . . .

The author of this document, Pery Broad, is charged with
having taken part in selecting prisoners for the gas chambers and
with killing individual prisoners by shooting in the back of the
neck. He is a technician, a man of 43, born in Rio de Janeiro,

son of a Brazilian citizen and a German mother. At Auschwitz, Broad became a member of the Political Division. Witnesses described him as an 'opaque personality', cruel at times, detached at others; 'We never knew whether he was filled with hatred for us or with pity.' When he was asked if he stood by his report, he hemmed and hawed and finally said yes.

Broad's detachment is very strange. (It may be typical.) There is not a hint that he, the accuser, the compassionate narrator, was in fact a member of the oppressor caste. He describes a 'clean-up', generally held on Saturday morning. High-ranking SS would assemble in the main office of the block.

They descend. A bunker is laboriously unlocked. The stench released is overpowering. A guard howls, *Achtung!* The prisoners stand up. Some can hardly do so. The candidates for death are led upstairs into a washroom where they are made to undress; fellow prisoners ink their number in large figures on their naked chests to facilitate registration of the bodies in the crematorium . . . SS take up position in the yard. By the blackwashed wall, a man is waiting with a shovel. The victims are brought out at a run, two by two, stood face against the wall. Behind their backs, rifles are at the ready.

In the last seconds of their life many of these walking skeletons, emerged after months of sub-animal existence, hardly able to keep on their feet, cry out, 'Long Live Liberty! Long Live Poland!' Their executioners try to shut them up by a brutal blow or make an end of it with a quick bullet. Men or women, bent old men or youths, there was almost without exception the same picture of human beings gathering their last grain of strength for an upright death. Never an appeal, no whining for mercy; instead, often a last look of abysmal contempt which drove the guards to paroxysms of fury. Thus died Poles and Jews, the people whom Nazi propaganda had always presented as slave creatures.

Broad comes to the first mass gassing (of which he implies he was a witness). All entrances to the crematorium area had been blocked, even to highest-ranking personnel; offices of adjacent buildings had been cleared. Picked SS men were waiting on the ramp.

The train drew up. Men and women were discharged from cattle trucks. All wore large yellow stars. From their faces one could see that they had already been through a good deal. There were about 300, most of them elderly. A few guards with revolvers discreetly tucked in their pockets escorted them to the crematorium yard. SS were acting strictly to orders: not an unkind word was heard.

Grabner and Hossler were standing on the roof. Grabner called down to the apprehensive but unsuspecting crowd, 'You are going to have a bath and be disinfected, and afterward you'll be shown to your quarters where some warm soup will be waiting for you. Tomorrow you'll be given work, each according to his capacity or trade. Now get undressed here in the yard and leave your clothes on the ground.' Grabner's tone was warm and friendly; people willingly complied. They were immensely relieved that the anxieties of the journey were over and that their worst fears were not going to be fulfilled. They were looking forward to their soup. More reassuring advice came from the roof. 'Put your shoes next to your bundle of clothes so that you're sure of finding them again after your bath.' . . . 'Hot water? Certainly – hot showers.' 'What's your trade? . . . Cobbler? Splendid. We need one badly. Come and report to me tomorrow.' So last misgivings were dispersed. The first walked into the gas chamber – everything was scrupulously clean and bare; there was only a strange oppressive smell, and there were no perceivable water pipes and taps. Meanwhile those outside were pressing on, and the chamber was filling up with people followed by joking and chattering SS who kept an eye on the door. When the last was inside, the SS skipped. Suddenly the iron-and-rubber doors flung shut; heavy bolts fell. The people inside began to hammer against them in helpless terror. The doors were then screwed air-tight from outside. 'Don't get yourselves scalded in your baths,' an SS shouted.

The Disinfecting Squad on the roof took off a lid revealing an aperture with six holes in the ceiling of the chamber; people below screamed when they saw a head in a gas mask appear in the aperture. The disinfectors then opened some tin cans. The labels read ZYKLON – PEST-KILLER – POISON – TO BE OPENED BY TRAINED PERSONNEL ONLY. The cans were filled with blue grains, the size of peas. These were immediately poured through the holes in the ceiling, and the opening shut tight again. Grabner gave a signal to a truck driver who had drawn up in the yard below: the engine roared up and the noise helped to cover the cries of 300 people dying of asphyxiation. Grabner was studying his wristwatch with clinical interest. After about two minutes the cries had ebbed into a low humming moan. Most had already lost consciousness. After two more minutes Grabner lowered his watch. Everything was over. Everything was quiet. The truck had left. Detachments were beginning to collect the bundles of clothes left in the yard. So it began in the spring of 1942!

Transport after transport disappeared in the crematorium. Every day! Larger and larger numbers of victims arrived, and murder had to be organized on a larger scale. The chamber held too few, the burning of the bodies took too much time. Hitler was waiting with impatience for the liquidation of millions of French, Belgian, Dutch, German, Polish, Greek, Italian Jews. They arrived in their long trains from the collecting camps in France and Holland or straight from Antwerp, Warsaw, Salonika, Berlin . . . Birkenau had to expand.

Speed and secrecy were the slogans. The construction of four new crematoria was pushed on by all possible means. Two of them had subterranean gas chambers, fitted now with dummy pipes and showers, in which 4,000 people could be killed at one time. Each of these death factories had a large hall for undressing. Crematoria I & II boasted 15 ovens, each capable of burning up to four or five corpses in record time.

Auschwitz was so proud that the Construction Office publicly displayed photographs of the new crematoria in their lobby.

In 1943 the procedure at Birkenau changed. By then rumors about Auschwitz had seeped out. A large detachment of SS, now openly equipped with revolvers, whips and dogs, would be waiting to meet the transports on the ramp. Also on the ramp stood the selectors, generally a doctor accompanied by an SS officer. Searchlights were trained on the trucks as men, women and children in a state of great exhaustion, misery and fear were ordered out and driven past. By the moving of a hand the selector indicated the side they were to stand on - to one side those who looked fit enough to work for a few more months; to the other, the old, the sick, the weak.

Broad's report continues:

In the spring of 1944 Auschwitz was at its height. Endless trains came and went between Hungary and Birkenau: an order was out that all Hungarian Jews were to be destroyed in one quick blow. Sidings were installed so that the next train could draw in while the last one was still being unloaded. All four crematoria worked at full capacity. On an average, 10,000 men and women arrived daily. Some of them had gone mad on the journey from thirst or fear. Time and again the furnaces burned out, the chimneys split from being overworked. There was nothing for it but starting up the open fires again to burn up the arrears of corpses that lay heaped behind the crematoria walls.

Gas chambers were opened when the last groans had barely ceased, bodies barely dragged out before the next living batch was driven in. Höss had been given the Distinguished Service Cross First Class with Swords; he himself often urged on the – usually drunk – personnel. The Russians had already occupied the whole of Eastern Hungary; camp Lublin, Auschwitz's sister enterprise, was out of action in Soviet hands: there was no more time to be lost. The number of killed during those few weeks of spring must have been a half million.

That mental, moral and spiritual perversion, that barely conceivable degradation, that abomination in the centre of civilization – how was it possible? How could it ever be? Such hell is not created in a day; such evil, on such scale, must have long roots.

How did it begin?

Primarily, germinally, the capacity for cruelty must lie in our natures. Man's capacity for giving pain to man is staggering. Yet the cruel and the brutal are not an all-powerful mass. The men of Auschwitz were scum from the start, but the point is that the Third Reich deliberately trained and licensed that scum; it endowed its promising criminal with the personal power to maltreat not a pair of oxen on the farm but large numbers of human beings. On a lesser scale, it has always happened. It happened to Christians in Rome, to medieval prisoners, to heretics; it happened in the Star Chamber, in slave ships, in convict settlements and nineteenth-century penitentiaries. It is happening now. It is happening to political dissenters. In the Iron Curtain countries, in China, in Africa . . . It happens wherever the administration and the climate of society allow the use of violence for ideological, political or economic ends.

It is well to realize this when thinking about Nazi Germany; it is well to realize, too, that Nazi Germany went farthest. There was the ideology that was a monstrous insult to every human and religious value; there was the hubristic abuse of science, the abuse of German talents for organization and hard work; there was the sheer size of the terror, the ultimate madness of will. If a child, with history book in hand, were to ask one day, Was that the very worst that ever happened?, the answer may have to be, Yes.

A beginning of the tragedy can be found in the 1920s. (There were earlier steps, of course, such as the First World War, the Franco-Prussian War, modern nationalism and, in turn, its origins in the Napoleonic Wars, the impoverishment and brutalization inflicted by the Thirty Years' War – the historical treadmill is unending.) In the 1920s Germans first listened to the vile ravings, and many found them agreeable and went to vote accordingly or joined the organizations that provided them with hope, aggression, soup and boots. The beginning was made manifest when the raving voice became the government of Germany.

Toward the end of the Weimar Republic, Germany was a country politically split and in economic distress, unused to, and uneasy under, the processes of parliamentary democracy. Governments were formed, and failed; so did the banks. The unemployment rate rose. In the last free elections, in November, 1932, the National-Socialist party polled 33.2 percent of the vote. Bad enough, but not enough for Hitler's party to be called to govern. Nevertheless, through a web of intrigue, misplaced self-interest, weakness and opportunism in high places, Hitler became Chancellor of Germany in January, 1933. He was in power; but it was mere constitutional power, and the government he headed was a coalition with but two Nazi Party members in the cabinet. He found that he had to consider the bureaucracy, the army and the business world; in fact, he had to conform to the lawful administration of the country. The opportunity for a breakthrough was presented four weeks later by the Reichstag fire of February 27, only six days before the next general elections. Hitler proclaimed that the fire was the signal for a Communist revolution, and he was able to issue a decree, the *Decree for the Protection of People and State*, which ordered a temporary emergency. That decree was never rescinded. The emergency was to last until the end of Nazi rule in 1945.

Overnight the first terror was on. The SA, the Brownshirts (who in those days played a more active part than the SS) were enrolled as auxiliary police. The beatings began, the arrests at dawn, the suppression of newspapers, dispersal of meetings, intimidation at the polls. People by the hundreds began to disappear into the first detention camps.

In spite of the terror, more than half the Germans voted against Hitler on March 5. And surely this, too, ought to be remembered. The Nazis got 43.9 percent of the total vote. What Hitler wanted was a clear two-thirds majority in order to pass an enabling act through the Reichstag. He got the majority by having the 81 elected Communist members arrested and thus prevented from taking their seats, and by scaring the centre parties into compliance or abstention. Only the Social Democrats remained opposed. The Enabling Act was passed on March 23. Hitler was in command. The rule of law ended.

From then on Hitler was able to by-pass – with sham legality – the still existing legal order. He was able to create the Gestapo, the concentration camps and, ultimately, the apparatus for the Final Solution. Hitler's hostility to law was a significant personal characteristic. He used to fall into a rage whenever it was pointed out to him that his orders were against the constitution. He regarded any form of legislation, even his own, as politically unwise, a restriction of his freedom of manoeuvre. (It was for this reason that there never was a National Socialist criminal code in force. One was drafted and completed by 1936 but was never promulgated. Thus Bismarck's Criminal Code of 1871 remained uninterruptedly the law of the land, a point that is of some importance in connection with the legality of the Frankfurt trial.) Hitler often spoke of his historical task of building an authority that was not founded on common law or moral law: all human beings were to be at the total disposal of the Führer power, *Führergewalt*; on principle, there were to be no basic guarantees, no Magna Charta, no Bill of Rights.

Back in the 1930s the Nazis proceeded gradually. Their political opponents were put out of action one by one. First the Communists; then the trade unions; then, in turn, while the next victim was looking on, the Social Democrats, the democratic centre parties, the churches, the aristocracy; even Jehovah's Witnesses came to be locked up in droves.

The first camps, the 'wild camps' as they were called in the early days in 1933, were private prisons improvised by the SA in disused barracks and in vacant cellars. Torture, not mere beating and bullying but extreme torture, took place.

Excesses, people said; a young movement, it'll soon get normal again.

It never got normal again.

By June of 1933 there were in existence in Prussia alone six official camps, holding some 14,000 people. They were run then by the SA, SS and a number of ex-soldiers. It was impressed upon them that they were front-line troops in peacetime, the enemy being the prisoners behind the barbed wire who must be treated with the utmost, but impersonal, hardness. 'Any leniency, any pity towards the enemies of the state is unworthy of an SS man,' they were harangued by Theodor Eicke, a violent man who had been both a convict and a mental patient and was now Inspector General of Concentration Camps. 'Softies have no place in our ranks and would do better to retire into a monastery. We have use only for hard, decided men who obey every order mercilessly.'

Inevitably the concentration camps became the magnet that

attracted the most corrupt and brutalized elements of the population. Himmler counted on and covered up 'excesses' whenever the lawful administration attempted to intervene. In one case, for example, criminal proceedings were initiated against the commandant, a Gestapo official and 21 SS men of camp Hohenstein in Saxony for 'grave ill-treatment of prisoners'. The Nazi gauleiter of Saxony wrote to Berlin to have the prosecution quashed. The minister of justice, Franz Gürtner, wrote in answer on January 8, 1935:

> The nature of the ill-treatment shows a degree of cruelty and callousness in the accused that is entirely foreign to German feeling. For atrocities of such oriental and sadistic character no explanation or excuses can be found.

A trial took place; the accused were convicted and given light prison sentences. In consequence, the prosecution attorney and two jurors, the three of them Nazis, were expelled from the party. Hitler personally reprieved the convicted men.

In the same year Wilhelm Frick, the minister of the interior, alarmed by the high number of camp prisoners, ordered an inquiry into the cases of all persons held beyond six months. The order was returned to him by Himmler:

'Submitted to the Führer 20th Feb. 1935. *The prisoners will remain.* H.H.'

In 1938, 60,000 people were in camps. With the war came the ghastly escalation. The prisoners were no longer chiefly Germans, but Czechs, Poles, Belgians, Dutchmen, Frenchmen, Russians, Greeks, Croats, Serbs.

Buchenwald and Sachsenhausen became overcrowded during the winter; many new camps, Auschwitz among them, were founded in 1940. In December, 1942, there were 88,000 prisoners in the camps – by next August there were 224,000. The monstrous increase went on. Five hundred thousand by August, 1944. Finally, on January 15, 1945, there were counted 511,000 men and 202,000 women – 713,000 prisoners in all. The staff required to guard them numbered 40,000.

MANY, MANY – though by no means all – were Jews.

Anti-Semitism had been official government policy from the early days. The belief in race as the determining factor of human quality, apart from being false and wicked, is a hopeless and defeatist creed. There is no room for grace. The Nazis tried to establish a kind of perverted Calvinism in this world – damnation by birth.

In the spring of 1933 the windows of Jewish-owned shops were smashed in many towns; at Breslau the SA policed the entrances to the courthouses, blocking admittance to Jewish judges and lawyers. Two weeks later, all Jewish judges and attorneys in Germany were officially requested to apply for indefinite leave. In May, Jewish doctors were forbidden to treat non-Jewish patients; in July, Jews were banned from jury duty; in September, Jewish artists and musicians were excluded from performing in concerts, films and on the stage; writers could no longer publish. Next, farming was forbidden to all who could not prove freedom from any Jewish strain back to the year 1800.

In September, 1935, came the Nuremberg Decrees for the Protection of the Blood. *Blutshutzgesetz*, as that repulsive idea was named. All Jews had to leave the civil service. They lost the vote (for what it was worth). Marriage, and sexual intercourse, with a non-Jew became a criminal offence. Jewish families were even forbidden to employ a non-Jewish woman servant below the age of 45. Soon after came an order to the effect that the names of Jewish war dead must in the future be omitted from memorials. By 1938, Jews had to carry special identification cards; men had to add Israel, and women, Sarah, to their given names.

On November 7, 1938, a 17-year-old Jewish boy, Herschel Grynszpan, shot a German Embassy secretary in Paris. In the aftermath 20,000 Jews from all walks of life were taken from their homes and thrown into the camps, synagogues were set afire all over Germany, and there was 'spontaneous' looting of 7,000 Jewish shops, 'spontaneous' killing of Jews in the streets. Yet the British chargé d'affaires wrote at the time:

I have not met a single German who does not disapprove . . . of what has been going on. But I am afraid that unqualified condemnation even on the part of declared National Socialists and high army officers will not have the slightest influence on the gang of lunatics who are ruling Nazi Germany at present.

The lunatics, instead, were giving another turn to the screw. Compulsory sale of all Jewish businesses; compulsory sale of land. Exclusion of Jews from all German schools and universities. Prohibition to go to theatres, concerts, cinemas, museums, to use sports grounds, beaches or swimming pools.

Then came confiscation of driving licences. The order to hand over gold, precious stones and pearls. The order permitting landlords to cancel leases of their Jewish tenants. The abolition of all civil-service and retirement pensions.

The war began. With it, new degrees of civic savagery. By 1942 the daily life of such Jews as were still at liberty in Germany had become wholly intolerable. They had to give up their radios and their telephones; they were forbidden to use public telephone booths or vending machines. They were not allowed to ride in public transport.

Jewish ration-cards were marked J, and they received: no clothes coupon whatsoever (after 1940); no tobacco and no egg ration (after June, 1942); no meat; no processed meat; no wheat products (October, 1942); no milk for children (1942).

Jews were ordered to: buy their food between the hours of 4–5 p.m. only (1940); give up all furs and non-essential warm clothing (January, 1942); mark the outside of their dwellings with a yellow star (April, 1942); hand over all electrical and optical appliances, bicycles, typewriters, phonograph records, etc. (June, 1942).

Jews were not allowed to: walk in public parks or gardens; eat and drink in restaurants, cafés, bars; subscribe to newspapers and periodicals; buy books; keep a dog, a cat, a canary, or any pet whatsoever.

The Jews in Germany had lost every civic, legal or human right. The sub-humanization process that had begun from both ends – executioners and victims – was about completed. After such preparation, the Final Solution had moved into the realm of the conceivable.

AT FRANKFURT the reading of the Broad Report ended in June of 1964. The trial continued for over one more year. Three hundred and sixty witnesses were heard in all; the tale they bore was substantially the same: each man and woman in that long, sad, restrained file recalled a sea of suffering and horror. To repeat it here in dry print would stun the mind. What was inflicted and endured at Auschwitz cannot be faced by normal human consciousness for long; the heart cannot take in pain on such a scale, the brain cannot contend with wickedness so measureless and so diseased. Pity and anger are inadequate. The law is inadequate – the law is not, and should not, be shaped to grapple with enormities such as these. Comment is inadequate. Expiation will be inadequate. And yet, letting it go, looking aside, would be an offence against justice, morality, the sense of fate itself.

That is why the Frankfurt trial had to go on to the weary end. Even when the events themselves were proved, far beyond the most unreasonable doubt, the court's task remained to prove – or disprove – link by link the guilt of the individual men accused. No single witness's story was enough; it was but a piece in a vast and intricate mosaic; it had to be checked, collated, corroborated by other witnesses, by documents, by dates. Had that man been in that place, on that duty, at that time? Was that witness able, personally, physically, to see that act? What was the distance? Was there a crack from which you had a view of the Black Wall? (And it must be remembered that only murder was involved; the time for prosecution for maltreatment, cruelty, torture – unless it caused death – had already lapsed by an old German statute of limitations.) In its determination to search for the truth, the court made a trip to Auschwitz in December, 1964; among the accused, only Dr Lucas chose to revisit the camp.

The courtroom evidence, necessarily, was presented piecemeal. Witnesses came, or failed to come on time, from Poland, Israel, France, East Berlin, the United States. Timing was not in the court's control. Many witnesses – survivors, attempting to recollect, after 20 years, events experienced in circumstances of unparalleled stress – failed to identify their man. 'I don't know . . . he used to be in uniform . . . he must have changed.' The judge later summed up the court's difficulties:

> In an ordinary murder case, not only are memories fresh, we moreover have the body, the medical evidence, the evidence of fingerprints, footprints, many material clues . . . All these were lacking here. Here, our unhappy witnesses often did not know the day, the month, the year, deprived as they had been at Auschwitz of the ordinary props to memory: they had no watches, no calendars . . .
>
> No wonder then that . . . sometimes their evidence, if patently true in essence, was not solid enough to convict in a court of law.

The accused themselves, who were frequently called upon to elucidate, were ready to admit that terrible things did happen, but – and here they always became eloquent – not when *I* was there. *I* was away – on sick leave, off duty, transferred; it happened on another day, in another block, under another man. The other man was not named. They stuck together.

If little so far has been said about the defence, it is because they were unable to contribute much of value to the case. Their role was not an easy one; they did, as was their duty, what they could. They contested evidence, exposed contradictions, shook some witnesses. For the most part they had to fall back on technical points and rhetorical lines – the accused were a few of many, were small men drawn into the vortex of history, had obeyed orders.

That vexed question of orders was submitted to expert evidence and much debate. The judge read out the section of German Army regulations (never rescinded) that forbids the carrying out of orders of a criminal nature. (Many people, among them court police, showed genuine surprise.) What was less clear was what actually happened to a member of the SS who refused such orders. Hans Buchheim, a German historian called as an expert witness, denied the common contention that refusal to obey orders necessarily entailed prison or death. 'The arbitrariness which threatened every citizen from the SS was not practised on their own kind.'

There was one other element that came to light again during the trial – the ugly link between German industry and the concentration camps – and it aroused very mixed emotions. During the war, as is known, German firms set up subsidiary factories in the vicinity of Auschwitz and some other camps. These were worked by forced labour, prisoners under supervision of the SS – 50,000 men at one time in an I.G. Farben works alone. Some of the firms engaged in war production had little freedom of choice; others, notably some directors of I.G. Farben, had themselves approached the SS. The handful of executives who gave evidence at Frankfurt made sad hearing.

There was for instance chief engineer Kurt Bundzus, who had been engaged in recruiting prisoners for a Siemens-Schuckert factory in 1944. To be of any use at all, he said, they needed feeding. His description is involved and remote. 'Their condition was such that I had to tell myself that some weeks of feeding would remain without effect on their capacity to do a day's work.'

Then there was a Dr Carl Albert Krauch, ex-chairman of I.G. Farben, who had been sentenced to six years in prison by the Nuremberg Tribunal as an accessory in the use of slave labour. He was asked if it was true that prisoners who had grown too weak to work were selected to be killed according to an arrangement with I.G. Farben.

Dr Krauch: This was not confirmed by findings at the Nuremberg trials.
Question: What do *you* know about agreements between I.G.F. and the camp in regard to prisoners who could no longer work?
Dr Krauch: Nothing to my recollection.
Question: Did you know about selections?
Dr Krauch: I was not informed.
Question: Did you know who ran the camp? Who gave the orders?

Dr Krauch: I did not know.
Question: Did you meet Adjutant Mulka?
Dr Krauch: Only from this trial.

'I walked through the works once,' the witness adds, 'and had the impression that there was no difference between those people and other foreign labour. The sick received treatment, if someone had appendicitis, for instance. It was in our interest to keep skilled workmen alive.'

HOW MANY Germans knew? Germans in the interior who did not see and smell the fires? They knew a lot, of course. The camps were feared; you cannot fear what you do not know exists. They saw things happening to Jews; they knew that neighbours – Jews and socialists and priests and the man who had criticized the Goebbels speech – disappeared. There were rumours about far-off places where nameless things were happening. The extermination camps were a state secret of the highest classification. Correspondence was in code. There were leaks, inevitably, through men on leave and local populations. Yet all in all it was a fiercely guarded (and scarcely credible) secret in a gagged country in time of war, and I think one must assume that the mass of Germans did not know of the death camps.

Yet what *was* known was terrible enough. Why did not more Germans react, recoil, cry out in 1933, in '34, in '35, before it was too late? Why was there not more revulsion, more clear-cut condemnation, why no effective protest, then, in government offices, big business, the army, the foreign service? It will never be an easy matter to judge.

MANY, FAR too many things heard during those 183 days of the trial haunt the mind. There was the witness who saw four- and five-year-olds hold up their arms: '*Block-capo*, please look how strong we are'; the witness who saw Kaduk drive children who were begging for their lives into the gas at pistol point; the boy who wrote in blood upon a wall 'Andreas Rapaport – lived sixteen years.' The old man from Haifa who had been dragged to Auschwitz with wife, two children, mother, sister, brother, his in-laws and their children, 'because I was a Jew'. The judge asked him, 'And are you the only one who remained?' And the old man standing there alone, saying, 'Yes.'

There is much still that cannot be told here that belongs for ever to the history of Auschwitz. The individual heroism, the acts of kindness and self-sacrifice by men and women whose spirit surpassed the limits of the human condition as they stayed good and brave and charitable in extreme hunger, bodily weakness and degradation; the rabbis and priests who remained a source of strength and faith; the – extremely few – successful escapes; the breakdowns, the disorganization that so ironically dogged those untiring administrators; the uneasy final weeks, the last ghostly roll call on January 17, 1945: 60,020 prisoners, and the evacuation before the advancing Russians, in the bitter winter weather, through the desolate landscape . . .

The closing speeches began in Frankfurt on May 7, 1965. They occupied 30 days. The four prosecutors spoke, the 18 defence counsel spoke. Nothing new was said. The prosecution asked for life sentences in most cases, and for the acquittal of Johann Schoberth, former guard, and Arthur Breitwieser, former member of the disinfection division, for 'lack of evidence'. The accused have the last word. The judge instructed them: 'It is your right. It is not a duty. But I am asking each one of you to reflect most earnestly whether you do not wish to break, at this last minute, the ice of silence. We should have come a great deal nearer to the truth had you not so obstinately remained behind that wall. Perhaps some of you have realized in the course of these proceedings that we are concerned here not with revenge but with expiation.' Mulka rose first. His response was a few stilted sentences.

'Venerable Court . . . I concur subjectively, objectively and legally with the submissions of my counsel . . . It only remains for me to express my . . . confidence in a just decision.'

Boger: 'Throughout National Socialist rule there existed for me only one consideration – to carry out the orders of my superiors to the limit. I came to Auschwitz without my volition. I see today that the idea I adhered to brought harm and was false. I carried out third-degree interrogations as ordered. I did not then regard Auschwitz as a cruel place for the destruction of European Jewry; my overriding concern was the fight against Polish resistance and Bolshevism.'

Stark, ex-member of the camp Gestapo: 'I was associated with the death of many people. After the war I often asked myself if I had become a criminal because as a believing National Socialist I had killed people. I never found the answer. I believed in the Führer, I wished to serve my people. Today I know that these ideas were false. I regret the wrong path I took then, but I cannot undo it.'

Schoberth, ex-guard: '. . . When Hitler came to power I was ten years old. I was brought up to be a good Nazi . . . I must ask you to consider what happened to people of my year. I was wounded four times, operated on eight times, decorated five times. I don't know what more I am supposed to say now. Aren't we, also, the victims of National Socialism?'

Dr Lucas: 'Most Venerable Court, the period of my life during which, against my will, I was assigned to Auschwitz is one that I cannot get over. Pressed into duty on the ramp, I naturally tried to spare the lives of as many prisoners as possible. But today, as then, I am moved to the question, And the others? I fought my way through to telling you the truth. So I can only hope that you will arrive at a judgment that will help me to free myself from this tangle and begin a new way of life.'

The court stands adjourned; public and reporters go home. Judges and jurors deliberate in privacy; presumably they meet daily, presumably they keep office hours. Nobody stands by with watch in hand. There is no pressure of fatigue, no pressure to go home, no drama. On August 19, 1965, the court reconvened.

It was a hot, gray, leaden morning. As on the opening day, the hall was crammed again with representatives of the world's press. Mulka looks aged; many look thinner. Of the 22 men originally accused, 20 are left. (One defendant, Heinrich Bischoff, died at home; another, Gerhard Neubert, had become ill but would be tried and convicted in 1966.) All but three are now in custody. Two of the jurors have been replaced by substitutes. The map of Auschwitz is still there.

One minute before half-past eight the judges came in. The chief judge immediately pronounced the verdicts and sentences in his firm, quiet voice. The court stood as it listened.

'In the name of the people, these have been found guilty:

'The accused Mulka guilty of being an accessory to collective murder in at least four cases of seven hundred and fifty men and women each;

'The accused Boger guilty of murder in at least one hundred and fourteen cases, and guilty of being an accessory to collective murder of at least one thousand men and women;

'The accused Broad guilty of being an accessory to collective murder in at least twenty-two cases, of which two cases of one thousand each;

'The accused Kaduk guilty of murder in ten cases, and guilty of collective murder in at least two cases, one of at least a thousand men and women and the other of two men;

'The accused Baretzki guilty of murder in five cases, and guilty of being an accessory to collective murder in at least eleven cases, of which one case of at least three thousand, five cases of at least one thousand, and five cases of at least fifty each;

'The accused Dr Lucas guilty of being an accessory to collective murder in at least six cases of a thousand each;

'The accused Klehr guilty of murder in at least four hundred and seventy-five cases and guilty of being an accessory to collective murder in at least six cases of at least two thousand six hundred and sixty men and women.'

In all there were 17 convictions. Then came the sentences. There were life sentences for Boger, Kaduk, Baretzki, Klehr, Hofmann and Bednarek; 14 years for Mulka; seven for

Adjutant Höcker; four years for Broad; three years and three months for Dr Lucas. The accused Schoberth, Breitwieser and the dentist Dr Schatz were acquitted for lack of evidence. The convicted men, who remained in court, showed no visible reactions.

Judge Hofmeyer then started the *Urteilsbegründung*, the post-verdict summing-up, which lasted through that day and the next. It took 11 hours. The judge began by saying that there had been an understandable desire to make this trial the basis for a historical analysis of the Third Reich and the political, psychological and social developments that led to the catastrophic events of Auschwitz; yet the court did not have the right to be tempted into such a multiplicity of issues.

'This trial has attracted attention well beyond the borders of this country. It has acquired the name of Auschwitz Trial; for this court it remained the criminal trial of *Mulka & Others*. And that means that the only determining factor of the verdict of the court is the evidence as to the guilt or innocence of the accused. The court was not entitled to conduct a political trial; even less was it entitled to conduct a show trial – a trial in which the outcome is a foregone conclusion and the proceedings are a farce staged for the general public. Anyone who has followed the proceedings here will know that . . . the court has laboured to get at the truth, nothing but the truth, and that has been the heart of the concern of these hearings.'

The judge then dealt with the defence contention that only the small fry were being held responsible here. It is true, he said, that the big men who planned it all are dead – Hitler and Himmler and Göring – but the small men also had been necessary to carry out the Final Solution.

Then he spoke of it all once again, in simple words, in the same quiet, rather homely voice.

'. . . The place that was Auschwitz . . . that hell inconceivable to any normal mind. The poor human beings arrived, their possessions were taken from them, their clothes; their hair was shorn; they were given a few rags, or even left stark naked. Here they were at the mercy of their cynical *capos* and SS guards, plagued by vermin, covered in sores, hungry day and night, beset by deadly fear of what sufferings the next hour might bring; forced to wear heavy clogs on their chafed bare feet, driven along roads like cattle to do hard, unaccustomed work; they were beaten, they were kicked, they were mocked, and in the evenings their guards rejoiced in making the exhausted creatures do exercises, do sport as it was called, until the poor martyred bodies fainted and this became an excuse to shoot them. That was their daily existence until life itself was taken from them in the gas chambers. There they died, naked, packed one against another, with their prisoners' numbers scrawled upon their skin, men separated from wives and children. It was death by suffocation, after a last struggle for air, the still living standing on the bodies of the dead. It was a cruel death. Outside, a doctor stood watching. Such was the fate of Jews and Christians, of Poles and Germans, of Russian prisoners of war and gipsies, of men and women from all of Europe at the Camp of Auschwitz . . . Even if all the men convicted here had been given the maximum penalty, there can never be an approximate retribution for what was done at Auschwitz. Human life is too short.'

And during the last minutes of the trial, Dr Hofmeyer, the judge who had done so much to keep the atmosphere cool, who had steered the court through so many clashes of temper and had never lost his own, allowed himself to break down. After having thanked the jury and his fellow judges, he said in a voice no longer quite audible or controlled that for nearly two years the bench had been under an almost unbearable emotional strain. 'No one who was here will ever be able to forget what he has heard . . .' Then the judge pulled himself up and icily addressed the convicted men. It was his duty, he said, to inform them of their right to appeal. All but one have done so.

We, too, should hear and not forget. This story is a part of our lives and time. It is irreversible for those to whom it happened, the unfortunate men and women who were plucked from home, from family, from cares and habits, from the entire normal context of human expectations. What was done cannot be undone.

What we can do is to honour them by memory, to mourn them, to think of them in sorrow and in awe. And we can learn. The SS man's words, 'At last we have the means,' are true now more than ever. Final solutions are within many a reach. We can remember Auschwitz and beware of listening to the siren song of expediency, beware of abrogating mercy, of setting aside the law. Beware of being sheep.

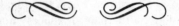

Catherine Caufield
In the Rainforest £4.99

'If I had an award to give I would give it to this book. *In the Rainforest* is
the epitome of detailed, on-the-ground, investigative journalism applied to
a problem that encompasses corruption, greed, disaster, and murder for the
sake of money and land. All this applies to the ecological rape of the
tropical forests. There is so much in this book that I could continue
praising. It should be required reading, cover to cover, for all those who
control the social, economic and ecological destiny of tropical moist
forests' NEW SCIENTIST

'Caufield gives admirable vignettes of local experiences a polished
journalistic treatment. When she is describing her meetings and discussion
with indigenous tribes of the Amazon, a pioneer farmer in Costa Rica or a
logger in the Philippines, she is at her best. Her book is refreshingly free of
jargon or irritating stylistic peculiarities.' THE OBSERVER

All Pan books are available at your local bookshop or newsagent, or can be ordered direct from the publisher. Indicate the number of copies required and fill in the form below.

Send to: **CS Department, Pan Books Ltd., P.O. Box 40, Basingstoke, Hants. RG21 2YT.**

or phone: 0256 469551 (Ansaphone), quoting title, author and Credit Card number.

Please enclose a remittance* to the value of the cover price plus: 60p for the first book plus 30p per copy for each additional book ordered to a maximum charge of £2.40 to cover postage and packing.

*Payment may be made in sterling by UK personal cheque, postal order, sterling draft or international money order, made payable to Pan Books Ltd.

Alternatively by Barclaycard/Access:

Card No.

Signature:

Applicable only in the UK and Republic of Ireland.

While every effort is made to keep prices low, it is sometimes necessary to increase prices at short notice. Pan Books reserve the right to show on covers and charge new retail prices which may differ from those advertised in the text or elsewhere.

NAME AND ADDRESS IN BLOCK LETTERS PLEASE:

....

Name————————————————————————————

Address————————————————————————————

————————————————————————————

————————————————————————————

————————————————————————————

3/87